Oprah, Celebrity and Formations of Self

Sherryl Wilson

Bournemouth Media School
Bournemouth University, UK

First published 2003 by
PALGRAVE MACMILLAN
Houndmills, Basingstoke, Hampshire RG21 6XS and
175 Fifth Avenue, New York, N.Y. 10010
Companies and representatives throughout the world

PALGRAVE MACMILLAN is the global academic imprint of the Palgrave
Macmillan division of St. Martin's Press, LLC and of Palgrave Macmillan Ltd.
Macmillan® is a registered trademark in the United States, United Kingdom
and other countries. Palgrave is a registered trademark in the European
Union and other countries.

ISBN 1–4039–1681–0 hardback

This book is printed on paper suitable for recycling and made from fully
managed and sustained forest sources.

A catalogue record for this book is available from the British Library.

Library of Congress Cataloging-in-Publication Data
Wilson, Sherryl, 1957–
    Oprah, celebrity, and formations of self / Sherryl Wilson.
        p.   cm.
    Includes bibliographical references and index.
    ISBN 1–4039–1681–0
    1. Winfrey, Oprah—Criticism and interpretation.   I. Title.

PN1992.4.W56W56 2003
791.45′028′092—dc21

                                                                    2003053272

10   9   8   7   6   5   4   3   2   1
12   11   10   09   08   07   06   05   04   03

Printed and bound in Great Britain by
Antony Rowe Ltd, Chippenham and Eastbourne

For Tom and Ella

Contents

List of Tables

Acknowledgements

The initial idea for this study germinated with help and support from Richard Maltby; I am grateful for his time and patience. The research was conducted in the School of Media and Cultural Studies, University of the West of England, Bristol, and the financial support the School gave me is much valued as is the friendship and encouragement I received from my colleagues there. In particular, I would like to thank Martin Barker who was generous with his time and encouragement in the early stages, Jon Dovey who injected enthusiasm, energy and humour at crucial moments, and Jane Arthurs whose interest, enthusiasm and friendship underlined the advice and guidance she gave me. Gillian Swanson and Lola Young offered invaluable criticism and advice while Denise Meredith demonstrated that she is patience personified when she read through earlier drafts; her attention to detail, and advice are much appreciated. Phil Hargreaves' IT wizardry saved me from insanity when the software I was using developed a mind of its own. Anthony Elliott's interest and support was also a central element in bringing this book to fruition. Finally, I want to say a big thank you to my friends, to my parents Bron and Wilf Wilson, to my sister Mandy Wilson, and to my children Tom and Ella Antebi: all have offered support in a variety of ways. For all of this, and to all these people, I am more grateful than I can properly articulate.

Introduction

The Oprah Winfrey Show: a popular phenomenon

'It was a mascara runnin' kinda day!' Talk show host Oprah Winfrey makes this declaration in a show dedicated to the celebration of inspirational teachers. The words are spoken in response to a clip shown of a previous programme in which we see Winfrey[1] in a tearful reunion with her 4th grade teacher, a woman who had been hugely influential for her young pupil. We learn that the teacher had been inspirational for Winfrey not only in fuelling the desire to learn, but also in helping her during difficult emotional times such as when her best friend killed herself. The teacher – Mrs Duncan – is brought onto the stage, introduced to the audience and is read a letter written by Winfrey. The letter reveals how much the older woman has meant to Winfrey, the profound impact she had had on her life, and the debt of gratitude felt as a result. Many hugs and tears mark the reunion. Looking back on this clip, Winfrey declares, 'It was a mascara runnin' kinda day!' and represents 'one of my all time favourite *Oprah* moments'. The image of running mascara underpins much that is associated with *The Oprah Winfrey Show*: female-centredness; emotional display; disclosure of intimate moments; a self laid bare. This reunion precedes and frames the salutes to teachers offered by audience members as they both actively endorse Winfrey's own sentiments as to the value of inspirational teachers and become a central element of the show itself.

Of course, the show is only one of a kind and belongs to a genre that attracts vilification in academic writing as well as in the media. Nonetheless, in America, as in other countries, the daytime television talk show is an extraordinarily popular phenomenon. Phil Donahue is credited with being the first television talk show host whose show, *Donahue*,

1

became the paradigmatic form for those that were to follow. *Donahue* first aired in 1968, after which the number of talk shows has proliferated; by 1995 'an average of fifteen such shows were being aired in the major US TV markets'.[2] The genre's format requires invited guests to disclose the most intimate aspects of themselves, recalling past and present difficulties and revealing often horrific life experiences to the camera, studio and home audiences for close scrutiny and judgement. Frequently, a guest therapist will offer a diagnosis of a situation, at the same time promoting a recent publication; the shows depend on a cultural acceptance of the validity of talk therapy. The conventional movement of the show is towards a resolution of emotional conflict, coinciding with the closure of the show, but with the anticipation that a new trauma, following the same conventions, will be delivered tomorrow or the next week.

The Oprah Winfrey Show first aired in 1986; the show and its host have since achieved iconic status. Although Oprah courts controversy – particularly over the ways in which she addresses, or fails to address, 'racial' issues[3] – she has attracted a dedicated fan base, of which many members claim that she has enriched their lives. Although Oprah's show is female-centred and the majority of her fans are women, she is of significance to male viewers also. Keith Warren posted a message on the fan website, Oprahwinfrey.de, saying that:

> Every time I am inspired by Oprah I think that it can't get any better than this, but then I will catch another show and she outdoes herself once more with her inspiration. She is truly a gift from God to the world ... [4]

The same website cites *Vanity Fair Magazine* stating that 'Oprah Winfrey arguably has more influence on the culture than any university president, politician, or religious leader, except perhaps the Pope'.[5] This is a huge claim to be made of an individual whose rise to prominence was through a form of television often described as trash TV. The success of *Oprah* has ensured that not only is Winfrey the 'undisputed queen of television talk shows [but also] the self-declared richest black woman in the world on the strength of it'.[6] The show does not just produce a fortune for its host; it is a lucrative commodity for its syndication company King World, generating about half of its profits – $180 million – in 1994.[7] Shattuc (1997) writes that:

> in May 1993 the *Oprah Winfrey Show* attracted a greater number of women viewers than network news programmes, nighttime talk

shows, morning network programmes, and any single daytime soap opera. More than fifteen million people were tuning in daily to watch Oprah Winfrey and her female studio audience debate personal issues with as much fury as an old-time revival meeting or the balanced-budget deliberations in the 1990s congress.[8]

By 1997, *Oprah* was watched by one in ten Americans and syndicated to 120 countries worldwide.[9]

Selfhood and *Oprah*

The central claim that this book makes is that the *Oprah* offers a construction of selfhood that is both recognisable to its audience, reflecting the fragmentation and dislocation characteristic of contemporary culture, but which also holds the attractive potential for a positive and meaningful existence. And, that the contradictions and conflicts inherent in this model are embodied by Oprah and contained through her performance as talk show host. Although *Oprah* does not deal solely with the traumatic and distressing – the mundane and banal often constitute programmes such as 'Dog Extravaganza' (BBC2, 22.5.96) and 'House Detectives' (Sky1, 26.7.96) – the show is most readily associated with scenes like the one in 'Teachers' Salute' described above. The programme most frequently presents a selfhood that emerges from relating stories of experiencing/overcoming problems of varying degrees. The revelation of a trauma is often accompanied by testimonies of endurance and survival that hinge on an individual's ability to transcend difficulty leading to a state – or partial state – of self-realisation. Repeatedly, it is Winfrey's self on display as she offers confession and testimony for public gaze and consumption, practices that are then mirrored by her guests or members of the studio audience as they recount their individual stories.

The show pivots on stories of invited guests that, firstly, reveal examples of a self under siege to the slings and arrows of outrageous fortune and secondly, the struggle to triumph over this adversity. Given this, an understanding of the ways in which self and identity are articulated on the show will lead us to a better understanding of its appeal to a mass audience. Therefore, the central questions addressed in this book are: What *are* the versions of selfhood that are serially represented on the programme? In other words, what models of self are constructed through the ways in which individuals are presented? A second, related question is: given that *Oprah* is a complex text that constructs versions of selfhood with widespread cultural impact in the United States, what kinds of cultural practices and traditions give rise to such a phenomenon as this show? In order to understand a cultural artefact, it is important to situate it within the social and historical context within which it emerges. For this reason it is important to position *Oprah* within a wider frame in order to identify the cultural practices embedded within the programme and which combine to produce the version(s) of self that is (are) displayed and articulated. Through these means we will be able to understand its appeal to a mass audience in the United States.[10]

It is also important to understand what *kind* of text *The Oprah Winfrey Show* is, and so Chapter 1 outlines the debate on television talk shows genre more generally. A number of critics do discuss *Oprah* specifically, but in order that we understand the concerns and issues that are related to these shows, the critical commentary encompasses a range of programmes.

Within this body of work, Foucault's formulation of confessional practice (1978) is frequently cited in order to explain and describe a paradigm of power relations that is observable within the programmes and in the subject positions that are formed through these. Foucault offers a tool for thinking about the process of confession, the spread of the confessional mode from the church and its employment in a series of relationships: 'children and parents, students and educators, patients and psychiatrists'.[11] He shows that the technique of confession has been appropriated by psychological models in which sexual 'truths' are seen as central to the 'truth' of the self. This then posits an essential or natural self that is discoverable through self-disclosure.

However, as Foucault argues, the idea of an essential self is problematic, and it is not my contention that the therapeutic strategies employed on *Oprah* work to uncover the truth of any individual. Rather, I am looking at therapeutic discourse as a cultural practice, one that appears both in academic writing and as a device in popular culture for the articulation of certain kinds of selfhood. Drawing on Foucauldian readings, the show may be seen as a technology for the production of subject positions. However, in analysing Oprah, we need to extend our attention beyond the technique of confession. There is a need to consider, for instance, the role of the equally complex cultural practice of testimony. I have noted that testimony is a textually important element of *Oprah* in that individuals articulate self-realisation and self-esteem; and, as Radstone (2001) has indicated, 'testimony needs to be mapped alongside and in relation to confession'.[12] This is undeveloped in the existing literature on the genre of talk shows. Those commentators that have appropriated Foucault – such as Shattuc (1997), Landman (1995), Young (1996) – do so with the aim of analysing the degree to which public confession works to normalise dominant social codes, and/or represents liberation from restrictive social practices (such as licence to speak the unspeakable). Useful as this approach is, it produces a polarised debate which, at present, hinges on a talk show-as-good-space/talk show-as-bad-space dichotomy. In order to advance our understanding of the show, I want to move beyond this dichotomy through a more nuanced recognition of the combination of cultural practices at work.

My own study accepts the popularity of *Oprah* as given and explores it from this position in order to understand the dynamics of the show and, therefore, its appeal to a mass audience. To reiterate my central questions: what models of self are represented on *Oprah*, and what kinds of cultural practices give rise to it? Because the show is a complex construct of conflicting traditions, cultural techniques and discourses, Bakhtin's notions of carnival and grotesque realism, dialogism and heteroglossia offer a way into thinking about the constellation of cultural practices that form the programme. The point at which Bakhtin becomes most useful is in my analysis of the Oprah persona in Chapter 5. His theory of the 'grotesque' opens up ways of thinking about Oprah, her body and her performance that stand at the heart of the programme. For this reason, I draw on Bakhtin's dialogic model of carnival – and related ideas of the grotesque – to explain the convergence of discourses on a television programme that has elements of what can be called 'grotesque performance' at the heart of it. This therefore does not represent a totalising model for this book, but can be used to address elements of *Oprah* that are as yet not fully recognised in contemporary accounts of the programme. The primary concepts drawn from Bakhtin are introduced here.

Firstly, the idea of dialogism is important to an understanding of the carnivalesque dynamics of *Oprah*. It acknowledges human interaction as creative, social, ideological and, crucially for my purposes here, historically specific. The dialogic approach sees language as a generative process that stems from social interaction:

> subjectivity is thus produced on the *'borderline'* where inner experience and social world meet, and they meet in signs – words...This borderzone of continuous interaction between individual consciousness, itself comprised of signs, and an outer world of signs is the location of all creative activity[13] (emphasis in original).

If we take this model and broaden its application to incorporate a system that includes the non-verbal, it becomes possible to apply it to *The*

Oprah Winfrey Show. The discourses produced on the programme are a result of a dialogic engagement between the discursive practices that shape the show – the television industry, entertainment conventions, the celebrity system, therapeutic sensibility and bourgeois expertise – and the individual everyday experiences of those who speak on the show and who watch from a distance at home.

Heteroglossia refers to the 'conflict between "centripetal" and "centrifugal", "official" and "unofficial" discourses... [It] foregrounds the clash of antagonistic forces'.[14] Heteroglossia, therefore, destroys the possibility of any unitary meaning in language. Official consciousness represents that which is in accord with stable, fully formed social values of morality, laws, of class and worldview; unofficial consciousness is also socially and historically determined but is incompletely formed, even as inner speech. Unofficial consciousness has therefore the potential to be livelier than the official and contains the possibility to 'ultimately burst asunder the system of ideology'.[15] Morris (1994) argues that the dialogue/conflict between official and unofficial consciousness lies at the heart of Bakhtin's theory of carnival.

I argue that *Oprah* operates as the borderzone in which the dialectical relation between the multiple, official discourses that both surrounds and structures the show (including Oprah's persona), and the unofficial discourses of the participants is played out. As a borderzone, the show offers a space of interaction between the outer social world with its norms, laws and values and the inner world of private experience. The discourses of the dominant culture meet and combine with those of the folk and the everyday to produce the (carnivalesque) process through which new forms of subjectivity are created, which are in part informed by hegemonic forces but which are also separate from them.

Bakhtin's work (1968) focuses on the Mediaeval Renaissance period, the transition of pre-modern to modern society, that produced a flowering of culture through the advent of the printing press, and through travel which resulted in new global relations. However, Bakhtin's assertion that every age brings about its own official speech lends a flexibility to his idea of the carnivalesque that enables a critique of contemporary cultural practices.[16] As aesthetic activity is the product of a dialogue between individuals, it is clear that the meaning given to any art form will have a cultural and historical specificity that marks its place in time. 'A new type of communication always creates new forms of speech or a new meaning given to old forms.'[17] I am not proposing here that *Oprah* is the re-creation of a televisual carnival, but that carnivalesque principles are in play on the show, enabling a folk language as well as the official discourses of the dominant culture to be articulated. This is particularly important when we consider the body of Oprah that is at the centre of this aesthetic activity. In turn, a consideration of Oprah-as-grotesque allows me to offer a formulation of *Oprah* as carnivalesque.

Cultural histories and cultural practices

Chapter 2 examines the cultural context in which the programme is produced and consumed. I argue that *Oprah* presents a paradigm of self that has its origins in black American culture and that the programme should be understood in relation to (and arising out of) the oral and literary traditions associated with that culture. This then combines with two other cultural practices evident in mainstream American culture to produce a text that is hybrid in form: confession and therapeutic cure, and commodification and the system of celebrity. I argue that one of the models of selfhood offered by a body of black American feminists is more deeply insinuated within *Oprah* than has been hitherto acknow-ledged. And that this model of self – in which individuals are placed in relation to others – is articulated with cultural practices of commodity and consumerism, the therapeutic and confession to produce a dynamic specific to the show.

In doing this, I turn to the fiction of Toni Morrison and Alice Walker because Winfrey is associated, through her acting roles in the film versions of their novels – *Beloved* (1998) and *The Color Purple* (1985) respectively. This has led me to explore the academic writings of these authors as well as the scholarly work that adopts a similar position such as Collins' *Black Feminist Thought* (1991), hooks' *Yearning: Race, Gender, and Cultural Politics* (1991) and Hine's *Hine Sight: Black Women and the Reconstruction of American History* (1994).[18]

I have already employed the term 'tradition' in relation to established cultural practices. However, this is a term that has to be used with caution. As Paul Gilroy points out, the idea of tradition signals what he describes as 'cultural insiderism' representing a cluster of 'rhetorical strategies' that supply a sense of absolute ethnic difference, national identity and cultural kinship.[19] This then suggests the possibility of a stable, rooted identity set within distinct, unchanging and non-porous boundaries. Through his concept of the black Atlantic, Gilroy (1993) demonstrates the fluid exchange of ideas and practices that occurs between nations and between groups of peoples. The black Atlantic therefore represents the 'rhizomorphic, fractural structure of [a] transcultural, international formation' which works against the (narrow) nationalistic address common in both English and African American studies.[20] Further, and with a relevance particular to my work, Gilroy argues that the legacy claimed by African Americans is only partly their 'absolute ethnic property'. Read through the concept of the black Atlantic, it is evident that this legacy also has significance for peoples of the Caribbean, Europe, Africa and America.[21]

I have indicated that I will be drawing on the nexus of cultural ideas and practices that emerge from within one African American tradition that foregrounds the possibility of active agency. This is not because I refute Gilroy's claims, but it is of significance that on her show Winfrey frequently describes herself as an African American. Through her film roles and her promotion of and admiration for work by black feminist writers such as Walker, Morrison, and Maya Angelou, Winfrey positions herself alongside people who articulate a particular view of self. This formulation of individual identity is then located within a shared history and experience. I need now to explain my use of the term 'tradition'.

I use tradition to signal the sets of experiences explored and explained by a group of people who see themselves as connected to one another. This is not to say that this book is drawing on a set of ideas that are exclusively the province of African Americans, or that the cluster of ideas used represents an impermeable membrane isolating the individuals that it surrounds: claims of essentialism are limiting and reductive. However, with all of the above qualifications in mind, I draw on a body of work and practices that emerge from within a particular group of people who define themselves as African American. This represents a methodological tool that I use as a 'chronotope' – 'an optic for reading texts as X-rays of the forces at work in the culture system from which they spring'[22] – through which to examine *Oprah*.

Oprah Winfrey is a woman who calls attention to her (black) skin colour not only on her programme, but also in extra-textual interviews that take place in a variety of media. For example, in a show that discusses her belief in the importance of spiritual wealth in relation to material wealth ('You Too Can Realise Your Dreams', Channel 5, 14.7.98) she says 'I was a Negro child. Now I'm an African American woman.' Reminding her audience that they 'know all the stories', she none-theless reiterates the fact that she 'came from the most segregated state – Mississippi'. This has a specific resonance, as the civil rights move-ment's struggle to overturn the Jim Crow laws is an element of recent American history. In another programme – 'Problems with Parenting' (Channel 5, 2.7.98) – she declares that as a child she thought that 'all white children were terrible', demonstrating a process of Othering premised on skin colour. During a television interview with Michael Parkinson, a British celebrity chat show host, (BBC1, 19.2.99) in which she was promoting the film *Beloved*, she discusses an incident that took place while on location in southern America and in a store. Waiting to be served, she realised that the colour of her skin rendered her invisible to the staff who worked there – until her face was recognised. Although the colour of her skin is not the sole way in which Oprah Winfrey defines herself, it clearly constitutes a significant element of her sense of selfhood.

The model of self articulated by these black feminist scholars can be juxtaposed with an alternative view of selfhood that has emerged from within the canon of American cultural criticism. I am placing my investigation of *Oprah* within the context of this work because it enables us to think through issues of commodity and consumption and their relation to ideas of the therapeutic. The relevance of this lies, in part, in the ways in which *Oprah* – and television talk shows – have been evaluated as the commodification of individual distress. In addition, the dominant discourse of this criticism also posits a disempowered self in relation to the social harm effected by the mass consumption of television shows more generally. Both of these positions are tied to the financial prerogatives of the television industry. The discourses of social harm and cultural anxiety are important for two main reasons. Firstly, the process of commercialism *does* influence the shape of the programme and the presentation of individuals within it. Secondly, in order to understand something of the construction of the Oprah persona, we need to acknowledge the part that economic systems play in creating a figure with mass popular appeal. This latter point is key as the Oprah construction lies at the core of the programme and therefore our understanding of *Oprah* depends, largely, on our understanding of Oprah.

This body of work articulates a generalised cultural anxiety that is tied to the culture of consumption, commodification, technological advance and the fragmentation of self-identity. It emerged from a group of intellectuals who fled from Europe in the 1930s and whose influence (through the dissemination of their ideas in universities) is mainly felt in two areas: the Frankfurt School and in psychoanalysis. Key intellectuals within the Frankfurt School, such as Theodore Adorno and Herbert Marcuse, have been highly influential in the debate concerning mass culture and high culture; those within the field of psychoanalysis, such as Eric Fromm and Erik Erikson, influenced observers of the national (social) character. The work on 'national character' by intellectuals such as Philip Rieff, David Riesman, and Christopher Lasch emerges from the former two schools of thought and engages psychoanalytic theories in the service of examining the American personality in relation to the apparent debilitating effects of mass media and consumerism.

Much post-Second World War writing concerning American culture within this body of thought conveys a sense of nihilism and an attendant loss of agency. These writers argue that there has been a loss of human individuality and difference amongst the sea of image-producing technology that has reduced life to the flat 'one-dimensional' surface that is (re)presentation. While consistently deploring the 'triumph of the therapeutic'[23], these influential post-war American cultural critics have variously deployed psychoanalytic models of mind to explore and articulate their argument. Tracking this particular line of thought will enable me to delineate a sense of anxiety that is evident from before the Second World War, but that appears to have increased in the post-war years. My particular focus will be on the model of self that these writers construct. However, these writings are present as objects of critical and historical analysis, and do not represent methodological prototypes for my own argument. I will not be drawing on psychoanalysis for my own examination of *Oprah*. Rather, I am following on from Mimi White, who does not advocate a psychoanalytic approach to cultural criticism but who suggests that the:

> profusion of the therapeutic in everyday and popular media culture might be seen as one manifestation of a larger cultural interest that is paralleled in the academic sphere in psychoanalytic and psychological discourses. In this light, the two spheres can be played off one against the other, mutually interrogating and illuminating, without subsuming one within the other.[24]

Thus, I am interested in identifying both the influence of psychoanalysis on the show itself and the way in which it has been evaluated.

A textual analysis of *Oprah*

The two conflicting traditions of thought discussed above will inform my textual analysis of *The Oprah Winfrey Show*. This will enable an examination of the versions of self articulated on the show and their relation to a wider set of cultural practices. I draw on a sample of 58 *Oprah* shows that were broadcast in the United Kingdom between October 1995 and July 1996.[25] The sample programmes that form the basis of my analysis constitute a random selection and have not been selected for any specific purpose – such as the examination of a particular recurring theme. This is done in order that I may investigate a broad and typical cross-section of shows that reflect the viewing experience of a regular audience. However, it should also be noted that these programmes were broadcast on British television. This means that the place occupied in the daytime schedule may well differ from that for American broadcast. In addition, a significant number of the shows I taped were broadcast on BBC2, a non-commercial television station, and so do not have the commercial breaks that form a part of the overall viewing experience for American audiences. Nonetheless, these limitations do not represent a substantial difficulty. Firstly, the shows in my sample are a part of the daytime television scheduling in Britain as they are in America, and secondly, evidence of commercial breaks within the programmes remain even when broadcast on non-commercial television. The reason for this is that Winfrey frequently signals the beginning of an advertising break and marks the return to the show through her reintroduction of that show's topic, in addition to supplying home audiences with information about conversation that has taken place while the show has been off air.

Textual analysis: confession, testimony and narrative

Conducting a textual analysis enables me to concentrate on (a) the form of self-expression that arises through the discursive practice of confession and the subject positions that are produced in relation to it, and (b) the narratives spoken by the guests. Chapter 3 focuses on a single programme, offering a detailed analysis of the confessional discourse that is central to *Oprah* and which functions as the foundation of the relationship between Oprah, her guests and the audience. In discussing this show, I draw on Foucault's discussion of confession as an 'agency of truth and power in Western society'.[26] White (1992) argues that 'confession and therapeutic discourse centrally figure as narrative and narrational strategies in television in the United States...Problems and their solutions are narrativized in terms of confessional relations...Self-identity and social recognition...hinge on participation in the process of mediated confession'.[27] Examining its history, Foucault argues that confession is a technology that is used in a range of practices. 'The confession has spread its effects far and wide. It plays a part in justice, medicine, education, family relationships, and love relations, in the most ordinary affairs of life...Western man has become a confessing animal.'[28] The act of confessing itself displays the power relations inherent in a process that operates to make visible, define, judge, codify, normalise and to exclude.

> The confession is a ritual of discourse in which the speaking subject is also the subject of the statement; it is also a ritual that unfolds within a power relationship, for one does not confess without the presence (or virtual presence) of a partner who is not simply interlocutor but the authority who requires the confession, prescribes and appreciates it, and intervenes in order to judge, punish, forgive, console and reconcile; a ritual in which the truth is corroborated by the obstacles and resistances it has had to surmount in order to be formulated; and finally, a ritual in which the expression alone, independently of its external consequences, produces intrinsic modifications in the person who articulates it: it exonerates, redeems, and purifies him; it unburdens him of his wrongs, liberates him, and promises salvation.[29]

The 'ritual of discourse' that takes place between Winfrey and her audience, and between the guests and Winfrey will be familiar to participants and audience alike – as White says 'All [television] viewers are always already inexorably caught up in the confessional mode...'.[30] Winfrey is the authority within the 'power relationship' to whom confession is offered, but she also moves from this position to that of confessor. By putting herself in this one-down position – the means by which individuals can be seen to be placing themselves in a position of less, rather than more, power – she effaces her star persona, conveying a sense of equality. Although both she and her audiences are aware that this is a fictitious relationship, it contributes to the sense of intimacy engendered by the confessional exchange and validates Winfrey's claim to be Every Woman – a declaration she makes of herself in the shows. In addition, this shift endows Winfrey with another form of power and authority, one that derives from personal experience: I know because I have been there too.

Related to this is the practice of testimony that is also a key aspect of the staging of individual narratives – this is addressed in Chapter 4. A small sample of *Oprah* shows is used to examine closely the structure of the guest's narratives and the placement of self within them. Here, I look at the ways in which stories are used to position the speaker, and at the positions adopted. Although parts of the narratives supplied by Winfrey and her guests may concern feelings of worthlessness, fear or shame, the expression of this is not always confessional in nature as redemption and exoneration is often neither sought nor offered. Thus, it will become evident that on *Oprah* the practice of confession is more tempered by testimonial discourse than has hitherto been acknowledged, and that the practice of testimony is key in the enactment of empowerment. This occurs through the claiming of knowledge and, subsequently, self-esteem.

Jane Shattuc discusses the testimonial nature of the discourse heard on such programmes in relation to the emancipatory practices of feminism and the links to religious practices:

> Because the shows are public arenas they do not evoke the intimacy and thoroughness of therapy or even consciousness raising groups. But because of their ties to a social ideology such as feminism, their discursive structure involves testimonials rather than confessions...The testimonial or witnessing has a long history in American fundamentalism and media evangelism. And it has been reinvigorated in the twelve-step movement, a secular model of witnessing. The original religious sense of the practice means the public testimony given by Christian witnesses to Christ and his saving power. Within evangelism the act of standing up and speaking one's religious experience is a social obligation...[31]

Although reciting one's story is clearly not therapy; the engagement of the guest expert/therapist within the narrative is merely a *representation* of therapeutic practice. However, Shattuc's reflections on the testimonial are pertinent here. The tradition of evangelism is what gives form and meaning to the testimonials heard on *Oprah*, albeit in a secular mode. The speakers stand and bear witness to the healing powers of self-renewal and regeneration. The history of religious confessional and testimonial practices is long and complex and will not be discussed here. However, I will be making links between the practice of testimony in the black church along with the call and response paradigm, demonstrating that it offers a useful insight into the dynamics of *The Oprah Winfrey Show*. My argument is that the process of confession and testimony offers the means of voicing a self that is empowered. This opens up a way of thinking about *Oprah* as a forum for 'talking back' described by hooks (1990) thus:

> Moving from silence into speech is for the oppressed, the colonised, the exploited, and those who stand and struggle side by side, a gesture of defiance that heals, that makes new life, and new growth possible.

It is the act of speech, of 'talking back' that is no mere gesture of empty words, that is the expression of moving from object to subject, that is the liberated voice.[32]

It is important to note here that in the guests' narratives, self-realisation and self-esteem mark the movement from victim to survivor; this is a repeating pattern of the stories recounted on the show. Although not of direct influence, Propp's structural account (1928) of recurring narrative patterns in folktales[33] has suggested a way of thinking about stories and the meanings that are inherent within a repeating form. So, rather than undertaking a content analysis of the guests' stories, I look at the emergent patterns that the narratives form over a series of shows and how they work to create an overarching meaning.

Textual analysis: celebrity and Oprah

The construction of the Oprah persona that is presented on the programme itself and enhanced through extra-textual material is examined in Chapter 5. It is my contention that the persona of any talk show host supplies an inflection to an otherwise formulaic product and is therefore central to the meanings generated by that programme. The Oprah persona is highly complex and structured to provide a meaningful point of reference to a 'racially' mixed audience. She embodies a series of conflicting and contradictory cultural formations: the constructions of self that arise from the African American community with which she aligns herself, the culture of anxiety and the therapeutic. These are all bound up with the system of celebrity that operates as a manifestation of the power and mobility of capital in the interests of consumerism and profit. I examine the ways in which Oprah negotiates these conflicts and the contradiction of being simultaneously extra-ordinary (a celebrity) and ordinary. I will reflect on the degree to which the notion of spectacle, with all its postmodern connotations, impacts on the presentation of self on *Oprah* and on the ways in which this is informed by the African American concepts of self-identity.

In considering the Oprah construction, I use Bakhtin's notion of 'grotesque realism' – the symbolic imagery of carnival – and which he insists is 'deeply positive'. This term is helpful in understanding the ways in which the conflicting, contradictory discourses combine to produce the Oprah persona and which produce the meaning(s) of the show itself. Ambivalent in its imagery, carnival is the affirmative articulation of the dual processes of death and becoming. Degradation, the essential axiom of grotesque realism, is the lowering of all that is high and ideal in order that something new may be born: grotesque imagery is a reflection of transformative possibilities. So, the principles of growth and regeneration are articulated not through the biological individual or bourgeois ego 'but in the people... who are continually growing and renewed'.[34] The grotesque body is that which is expressive of the death/birth cycle, is the embodiment of transformation and becoming.

Taken all together, carnival – with its dialogic relationship between official and unofficial culture, its frank language and behaviour, the authority of the folk and the creation of something new based on old forms – provides a framework that offers a way of thinking about the cultural practices, and their relations, that are mobilised during *The Oprah Winfrey Show*. At the centre of the show is Oprah's (grotesque) persona that is tied to the practice of sharing private experience, thereby broadening the base for a power that is political.

1
About Television Talk Shows

The purpose of this chapter is to provide a map of the existing debate on television talk shows within media studies, and to delineate the range of positions currently available within it. The reason for this is to firstly introduce the reader who may be unfamiliar with this field of study to the range of issues which, when considered collectively, can shed a bright light on the nature of confessional talk shows as well as the critical responses to them. So, while I may disagree with certain positions held, the talk show debate highlights the matrix of processes at play within the programmes.

Secondly, in outlining the work carried out by others, my own approach and methodology becomes apparent. Understanding the genre which is synonymous with Oprah Winfrey is an important starting point from which to uncover the nature of her celebrity persona. In examining the debate as it currently stands, I think we can begin to understand something of the complexity of the shows. Further, a survey of this nature will reveal the ways in which a study of the sort I am conducting for this book advances our understanding and knowledge of the dynamics that constitute *The Oprah Winfrey Show* and the Oprah celebrity persona. It should be noted that the debate does not engage with the production of celebrity *per se*, and that I am using it here as a building block towards developing an understanding of the nature of Oprah's celebrity. It is clear that the personality and mode of operation of the talk show host inflects their respective shows with specific meanings. Nonetheless, there are characteristics that are common to all; it is these that are explored in this chapter.

The Oprah Winfrey Show is a cultural phenomenon that has achieved iconic status in America; the programme itself is constituted through a number of conflicting discourses that work to produce a complex text that is polysemic in nature, difficult to read and hard to categorise. The show is situated within a highly contested genre of popular entertainment which, overall, is difficult to catalogue because although talk shows share some formal qualities, individual programmes vary widely. This variation has a lot to do with the persona of the host who facilitates the proceedings and the relationship they engender with their studio guests and audiences. In addition, the shows have changed over the past twenty years.[1] Nonetheless, within the body of cultural criticism on television talk shows, there is an emergent literature that has formulated a description of the genre. Jane Shattuc supplies a constructive typology that distinguishes issue-oriented talk shows, such as *Oprah*, *Geraldo*, *Sally Jessie Raphael* and *Donahue*, from the rash of more sensational shows which date from 1991 with the *Jerry Springer Show*, *Jenny Jones*, *Montel Williams* and *Ricki Lake* (1993). Shattuc (1997) describes issue-oriented shows as those that can be formally characterised in the following ways: content is sourced from personal experiences that reflect contemporary social issues; active audience participation; the 'moral authority' that resides in the host and/or guest expert; by their address to a female audience; and by being produced by non-network companies and broadcast on network affiliated stations.[2]

Whilst Shattuc usefully delineates the characteristics of issue-orientated shows and separates them from the later, more sensational form, the wider debate on talk shows often does not draw such distinctions. The debate is caught in a set of oppositional judgements. On the one hand, there is the body of writing that derides talk shows, framing them as trashy manifestations of mass/popular culture, exploiting the participants for commercial gain, and/or that they work to recuperate the individual within dominant discourse. On the other, there are those who see talk shows as a discursive space for the construction of a positive self-identity, a site in which marginalised voices not usually given a public platform can make themselves heard. This is a frequent dichotomy structuring cultural criticism and the discussion on popular culture, ideology and politics. However, there is something missing from these accounts of the talk show genre. In adhering to a set of positions defined through the high culture/low culture dialectic,[3] the questions of *how* these shows are constructed and what sorts of meanings can be attributed to them remain muted. In addition, the conflation of the earlier, issue-oriented shows with the later, more sensational programmes occludes certain characteristics that are important in the consideration of them as cultural texts. As Shattuc demonstrates in *The Talking Cure* (1997), the prevalence of talk shows on daytime television has grown significantly over the past twenty years. The question of why this might be the case aside from acknowledging the political economy of the television industry remains only partially answered. To remain within the good space/bad space binary is to restrict our understanding of talk shows, so a move away from this dichotomy is needed in order to develop a more complex understanding of the shows' construction and of their function in popular culture.

As well as adhering to one or other position within the dichotomy, there is a tendency for commentators to identify and single out a single element of a show that is then drawn on to offer a more generalised reading of what functions the programmes perform. The focus variously rests on the social effects of talk shows, the representation of racial and/ or sexual identities, the role of confessional discourse and the therapeutic. All of these positions provide some useful insights on the talk show genre, but in the eagerness to apportion judgement, gaps remain, preventing a broader understanding of this cultural form. Another problem is the single-issue focus. On the one hand, exploring a talk show through its presentation of sexuality, 'race', or gender relations does at least open up a dialogue through which the programmes can be conceptualised in relation to popular culture. On the other hand, on *Oprah* a single issue is frequently dealt with in a variety of ways over a range of programmes: this is presumably because of the commercial need to address a variegated audience. So, meaning accrues over time and, I would argue, hinges on the ways in which the host mediates the issues presented and on his/her relation with the guests and audience. This brings me to a further problem in attempting to define the meaning inherent within a show: that of the audience. It is beyond the scope of this book to incorporate empirical research on audience responses to *Oprah*, but it does have to be acknowledged that we cannot assume what the audience is doing with these texts, what meanings are being generated, without actually asking it.[4] Indeed, there is a difficulty in knowing whom it is that comprises the audience beyond the demographics offered by commercial companies such as A.C. Nielson. However, with this – very significant – qualification in mind, I would posit that it is more fruitful to explore *Oprah* across the range of issues and their representation, as this would more closely resemble the practice and experience of regular viewers.

Frequently positioned as trash TV, talk shows are cited as representing the worst excesses of cheap television, signalling the 'dumbing down' of culture. This arguably is where moral judgements are most explicit: frequently alarmist in tone, commentaries denigrate talk shows on the grounds that they transgress boundaries of 'good taste', inspire and require 'bad' behaviour, publicise that which should remain within the private realm and signify a cultural pollutant. Vicki Abt and Mel Seesholtz offer a clear example of this position; their work will be discussed in some detail below. The 'trash TV' position does have some justification. Talk shows *are* cheap television, attract good viewing figures and represent a sound financial proposition for producers. An argument could be made, then, that display of private matters for public spectacle and commercial gain reduces individual dis-ease to a commodity, a process in which the consumers (viewers) are commodified as well. The economics of the television industry are beyond refutation and are intrinsic to the production of talk shows. Nonetheless, we are left with questions such as who are the arbiters of taste and by what criteria are they (self) selected, and on what grounds is the display of emotion deemed unacceptable in the public sphere? This position can tell us something about the prevalence of ideas that are connected to the cultural anxiety articulated by the elite cultural critics which will be discussed in Chapter 2 – and the role of television within this – but it tells us little about the programmes themselves. Another angle in the trash TV position is that which posits talk shows as a vehicle that works to reincorporate aberrant personalities into hegemonic discourse. Therapy and confessional discourse is seen by some as the means of recuperation. The problem articulated here is twofold. Firstly, the therapeutic is too closely aligned with individualism to be of value in the production of a wider political debate. In assuming that an individual has sole corrective responsibility, the focus remains at the microlevel, leaving social practices that give rise to inequality, poverty, abuse and gender inequity unchallenged. The second problem identified in this position is the normative function of therapeutic and confessional discourse. As a normative corrective to the kinds of 'dysfunctions' displayed on the shows, the therapeutic strategy works to create subject positions that reinforce hegemonic cultural and social values. Landman (1995, 1996), Epstein and Steinberg (1995) and McLaughlin (1993)[5] are among those who take this view; their work will also be considered in detail below.

It is certainly the case that in presenting individuals as the authors of their own fate – which *Oprah* most definitely does – the broader cultural and social attitudes do often go unchallenged. However, if what is meant by the term 'political activity' is shifted, the focus on the individual can be seen in a different light. Cruikshank's commentary (1993) on the self-esteem project of the California Task Force provides a different perspective. This is a political project that is premised on the idea that the self-esteem fostered in an individual can have a profoundly positive impact on the social body as a whole. Strategies of empowerment and self-help enable a politically active self that is linked to goals of social order and stability.[6] The idea that individuals can experience empowerment through self-esteem may be self-evident. But Cruikshank takes this further by suggesting that self-esteem constitutes a form of power that produces an agency that actively and positively impacts on the wider social context. This, I would argue, more closely resembles the processes of self-expression that take place on *The Oprah Winfrey Show*, and is closely tied to Oprah's celebrity persona.

There are commentators such as Wayne Munson, Donal Carbaugh and Paolo Carpignano *et al.* who see talk shows as emancipatory, as a site of empowerment in that they open up a public forum for debate in which the everyday experience of individuals is the privileged discourse. Here, talk shows represent a space of radical possibilities, whether on the grounds that they allow for the frank discussion of sex and sexuality, employ a feminist framework, or facilitate an emotional intelligence. Within the shows, emotion and emotional issues are seen to emphasise the link between affect and self-identity, which are therefore lent an authority otherwise absent from much mainstream popular culture; it is this that forms the locus of political content. This is an argument that is closer to my own. The shows do indeed foster an emotional literacy that is traditionally the province of the feminine; the role of emotional talk is important and should not be dismissed. However, as stated earlier, the shows are constructed for a female audience, therefore, we cannot be too surprised that emotions provide both a language and currency for evaluating self and relationships with others. In relation to the wider, feminist debate, what I am interested in is the degree to which some aspects of the black feminist movement are implicated in *Oprah* and the degree to which these have shaped the form and content of the presentation of self.

The role of the expert in relation to the lay guest is more problematic. On *Oprah*, the expert voice is on occasions used to frame and explain the account of experience offered by a participant as well as to offer prescriptive advice. However, there are other instances where the voice of the lay individual is most prominently heard and without the need for bourgeois, expert validation. This will be explored further in my textual analysis in Chapters 3–5.

Most interesting of all the literature on the genre of talk shows is that which is ambivalent in response. Without explicitly doing so, writers such as Shattuc (1997), Landman (1996) and Gamson (1998a)[7] identify the complex, polysemic nature of the texts. Here, it is recognised that talk shows frequently perform contradictory functions: the shows can be emancipatory *and* exploitative, feminist *and* apolitical. Talk shows *are* ambivalent texts but what can we make of this? In fact, this ambivalence illuminates one of the more interesting aspects of Oprah: the ways in which she manages and contains conflicting discourses; the ways in which her persona is the embodiment of these conflicts. It is from here that the Bakhtinian idea of the carnivalesque supplies us with a language through which to discuss and understand the genre and Oprah. It is my contention that these shows cannot be properly understood without situating them within the set of historical and cultural practices that give form to them and through which they may be read. These discursive practices converge and combine to produce a cultural form that is carnivalesque in nature.

The review of the critical literature, rather than focusing on *The Oprah Winfrey Show*, encompasses a range of shows within the genre. This is because relatively little writing is devoted solely to *Oprah*, rather, the show is more often grouped with other programmes – as is particularly the case for writers within the trash TV position. Through just a cursory glance at a range of programmes across the genre, it becomes obvious that while they operate under the same rubric – the disclosure of a deeply personal aspect of an individual life – the shows do in fact differ in tone and style. These differences are largely defined by and through the host, and are dependent on target audiences. Although this is hinted at in the literature through a comparison of the values lent by, for example, Phil Donahue (white, male, liberal) as distinct from those offered by Oprah Winfrey (black, female, feminist), this difference remains undeveloped.

Trash TV and the public display of emotional talk

Social effects of talk shows

There is a collection of critical material that analyses the impact of talk shows on the social body. This is located within the field of media studies that has already provided an extensive literature on representation, ideology, power, and subjectivity and subversion. The growth of television talk shows has prompted a debate that adopts a variety of positions. One – Frankfurt School influenced[8] – is that which signals alarm at the growth and prevalence of talk shows on the grounds that they constitute a cultural pollutant. Here, links are made between popular therapy, TV and social harm. Teresa Keller is, like me, interested in how trash TV has come to be framed and further asks if the concern over it is justified. She considers which shows are commonly thought of as trash: are they really trash and if so, why?[9] Keller's work (1993) provides a useful starting point in that she delineates characteristics that mark this form of television, presenting points of reference from which to consider more specific issues.

Keller's perspective is formed by the public debate that arose during the 1990s over the apparent growth of trash television, a term that is interchanged with 'tabloid', 'shock' and 'reality' TV, all forms that exploit fear by privileging the emotional over the rational. Whilst not offering any analysis of the conditions that gave rise to such programming, Keller does delineate elements that combine to produce this degraded form of television, singling out news magazine programmes and talk shows as the worst proponents of trash TV. For Keller, a genre is defined as trashy by a content of sex and violence, when boundaries between news and entertainment are blurred, by sensational language and the accompanying music that prescribes audience response, and by the re-creations of actual events. I would add to this that programmes characterised as trash are frequently cheap to produce and have an emotional component at their core thereby foregrounding subjectivity.[10] Thus these programmes attract the charge of commercial exploitation of the emotionally vulnerable.

However useful in pointing out the defining aesthetics of trash TV, Keller's work has its limits. Although she disparages the apparent blurring of the boundaries between news and entertainment, she herself conflates news magazine programmes with talk shows. Keller concludes:

> Not all talk shows and news/magazines are trash, and content varies among episodes. Oprah, Phil, Sally, and Geraldo do all address serious topics and often make a useful contribution to television fare. But there are unattractive qualities among editions of these shows...when they aim for emotional rather than intellectual response. They exploit fear...Stories are woven around a small part of the truth, often focussing on minute details of sex and sexual dysfunction, of murder, rape, incest and other examples of human disregard for other human life and dignity...But in the United States, our basic philosophy is that if we err, we err on the side of freedom. Some television is trash, but we just have to grin and bear it...and maintain confidence that individual values and good taste will prevail.[11]

While Keller's typology of trash TV is helpful in identifying characteristics that mark it, she constructs her argument with broad brush-strokes that conflate a range of programmes across genres and that leave talk shows underdescribed. The complex nature of talk shows is thus effaced. She avoids an interrogation of the notion of 'good taste', who the arbiters of taste may be, or what meaning may lie in the reliance on the emotional – a sign of bad taste in Keller's formulations. The 'useful contribution' that a number of talk shows offer is swept aside or negated through Keller's insistence that the emotional signals degradation, a trivialisation of serious matters that, in her terms, require an intellectual (rational) response.

The display of emotional life

If we sweep aside the emotion in the talk show, we would be very limited in our understanding of the Oprah as her persona is constructed through appeals to precisely this; emotional responses to life experiences form the basis on which the show is built. Eva Illouz offers a way out of this stalemate. Recognising that emotional intimacy is a theme 'somewhat neglected by many students of talk shows'[12] she takes a range of issue-oriented shows and looks for emergent 'patterns of meaning'[13] through which to examine emotional discourse and the meaning in the deployment of affect. Situating her analysis within the social and cultural context 'from which talk shows emerge and in which they in turn make sense' Illouz (1999) employs an 'eclectic strategy by bouncing the codes and conventions of talk shows against the backdrop of contemporary political ideas, recent transformations of the family...and the transformations that modernity has brought to processes of identity formation'.[14] The result of her analysis reveals broad – rather than specific – patterns of meaning, demonstrating that emotional talk is a way of framing embattled relations that threaten the integrity of the self. This, Illouz argues, is what lends both moral and cultural meaning to talk shows. As a structure for understanding the relationship between self and others, the emotions in talk shows, 'and perhaps in America at large', offer ways of talking about 'a broken (or longed for) social solidarity'.[15] Emotion becomes the only reliable currency once moral prescriptions can no longer be relied upon; it takes the place of legal and moral frameworks with which to make sense of the struggles of everyday life in the age of late capitalism. And talk shows, responding to this perceived yearning for social solidarity, are a 'unique cultural forum because they dwell on emotions as a...component of interactions'.[16]

Illouz's hermeneutic analysis opens up the possibility of thinking about the emotional currency – frequently evoked as the (bad) opposite of reasoned debate – of talk shows. Her work demonstrates the validity of emotional talk on television and the cultural/political uses to which it may be put. Emotions frequently underpin the narratives recounted on *Oprah* according them with meaning, and by extension they operate to validate the speaker. The significance of this will be discussed in Chapter 4. Illouz's position offers us a more textured approach to understanding talk shows than that proffered by Keller. As she (Illouz) states 'a critical evaluation of popular culture can properly take place only *after we have elucidated its meanings*'[17] (emphasis in original).

The free flow of emotional expression on *The Oprah Winfrey Show* does stand in place of political interrogation of social and cultural conditions. However, I would argue that this, rather than signalling a loss of moral framework, actually constitutes a moral code that places self in relationship with significant others and is a morality that pervades the majority of the shows. Nonetheless, in order to 'elucidate the meanings' that are specific to *Oprah*, I would argue that we need not just look to the participants' stories – which *are* invested with emotion – but also to the relationship between Winfrey and her guests and viewers. This is also the result of an emotional engagement that becomes embodied within the persona of the host and is key to our understanding the meanings generated by the show. This is examined in detail in Chapter 5.

Keller's position equating emotion with trivia, is interesting for the way in which it exposes the value systems structuring patriarchal culture. In line with this is the authoritative voice of the (academic) expert who pillories talk shows on the premise that 'ordinary' people talking publicly about troubling private and personal issues is a mark of cultural degradation. This is a voice that assumes a moral guardianship, raising issues of power that are left unproblematised.

The apparent denigration of cultural values signalled by the display of emotion is expanded in Vicki Abt and Mel Seesholtz's 'The Shameless World of Phil, Sally and Oprah: Television Talk Shows and the Deconstructing of Society'.[18] Here we have a clear summary of the objections that are frequently raised about talk shows and that represent a debate around the issue of power but without naming it as such. In other words, these arguments are unself-consciously premised on the assumption that the voice of the intellectual and/or clinical practitioner should be heard over that of the lay individual. That the shows may offer the (empowering) possibility of self-definition is ignored or implicitly refuted in the overarching concern for maintaining a bourgeois morality that is predicated on the separation of the private/public spheres.

Assuming this position, Abt and Seesholtz wonder what 'this constant attention [by "Phil", "Sally" and "Oprah"] to the fringes of society, to those who break rules, is doing to our society's ability to define and constrain deviance'. Adopting a polemical rhetoric, Abt and Seesholtz (1994) state that:

> One thing seems fairly certain: law abiding, privacy-loving, ordinary people who have had reasonably happy childhoods and are satisfied with their lives, probably won't get to tell their stories to Phil, Sally or Oprah. But if they did get on a television talk show, they would have to highlight the problematic aspects of their lives. Television is not interested in adequately reflecting or representing social reality, but in trivializing its underside for fun and profit.[19]

Abt and Seesholtz seem to believe that society's 'underside' exists separately from 'social reality' which, for them, is conceptualised as a series of rules that operate to ensure normative behaviour. 'Society is a result, then, of its boundaries, of what it will and won't allow. Shame, guilt, embarrassment are controlling feelings that arise from "speaking the unspeakable" and from violating cultural taboos...As we watch, listen and are entertained television is rewriting our cultural scripts, altering our perceptions...'.[20] Taking issue with the questions asked by the audience – which are 'often rude by conventional standards' – they see that the 'most problematic part of this is the generally non-judgmental tenor of the dialogue between the "guests" and the audience. Society's conventions are flouted with impunity'.[21] This, they argue, is leading to a collapse of cultural distinctions between public and private, truth and falsehood, good and evil, normal and abnormal.

The binary logic of this position forecloses the possibility of any discussion with respect to the nature of power, its loci and its distribution in a patriarchal, capitalist system. What the position articulated here by Abt and Seesholtz does offer us is evidence of a cultural anxiety that stems from considering the social and moral effects of mass culture. Further, this position demonstrates that, even though described as empty of meaning, talk show contents are seen to exert a powerful influence, albeit a negative one. One problem here is that they leave the hosts undifferentiated. As stated above and as we will see, the Oprah persona impacts heavily on the meanings generated by the shows, and therefore, the hosts do indeed require as much analysis as the content offered by the guests and experts.

Key to all of this is a concern with financial profit. Himmelstein (1984) argues that talk shows epitomise television's exploitation of the American myth of the individual, in which celebrity, status and success are signs of having Arrived. In order to feed the appetite of commercialism, television forever seeks out the bizarre, the glamorous and the exotic.[22] Himmelstein, Abt and Seesholtz argue that the process of commercialism – television's drive for profit – is the source of the proliferating display of 'deviant sub-cultures' and broken taboos, which indicate a degeneration of social and cultural values. This position conflates 'bad taste' and the 'rude' with 'social harm' that in turn is bound up with the commercial. This leaves us with the need to disentangle the disparate elements that form their arguments before we can achieve a greater understanding of talk shows.

Joshua Gamson's response to the *Jerry Springer Show* provides a clue as to the root of the antipathy towards a public display of private difficulties that troubles commentators such as Keller, Himmelstein, Abt and Seesholtz. Focusing on representations of sexualities, Gamson (1998b) conducted audience and participant response research from which he concludes that: 'talk shows are, as prime purveyor of public visibility of sex and gender nonconformity, terrific foci for the anxieties and hostilities that a queer presence provokes'.[23] The public declaration of sexual status speaks to concerns of taste, inextricably bound with middle-class anxieties over who should populate the public space of talk shows, provoking outrage at moral indecency. On the other hand, talk shows provide a narrow opening in which 'freaks' talk back 'even if the freak refuses that term'.[24] The real point, Gamson (1995) argues, is not the shows themselves, but the limits placed on the positions of those speaking – as expert, freak, or rowdy. 'You know you're in trouble when Sally Jessy Raphael (strained smile and forced tear behind red glasses) seems your best bet for being heard, understood, respected and protected. That for some of us the loopy, hollow light of talk shows seems a safe, shielding haven should give us all pause.'[25]

Gamson's position signals a move in the debate away from the emphases on social harm in emotional display and towards a conceptualisation of talk shows as a public arena in which to make one's self heard. This is also evident in the work of Aaron Fogel, Donal Carbaugh and Wayne Munson whose position is one that moves us away from entertainment, commercialism and social harm and towards a consideration of talk shows as public space and public debate. They are nonetheless linked with those concerned with social harm through their preoccupations in the field of cultural commentary. Here talk shows are seen as the site for the rehearsal of national character and identity. Although this American character is left unproblematised and is posited as a universal, we can see that the *debate itself* becomes a site for articulating identity.

Public space/public debate

Fogel (1986) describes talk shows as the 'controlling contemporary form of public discourse' arguing that to understand America 'we need first to learn how to read talk shows'.[26] Fogel does this by locating talk shows within the literary tradition of Ralph Waldo Emerson's transcendentalism, which couples a belief in the self-reliant individual with the possibility of escape from established values and materialism. It should be stated that the talk shows Fogel refers to are celebrity chat shows and not those of a confessional nature, but his identification of transcendentalism speaks to a key American historical and cultural theme. This view is echoed by Donal Carbaugh who *has* done a very detailed analysis of speech on *Donahue*,[27] which he sees as a powerful and complex cultural symbol of contemporary American life. Positioning his work as ethnographic, Carbaugh (1989) centres his discussion on the cultural narrative that forms a dominant discourse in America, one which we will see in the following chapter is largely the product of white and middle-class men. His argument is that symbolised by the notion of individual rights – to speak, to hold opinions, to disagree – 'American conversation' loudly affirms 'a common humanity of persons as individuals, with a separate humanness for each ... When there is a rub or injury done, its sense tends to be heard and resolved in terms of the individual'.[28] Whilst some talk show commentators argue that the emphasis on individualism empties out any potential for politicising the speech, Carbaugh maintains that this talk is actually grounded in the political as it draws on concepts enshrined in the Constitution and the Bill of Rights.[29]

More broadly, Carbaugh's analysis represents an example of the ways in which the significance of talk shows is not ignored or neglected but expanded to take on the common cultural values embedded within the American liberal tradition. Carbaugh concedes that class and gender do impact on discourse but his work favours seeking out common meanings embedded in *Donahue* rather than looking at specific inflections. We could ask: whose 'common meanings' are they; are they common to all?

The notion of common meanings also marks Wayne Munson's position. He conceptualises talk shows within the frame of community and difference, defining the programmes as 'outposts for the disaffected since the 1960s'.[30] Munson's strategy (1993) is to interpret the shows by drawing on the ideas around postmodernism: 'a broad cultural definition characterising the West, particularly the United States, in the latter half of the twentieth century', represented by and through 'a crisis in philosophy, knowability and technology ... '.[31] In general, Munson sees talk shows as creating a 'hyperlocal or cyberspatial "place" in which new lines are being drawn as old ones are erased'. This of course is the very thing that Abt and Seesholtz object to, but Munson sees this in a more positive light. For him, talk shows signal the creation of new, 'and the least understood' neighbourhoods in America. He argues that audience contribution through which spectatorship is transformed into participation, the dependence on intertextual cognition and the sense of alliances being (re)formed, all works to create a community in which knowledge is not the sole province of established institutional circuits. Munson concedes that this knowledge is exploited as a commodity, but argues that this does not impede the generation of understanding through the participation in spectacle and narrative within an accessible and friendly media. 'The talk show has come to occupy a thankless position; as eminently useful, efficient, and integrated into public discourse as it has become, it still gets "no respect" ' because:

> its rule-and-boundary blurring efficiency in response to an accelerated image economy is frightening, a harbinger of chaos to the many who fear the media's power, but who also fail to see that the talk show positively *structures* chaos, just as chaos structures *it*[32] (emphasis in original).

Interestingly, and unlike Abt and Seesholtz, Munson marks *Oprah* as different from the range of talk shows within the genre. This show, he argues, acts out Winfrey's belief in taking control of one's destiny as a catalyst of growth. Winfrey is 'a signifier of progress, perfectibility and control' made manifest through the development of her own production company, Harpo Productions, 'and diversifying into films that voice the experience of blacks and women who were once excluded ... from modernity'.[33] Munson challenges Harrison's[34] assertion (1989) that Winfrey's New Age philosophy is dangerous and incoherent, that her show gives people an experience in lieu of having to think, that it masks a passive unquestioning of a programme which is more about

Oprah than anything else. Munson argues that she (Harrison) is trotting out old and questionable assumptions about the media's exploitation of the 'vulnerable female/child spectator'.[35]

This response to Harrison links back to the earlier discussion of social harm. But for me, more interesting is the gendered account of community. We can see that, in this formulation, the theme of emotion has faded from the debate. If we accept that emotion is seen as belonging to the realm of the feminine, what are we to make of the debate that ignores this constitutional element that is fundamental to talk shows? For Fogel, Carbaugh and Munson the meaning of talk shows resides in the articulation of an American identity. But I think that we have to conclude that this is one particular form of cultural character and not one that necessarily includes women. Neither can we assume that ethnic minorities, gays and lesbians and other marginalised groups are represented in this view.

Munson picks up on the 'vulnerable female/child' discourse, but this relates to the trash TV position rather than to talk shows *per se*. However, one aspect of Munson's work leads us into areas of the debate which highlight this problem. His view that knowledge is not solely located within the realm of established institutional circuits has been more precisely explored through the employment of Habermas' notion of the public sphere in order to examine the impact of expert voices on talk shows. This has the advantage of being more productive than the moralising perspective adopted by those who are concerned with social effects, and more focused than the generalised accounts offered by Fogel, Carbaugh and Munson. Further, this approach has given rise to an interesting debate that enlarges our understanding of talk shows whilst simultaneously pointing up inherent limitations. Whilst the problem of a blindness in relation to gender issues discussed above is not addressed explicitly, it comes to light in the tension between critics who adopt the same theoretical frame but who form opposing positions within this.

Firstly, we are shown how Habermas may supply the theoretical frame through which to explore the idea and implications of positioning talk shows as a (new) public space. This position is held in response to 'conservative ideologues and Leftist cultural critics' who see the mass media 'as the reason for the degradation of public life'.[36] In their influential article 'Chatter in the Age of Electronic Reproduction', Paolo Carpignano, Robin Anderson, Stanley Aronowitz and William Difazio reformulate Habermas' idea of the democratic public space to argue that talk shows constitute a new public space. For Carpignano *et al.* (1990), talk shows represent a site of discursive struggle that offers the potential for empowerment. This empowerment, they argue, emerges through discourse which is based on (proletarian) common sense and which, crucially, is privileged over expertise.

The argument has its attractions: its affirmation of lay voices provides a counterbalance to the rather alarmist and nihilistic position that denounces talk shows *precisely because* they are constituted by and through 'ordinary' individuals with their messy problems. However, Lisa McLaughlin offers a different reading based on Habermas' formulation through which to counter Carpignano *et al.* – and, by implication, Fairclough, Livingstone and Lunt. Her response to Carpignano *et al.* reminds us to be cautious in celebrating the democratic and liberating potential of talk shows. At the same time, she demonstrates the problematic with the either/or binary mentioned above. McLaughlin's method is to focus on 'sex work and its pervasive presence as a topic on daytime talk shows' in order to examine how precisely expertise mediates the stories recounted by the guests. Her work here reveals the continuance of patriarchal discourses that position women as the lesser Other.[37]

Firstly, McLaughlin questions Carpignano *et al.*'s definition of 'common sense' – and by extension, the utopian vision of a democratic, communal public. In 'Chatter in the Age of Electronic Reproduction' common sense is seen as divorced from the discourse of expertise. However, McLaughlin counters this by arguing that '[d]ividing practices informed by social norms spring from expert knowledge and enter a public space as practical advice that normalizes and dichotomizes, thus reinforcing expert knowledge'.[38] Agreeing with Carpignano *et al.* that talk shows operate as a forum for controversy, confession and testimonial, the programmes rarely, McLaughlin argues, function as a site of empowering or resisting discourse. The problem is, she argues, not in locating the presence of female voices and/or their feminist inspired arguments but in the degree to which feminist discourse represents a challenge to the traditional representational apparatus.[39]

> The talk show represents an intersection of discourses, none of which exists apart from the social structure, so that it is unlikely that the structural transformation [of the public sphere] provides new discursive practices that are so external to traditional modes of political and ideological representations that they are able to militate against them ... Ultimately ... talk television ... is no more empowering than locating Madonna on the cutting edge of feminism.[40]

McLaughlin's approach usefully problematises utopian notions of the free and democratic nature of talk shows. Her analysis of sex talk moves us away from the generalised moralising of Himmelstein, Abt and Seesholtz and also reminds us that a female orientated genre does not necessarily equal liberation from the patriarchal order. She is right to suggest that institutional interests are integral to the talk show structure; the political economy of the television industry is inextricable from the shows themselves. And her position on the formation of 'common sense' is persuasive. However, it is also the case that articulation of personal narratives is a means of empowerment for individuals or groups of people otherwise marginalised from the mainstream, as suggested by Gamson. The tension between Carpignano *et al.* and McLaughlin underlines the shortcomings of the either/or dichotomy that characterises much of what has been written about the genre. It is clear that both positions have merit and can be convincingly substantiated. Left undeveloped is the ambivalent nature of the shows, an ambivalence that becomes even more problematic when we look at research that has been conducted with audiences and participants.

Livingstone and Lunt's influential work (1994) examines the plausibility of the position that sees talk shows as a public space that offers new opportunities to question power. Citing Carbaugh's declaration that talk shows offer a location in which 'millions gather daily to talk' offering a 'cultural performance of identity',[41] they consider the construction of identity that hinges on the social reformulation of public knowledge. Livingstone and Lunt's method is to combine analysis of a range of talk shows with interviews with audience members and participants. They conclude that talk shows mark a shift in the relationship between experts and laity, identifying a *loss* of authority on behalf of the expert as he/she speaks for others, whereas the guest, who speaks for him/herself represents the voice of the 'authentic'. This formulation raises issues of authenticity and 'truth' which are seen to be constructed through the narration of one's own experiences, and the credibility of which is privileged over that of the expert who often has to defend their position.[42] The work carried out by Priest (1997) supports this view. Her study of *Donahue*[43] participants reveals that the programme is used as a platform from which to challenge their (largely) deviant status. Many of Priest's respondents reported generalised feelings of empowerment arising from the audiences response to them and from the legitimacy lent in appearing on national television. For the majority of the participants, the reinscription of self as valid outweighs the negative repercussions experienced as a result of public disclosure.

So, Livingstone and Lunt's work is innovative in that it combines textual and audience analysis, and Priest's findings lend further weight to their argument, which sees the lay voice as privileged. Consequently, what emerges from the debate as it has been mapped out above is that it is possible to credibly refute *and* endorse the political potential of talk shows; both positions illuminate aspects of the programmes that remain occluded in the more generalised discussion of them. But it is also evident that this does not *extend* our understanding of talk shows as a popular form.

A way out of this bind is through the development of an understanding of the stories recounted by guests through a close examination of those narratives in order to see what they are a performance of. I argue that at the heart of the narrative performance is an articulation of self that we need to recognise and understand within a range of (conflicting) cultural discourses. This is the point at which understanding the host's persona becomes crucial: it is through the embodied values of a show's host that participants' stories are mediated and inscribed with meaning. Therefore, the confessions and testimonies articulated on the programmes cannot be divorced from the host persona itself. This must necessarily impact on the degree to which talk is liberated from or circumscribed by official (normative) discourse. It is the convergence of these discourses that create a text that is ambivalent and therefore difficult to read.

The position occupied by Gamson again offers a way out of this catch in that his work addresses both the 'bad taste' that is displayed in talk shows and the formation of identity that occurs in this public space. Gamson's response to *Jerry Springer* is to compare it with other shows in the genre: 'While on sanitised, "proper" talk shows like *Oprah* ... people are kissing each other's butts, on Springer's, refreshingly, people are kicking them.' He continues:

> There is an understandable pleasure in that. There is a distinct thrill in watching those rules get broken, not just for a pseudo-rebellious middle-class guy like me, but especially for classes of people rarely seen on television, who, when they are seen, are often told that they are 'trash' to be cleared off the screen ...[44]

The outrageousness that has made *Springer* such a hit is, Gamson argues, a move against the imposition of rules designed by some people to keep other people in their place. Here he develops the argument expressed in his earlier paper: 'the sad part of such a situation is ... actually a serious problem'.[45] The public space of television 'is not a very open one' and despite Springer's claims of First Amendment rights and that his show offers a forum for the disenfranchised, *Springer* remains 'a pitifully narrow, cruddy little spot in which speaking isn't really even an option'. And what is 'scary' is not the screeching of the participants but that this is the 'best deal on the table'.[46]

In fact, *Springer* is not the 'best deal on the table' but Gamson helps to pinpoint the need to explore the ways in which identity is constructed and displayed on talk shows and the potential this has for the (dis)empowerment of the otherwise silenced. What makes *Springer* a 'cruddy little spot' I imagine, are the acts of violence and strings of expletives – tastefully bleeped out – that constitute the main fare no matter what the (almost always bizarre) topic of the day. To be sure, *Springer* represents the most extreme display of 'bad taste' deplored by some, but how is this affected by emphasising the issue as one of a *public* deployment of confession and testimony? Illouz's work on the meaning supplied through the emotional content of talk shows supplies us with some of the answers to this. Given that emotion is key in the narrative performances of the participants, we need to take this aspect of the shows more seriously than those who decry the programmes *because* of their recourse to emotional dialogue. However, the patterns of meaning that Illouz identifies need to be considered further within the confessional and testimonial discourses that give shape and form to the guests' narratives. These in turn are inextricably linked with notions of the therapeutic (which itself constitutes a key discourse within American culture, both in popular form and in academic cultural criticism). There already exists a range of positions that centre on the therapeutic strategies of talk shows and the ways in which identity is constructed through this. This body of work is the focus of the next section.

Confession, testimony, trash and the therapeutic

Carpignano *et al.* point out that talk shows do not follow the 'structural balance' of a news debate which aims to inform. Rather, they argue, 'the purpose of the talk show is not cognitive but therapeutic. The structure of the talk show is not a balance of viewpoints but a serial association of testimonials'.[47] As I have already indicated, testimony exists alongside confessional practice and is certainly central to the talk show structure, but this discussion is for later. For now I want to map out the ways in which the therapeutic has been analysed and which stand counter to the findings of Priest, Livingstone and Lunt, and to the optimistic conception of empowerment articulated by Carpignano *et al*.

What seems to be at the centre of the problem attributed to 'television therapy' is commodification. Himmelstein argues that the commercial hijacking of psychological discourse helps to 'legitimise the public media commodification of the psyche', and decries *Donahue* for being 'mid-western-pious-soul-searching-group psychotherapy'[48] pandering to a self-help generation in search of easy solutions to complex questions and personal identities. The flattening out of critical faculties that is identified as a social effect is a familiar Frankfurt School position, but is one that Himmelstein does not enlarge on. However, we can return to the work of Abt and Seesholtz for a more detailed argument about the (damaging) enmeshment of commercialism, therapy and popular television. What we learn from this is the ways in which economic processes are seen to impact on the representation of self through therapeutic discourse.

According to Abt and Seesholtz, when their first article, 'The Shameless World' cited above, was published, 'it triggered a largely unanticipated international reaction against the contemporary confrontational chat show syndicated and popularised by Oprah Winfrey in 1986'.[49] This reaction was made manifest by significant changes in the programme's formats, one of which Abt and Seesholtz welcome – namely, Winfrey dedicating two of her shows to discuss their opposition to the genre. The appreciation expressed by these two academics of having their work form the focus of two programmes within a much despised genre is contradictory and rather bizarre. Abt and Seesholtz clearly indicate a positive potential within the interactive participatory format of talk shows which, on this occasion, has brought their academic work to a popular audience. This raises the question that if participating on *Oprah* offers them the benefit of having *their voices heard by a mass audience* why would this be any different for other participants? The answer is supplied later in their treatment of the therapeutic inflection of talk shows which is premised on legitimate knowledge, who can claim to have it and how it is mediated, linking us back to the Carpignano/ McLaughlin debate.

Happy though they are with Winfrey's response to their criticism, most of the consequent changes are identified as self-serving. Rather than shifting ground, Abt and Seesholtz remain entrenched within their negative social effect position. They argue that the offers of therapeutic after care for guests who reveal trauma on the shows, and the follow-up shows that track the fortunes of guests, work to present a veneer of caring that obscures the fact that the sole object of any of these shows is revenue. In addition, '[t]he much-ballyhooed, so-called improvements actually exacerbate the situations and practices analyzed in "The Shameless World" '.[50] Now, four years after 'Shameless World' was published, shows are:

> taking on the mantle of "therapy" [and the host has] now metamorph-osed into the host *as* therapist ... [I]t is more critical than ever that we in the academic and clinical professions continue speaking out and writing about the implications of years of exposure to these hypocritical and illusory performances.[51]

Abt and Seesholtz argue that 'years of exposure' to faux therapy will lead to a trivialisation and misunderstanding of the therapeutic process. Properly trained and licensed clinicians, they argue, should restrict their practices to the confines of controlled clinical setting where the conventional therapeutic ethos of confidentiality, careful assessment and professional accountability can be maintained; and presumably, the unspeakable remains unspoken in the public arena.[52]

This concern over who has the right to speak and under what circum-stances is interesting. It is, of course, bound up with issues of power – as indicated by McLaughlin and Carpignano *et al.* What is particularly interesting in the case of Abt and Seesholtz is their unreflexive com-mentary that strives to maintain the bourgeois status quo in which 'real' experts police that which can be legitimately discussed in the public sphere.

In their 1998 publication the authors do engage, to some degree, with questions of power through their response to an article published by Grindstaff (1997)[53]. Grindstaff, an assistant university professor of communications, defends *The Jerry Springer Show* by arguing that cultural boundaries are arbitrary constructs to preserve class interests and protect the powerful. However, Abt and Seesholtz (1998) remark that:

> [h]er defence of this type of entertainment as a forum for the under represented seems a particularly egregious example of political correctness. Such a notion is like suggesting that minstrel shows gave African-Americans an empowering forum, or that circus shows empowered those with birth defects. These are all examples of carica-turing and making buffoons and freaks out of the powerless ... It would seem to us that the role of a communications professor,

indeed the academic community in general, should not be that of apologist for the patently obvious on most talk shows, but to explain how and why the shows work and who benefits from their success.[54]

While Abt and Seesholtz argue that it is important for work to be carried out in order to see who benefits from the shows and to understand their popularity, they themselves do not attempt this. Taking their cue from writers such as Christopher Lasch, Philip Rieff and Neil Postman,[55] they maintain that talk shows are a banal form of entertainment providing a source of huge profit for the producers. However, the point that they make about minstrel shows in relation to African Americans underlines a key argument in the debate as a whole: the possibility of self-representation. (The minstrel shows of course were not a mode of self-representation for black Americans but a caricature of racial stereotypes constructed by whites.)

I will, as previously stated, be situating my own analysis of *Oprah* within the discursive context which structures both the show and the responses to it, arguing that to view talk shows through the lens of one position is to eclipse other important dynamics that come into play. So far, the work discussed adopts a singular focus, but the debate does include work that takes an approach similar to the one I am proposing. This is the work carried out by Epstein and Steinberg (1998) whose paper 'American Dreamin': Discoursing Liberally on *The Oprah Winfrey Show*'[56] is altogether more interesting as it explores the multiple versions of the American dream that give form to and are produced within the programme. Epstein and Steinberg's separation of a number of 'versions' of the American cultural narrative rather than the universal of 'community' posited by Fogel and Munson is a useful contribution to an understanding of *Oprah* as a cultural form.

Their view is that 'the *Oprah Winfrey Show* can be read as a key site through which "America" as the dominant aspirational metaphor for "imagined community" is reproduced'.[57] Epstein and Steinberg identify the multiple forms of the American Dream and explore ways in which *Oprah* is framed by them, and the degree to which the show's discourse challenges the hegemonic status quo. The forms of American Dreaming explored are the therapeutic version, the family version, the female version and the civil rights version, all of which present as a common sense form of liberal politics. Interestingly, the transcendental version demarcated by Fogel is absent from the analysis here; this is because Epstein and Steinberg adopt a pessimistic position in relation to *Oprah*, one that refuses transcendental possibilities. However, their identification of disparate cultural narratives does draw our attention to the cultural and social context in which the show is produced. The complexity of *Oprah* is thus engaged with rather than effaced in the service of making broad generalised statements about harmful social effects.

Epstein and Steinberg argue that therapy is an American common sense – the American vernacular – and that 'it is virtually impossible to live in the United States without being interpellated into the therapeutic experience in some way'.[58] The focus on the individual within the therapy formula is nonetheless undercut by the public nature of the confessional practices which, in its aim of empowerment and positive action, is more closely aligned with feminist consciousness raising groups and church-based black civil rights movements. The latter two groups' emphasis on collectivity exists in tension with the individualistic premise of self-help which is threaded through the show resulting, often, in an ambivalence which may empower and educate 'but which can so easily degenerate into a destructive slanging match'.[59] Further, Epstein and Steinberg argue that notions of the therapeutic are framed by 'almost exclusively white, and by definition, middle-class' experts which reinforces 'white, middle-class, heterosexist' values that promote the possibility of 'healing your way to freedom'.[60]

There is much that I am in agreement with here. Epstein and Steinberg's overall acknowledgement of the complexity of *Oprah*, with its interplay of numerous discourses, successfully challenges the simplistic formulations articulated by Himmelstein, and Abt and Seesholtz. In addition, their argument is that the individualistic therapeutic strategies at play on *Oprah* are indeed transformed through the public nature of confessional discourse and are more closely aligned with 'feminist consciousness raising groups and church-based black civil rights movements'. Radical potential lies within the ethos of the liberal democracy – meaning the rights to free speech, legal equality and enfranchisement – which inform *Oprah*. But empowerment of the powerless, Epstein and Steinberg argue often slips into a recuperation that supports the powerful. 'The show's framework places significant obstacles in the way of substantive interrogation of the structural inequalities that make the American Dream a nightmare for so many, not only in the USA but throughout the world.'[61] As with other institutional practices that characterise American Dreaming, the therapeutic ideal goes uninterrogated, working to co-opt individuals back into the norm. Through this, Epstein and Steinberg are implicitly pointing to the ambivalent nature of the show, identifying the 'complex processes of hegemony through which the status quo is at one and the same time challenged and upheld'.[62] Although I too recognise the play of the therapeutic within the show, I think much more weight needs to be given to the influence of black American cultural practices.

Epstein and Steinberg's attention to the cultural contexts that give meaning to the various discourses on *Oprah* is recognition of the complexity of the show and of the ambivalence it articulates. We can see from their approach the ways in which cultural narratives impact on the formation of a cultural form. I also agree with their premise that if institutions such as therapy and heterosexual relationships *were* to be substantively challenged, 'the entire dynamic of *The Oprah Winfrey Show* would become immeasurably more radical and radicalising'.[63] However, we need to bear in mind that we are discussing a popular television show that has a mass and variegated audience. It does not, and, within the political economy of commercial television, cannot set itself up to be a forum for political debate and change. In Epstein and Steinberg's formulations, this represents a failure and political disability (which, within their frame of reference, it clearly is), but by itself this position does not fully explain the show's popular success. However, if we think of the programme in carnivalesque terms, we begin to see a different picture emerging from the ambivalence that marks the show. What becomes evident is that a series of conflicting discourses converge on the programme to create *something entirely new*. At the heart of this new creation is what can be described as the grotesque body of both the host and the guests whose performances embody the processes of death and regeneration. This process can also be seen in the self-esteem project discussed by Barbara Cruikshank and I would argue that *Oprah's* dynamic produces the same potential for political participation. Thus, the show operates simultaneously as commercial popular entertainment *and* as a politicised forum. Both of the elements are realised through the grotesque performances of the shows' participants and the host. This will be explored in more detail in Chapter 5 when I discuss the construction of the Oprah persona.

It is in TV therapy that we see instances of the spread of confessional practices, such as the migration that Michel Foucault identifies. Foucault's terms of analysis have been taken up by a number of commentators on the talk show genre and *Oprah*. For example, Landman (1996) argues, much as Epstein and Steinberg do, that therapy works to reincorporate the 'aberrant' individual identity within a normative frame. Her argument begins with the proposition that discourse on *The Oprah Winfrey Show* has a regulatory function, that the show exists as an arena 'where not "truth", but the realms of the affective and the subjective are policed'.[64] Nonetheless, she finds that her conclusions are 'ambivalent at best'.[65] Despite the show's tendency to circumscribe identity within the limits of a televisual format, the programme's inherent instability, its shifting tones and topics addressed, and its contradictions open up a space 'that reflects an openness to the complexity of experience that might otherwise be denied by the program's therapeutic and discursive tendencies'.[66] Landman does not state *why* an individual's testimony-as-truth is problematic, but her ambivalent conclusion is a reflection of the ambivalence inherent within the show itself.

Landman states that 'the solution to [the problem of identity] is equated with finding the "truth" ',[67] which, on *Oprah*, is reached through the discursive strategy of confession. She also recognises that there are ways in which the normative function of *Oprah* becomes disrupted, occurring at times when, as Donal Carbaugh argues in relation to *Donahue*,[68] oddness is celebrated indicating a uniqueness of identity. However, as liberatory as this might appear, the search for 'truth' is heavily circumvented by and through the act of testimony, an act that as Landman says, more accurately describes the verbal discourse of *Oprah* participants. The problem that Landman identifies with this is that, offered as a testimony, an individual's assertions are, have to be, accepted as the 'truth', foreclosing any further investigation. The appropriation of the therapeutic, reformulated to fit the conventions of confessional talk shows, further prohibits the search for 'truth'. Thus, Landman moves the debate away from concerns with social harm, instead becoming more interested in the kind of truthfulness displayed on the show.

Rather like McLaughlin, Landman's work contributes to the talk show debate by balancing 'the discussions of the chat show as an open and participatory arena with consideration of its "regulatory" functions – the juridical, "therapeutic", and confessional elements present in the narrative presentations of self that dominate this discursive arena'.[69] Landman explores *The Oprah Winfrey Show* through what she calls the 'storied voice' which engages individuals in a 'trial of identity'. This process both tests and evaluates identity positions through narratives of 'self positioning'.[70] Landman argues that the guests are caught up in what Foucault formulates as the spiral of pleasure and power in the confessional – formed through the pleasure in seeking out, questioning and monitoring, and the pleasure of evasion, 'showing off, scandalising or resisting'.[71] Thus, the guests' stories are simultaneously a mark of pleasurable exhibitionism and subjected to regulatory control. This latter aspect of the pleasure/power spiral is articulated through confession.

In the context of *Oprah*, this constitutes therapeutic discourse in which guests seek a 'moment of cure in the host and studio audience's response'.[72]

Landman's position is that on *Oprah* identity is constructed through narrations of self – and with this I agree. However, she is preoccupied by the idea of an authentic 'truth' as opposed to that truth which is bound up in the power/pleasure spiral and which determines the way in which identity can be read on the programme. This is a convincing argument, but the notion of 'truth' is problematic here. Landman is not so concerned with 'truth' and social harm/redemption but in the ways in which identity is given a test run and submitted to judgement. Her argument is that since identity on *Oprah* is constructed through therapy, confession and testimony, it (identity) becomes fixed on 'notions of "recovery" on the one hand . . . or victimhood on the other'.[73] Landman recognises Carpignano *et al.*'s proposition that the construction of identity mounts a challenge to the 'objective' truths that arise within a male dominated public space. However, she argues that a truth based on a person's need to 'find a "fit" or "fix" for their discomforting experiences' arises in its place.[74] And the testimonial nature of an individual's narrative forecloses the possibility of interrogating the 'truth'. Landman does not state this, but the inference here is that the dominant discursive structures that promote this form of 'truth' telling – patriarchy, therapy, expertise – prevail. This of course is the premise of McLaughlin's argument, and so we remain caught in the empowerment/liberation dichotomy.

The findings of Priest, Livingstone and Lunt revealed possibilities of empowerment identified by participants. But what about other empirical work that is formulated within a Foucauldian frame? Linda Martin Alcott and Laura Gray-Rosendale identify themselves as incest survivors 'actively involved in the movement of survivors for justice and empowerment'.[75] Their concern is with the possibility that speech acts as a site which can bring liberation and empowerment but which is also the locus of struggle that confirms hegemonic discourse. Here, they examine 'survivor discourse' on 'numerous episodes' of *Donahue, Geraldo, Sally Jessy Raphael* 'and to a lesser extent', *The Oprah Winfrey Show*.[76] Their examination of the show's structure reveals close ups of survivors who tell their tales, the questioning by the host, questions from the audience and finally the explanations offered by the 'sympathetic but dispassionate'[77] expert. Alcott and Gray-Rosendale (1996) point out that it is the survivors – rather than the perpetrators – who are the guests and who have to explain and defend themselves, a practice that reduces survivors to the status of victims. The authors question the medium's ability to transform the speaker's status from one of victim to one of empowerment. On the one hand, giving voice to women and children who are victims of incest does challenge structures that are in place creating a silence around the subject. On the other hand, hegemonic positions are maintained through recourse to expert knowledge called in to determine the truth of the survivor's experience. However, Alcott and Gray-Rosendale echo Priest's findings. Although the survivors are positioned so that they have to explain and defend themselves, speaking on television talk shows can be powerful. This is the case for the members of the audience who are also survivors as well as the guests: the process names and validates their own experiences and goes some way towards exploding stereotypes.

Nonetheless, we find ourselves caught up in the now familiar loop when Alcott and Gray-Rosendale state that this transgressive potential becomes lost when the survivor is reified as an object deserving pity and in need of expert help.

A particular point of interest for this book however, is that *The Oprah Winfrey Show* is seen to obstruct the recuperation of individuals' narratives because Winfrey's mode of operation reflects her own history as a survivor and works to close the gap between survivor and dispassionate expert. That Alcott and Gray-Rosendale isolate Winfrey in this way is, in my view, key to our understanding of *Oprah*, and is fundamental to the Oprah persona.

Alcott and Gray-Rosendale's position is closely linked to the theme of liberation/recuperation and public debate discussed earlier. Jane Shattuc takes this up further in her analysis of confessional and testimonial discourse as public display. Her work illuminates some of the difficulties that have prevented the debate on talk shows developing beyond the either/or binary. One of the problems is that Foucault is played off against Freudian concepts of the talking cure, resulting in ambivalent conclusions. As with Landman, Alcott and Gray-Rosendale, Shattuc draws our attention to the ways in which Foucault's analysis of confession may be used as a means of evaluating the processes at work on talk shows. Ultimately however, her position is confusing. On the one hand, she recognises the 'power hierarchy of interlocutor and confessor'[78] at play in confessional practice. 'It is important, then, to question the degree to which daytime talk shows take part in a larger power hierarchy that uses therapeutic concepts of "self-knowledge", "self-actualization", and "emotional freedom" to regiment and control viewers.'[79] On the other hand, the conventions of talk shows, she argues, spring from the feminist challenge to patriarchy, and 'although Foucault offers a cautionary model against a rush to characterize the shows as feminist, his critical stance does not allow for the possibility of emancipatory movements such as feminism'.[80] She states that daytime talk shows most clearly invoke Freud's 'talking cure' both through the 'free flow of talk' and by their emphasis – 'two thirds' of the shows' content – on psychological or sociological issues.[81] Shattuc then considers the degree to which recourse to therapeutic language upholds or subverts the authority of the expert and identifies a challenge to the top-down logic of therapist/patient relationship.

> Psychology is changing in the late twentieth century as therapy moves from the confessional to the public arena. Indeed, TV therapy is closer to testimonials of faith than to the guilt ridden whispers of the confessional. No longer is the therapeutic a matter of secrets pried from the unconscious. Rather, therapy is an ideology based on the power to affirm the survival of emotional weakness, repression, and subordination – all sensibilities derived from feminist theory.[82]

Here Shattuc is conflating the therapeutic hue of *Oprah* (or any talk show) with therapy *itself*. The two are not the same. Shattuc herself states that it would be misleading to liken TV therapy to Freud's talking cure, but she argues that daytime talk shows have reinvented 'talking as a curative as a consequence of ego psychology and the American cultural psychology ... [that evolved] out of the anti-authoritarian post-World War II climate ...'.[83] More importantly for our purposes here, the Foucauldian perspective fades from her argument and she fails to fully address the question: how far does a popularisation of psychological discourse enable a re-articulation of self freed from the imposition of the dominant codes and prescriptive ways of being? What Shattuc's work does do for us is to underline the shift between the private confession and the public display that is TV confession which, as she rightly points out, is more testimonial than 'guilt ridden whispers'. As it is my intention to demonstrate the centrality of a black feminist perspective both to the Oprah persona and to the show as a whole, it is pertinent to test out the available models that discuss the political impact of *Oprah* through the issue of 'race'. A note of interest at this point is that (with one exception) all those who explore 'race' and 'racial' representation look to *The Oprah Winfrey Show* for their analysis. This not because Winfrey is the sole black talk show host in America: Montel Williams – a black American male – hosts his own programme along lines similar to those of *Oprah*. At times the reason for drawing on Winfrey is clear in that the critics are concerned with black feminism. However, the focus on *Oprah* works to absolve other (white) talk show hosts from the burden of responsibility for 'racial' representation and displaces it to Winfrey. This observation indicates a debate too complex to be explored in this book; my own reason, as explained in the Introduction, for focusing on a black feminist perspective is due to Winfrey's own alliance with a body of thinkers who represent a significant part of that field.

TV talk shows and 'race'

A black feminist perspective

One of the earlier (and one of the most complex) readings of *Oprah* is Gloria-Jean Masciarotte's much cited paper 'C'mon, Girl: Oprah Winfrey and the Discourse of Feminine Talk'.[84] In the same way as I do, Masciarotte questions the validity of cultural critics who 'read the talk show's overlapping, never-ending narratives as dangerously displacing the sense of authentic private psyche or the earlier self or soul'.[85] What is particularly interesting about Masciarotte's position is that it is not framed by the feminist debate as Shattuc's analysis is, but it does nonetheless recognise the centrality of emotion, of black feminist discourse and the ways in which it is translated for and played out in *Oprah*.

Masciarotte wonders if the antipathy felt by cultural critics towards Winfrey and her show is because they are frightened by 'all these women talking on, talking to, and talking about television ... [Is it because] they have invaded the Symbolic register and suggest a reconstellation of individual and social agency?'[86]

In order to analyse speech on *Oprah*, Masciarotte uses psychoanalytic theory together with analyses of African American narrative structures and 'signifying practices' identified by Gates Jr (1988).[87] Her argument is that Oprah Winfrey 'is not a simulated self, and so a fetish for the endless lack of consumer desire, but a tool or device of identity that organizes new antagonisms in the contemporary formations of democratic struggle'.[88] The talking subject here derives its ideological authority 'directly from the experience of gendered and oppressed identity as it was popularized by the liberal American women's movement' characterised by its 'rallying cry of the personal as political, in contradistinction to the analytical as political'.[89] This is fused with Winfrey's refusal of 'the essentialist algebra of hegemonic acceptance: black + woman = Mammy = m/Other = the absolutely Othered = the Other of us all' to produce a subjectivity encoded by the insistence of resistance 'and a reinterpretation of the marginal object into powerful subject'.[90] In Masciarotte's view (1991), *Oprah* is saturated with a politics that is inextricably linked with the personal. She notes that Winfrey's insistence on the authority and authenticity of lived experience precludes a descent into sentimentalism.

Like Illouz, Masciarotte asserts that the emotional content of the stories articulated on the show underpins the political act of speaking publicly through forcing a recognition of the difficulties that reside in lived experience; emotion works to validate individual experience and reject processes of normalisation. Opposition is not, Masciarotte argues, used to fix difference but rather to problematise it, and the function of the talk show is not to resolve difficulties but to create a space for the display of stories. These stories, mediated by Winfrey, refuse recuperation because they hang on Winfrey's own 'necessarily double-voice public identity as a large black woman: the matriarch of difference, the sign of negativity in bourgeois, white patriarchy; *and* at the same time as a rich, glamorous television producer/star'.[91]

This recognition of the ambivalence of Winfrey's public persona is, in my view, the most convincing formulation of Oprah and the impact that this then has on the ways in which stories are related and heard on her show. It enables us to consider the Oprah persona from beyond the either (good)/or (bad) position posited by the majority of commentators. Surprisingly Masciarotte's work has not been developed in the debate subsequent to the publication of 'C'mon, Girl' in 1991, despite the frequency with which it has been cited. This, despite the fact that Masciarotte, in a footnote, states that:

> [t]he talk show's absolute opposition to the confessional brings up an interesting area for further work – the changing pattern of Foucault's Repressive Hypothesis and the ideological work of public discourses as the construction of identity. While talk show participates in the discursive construction of identity – sexual, gendered, class and racial – it does not operate within the illusion of secrecy and privacy that makes confession the discursive fixing of the self.... The talk show does not promise forgiveness or even cure; and it does not value the private self. Perhaps its fixing is in the promise of citizenship in the public voice, thus making intimacy the ideological lure of the 1980s as sex was in the 1960s.[92]

Squire's 'Empowering Women? *The Oprah Winfrey Show*' (1994) also recognises the importance of black feminism in *Oprah* which is seen as a forum for the empowerment of women. The core for the analysis in this article is based on programmes aired over a two-week period throughout which the shows' contents remain 'fairly constant',[93] and examines a range of issues – gender, sexuality, class and 'race'. Squire argues that although Winfrey often endorses traditional notions of femininity – heterosexual, domesticated, nurturing – this is problematised by her deployment of black feminist issues, histories and writing, and by the 'super-realism' that characterises her shows. 'Super-realism' is Squire's term that identifies 'an unsettling combination of emotional and empirical excess that puts common assumptions about gendered subjectivities in doubt'.[94] *Oprah's* combined use of information and psychological formula to narrate the growth of an individual at times fails to integrate sufficiently to form a realist truth; and super-realism, 'a realism torn out of shape by excesses of emotion . . . disrupts the explanatory framework'.[95] The frequent practice on the shows of presenting visible 'racial' difference without comment could be, as Squire points out, 'television's caution about "race" ' but she argues that it actually works as 'anti-racist empowerment'.[96] For example, a mixed 'race' or black family will often be presented as 'a family'. The silence allows for 'racial' differences to appear but are 'refused legitimacy in the narratives'.[97] The combination of black feminist thought and this super-realist mode together rework conventional recourse to psychological explanations and cures, allowing the unspeakable to be spoken. In the process, Squire argues, *Oprah* is able to deal with complexities of gender, 'race' and class in ways that traditional feminism has been unable to do.

These writers draw out the ways in which the emotional content of talk shows provides a powerful mode through which selfhood can be expressed, understood and validated. This affirmative function of talk shows is underpinned in Masciarotte and Squire's analysis by the empowering nature of black feminist discourse. Nonetheless, Squire's position that silence = 'racial' empowerment is unconvincing in its unproblematic formulation: it does not address the complexity of the Oprah persona in the way that Masciarotte does. Rather, Squire's formulation leaves the black/white dichotomy in place without examining the interplay of discourses that emerges from it.

'Race' and representation

Unsurprisingly, Epstein and Steinberg (1995) disagree with Squire's argument that black feminism works to trouble easy and traditional assumptions about gender positions. They argue that the emphasis on healing erases a focus on gender politics, a silence endorsed by placing the responsibility for the healing on the woman; the show's insistence on heterosexuality framed by a therapeutic ethos undermines Winfrey's black feminist project.[98] This then, also stands counter to Masciarotte's optimistic claims that under the sign 'Oprah Winfrey' the subject is (positively) positioned at the site of contradiction, pulling 'at the threads of the dominant culture'.[99]

More forceful in condemnation of the management of 'race' on *Oprah* is Robert Ferguson's argument that takes the view that Winfrey capitulates to corporate interests. He states that the *Oprah* show broadcast from LA in the wake of the Rodney King riots in 1992, rather than meeting its objectives of discussing racism in America, racial issues were obscured by the apparatus of television production and eclipsed by discourses of free market capitalism. Ferguson (1998) approaches his subject through an examination of the ways in which Winfrey manages the contentious issues of racial tension and violence, and consequently, her orchestration of the angry black and Korean voices. His concern centres on the difficulty, as he sees it, experienced by the black and Korean members of the audience in articulating their disquiet:

> They are angry and operating in a discursive field in which most of them never find a voice. Thus they often become confused as they struggle to find words which fit into the fragmentation of a debate carried on at such speed...Winfrey is much more likely to empathise with the emotional drift of contributions than she is to pick up on the analytic or substantive content... [I]t would be a mistake to look only to Oprah Winfrey for the origins of the discourse which is under such stress in the programme. It is the discourse of a free America, of the American Dream, of postmodern capitalism...Oprah Winfrey is in the impossible position of having to maintain her credibility as an African-American while defending the hopes and aspirations of entrepreneurial capitalism against the onslaught of the dispossessed and the disillusioned.[100]

Ferguson's position identifies the strains evident in *Oprah*: the tension between those normally without a voice attempting to speak and the corporate interests that define and shape the platform from which to be heard. This is helpful in that it draws attention once again to the ever-present corporate interests, providing a significant context for our understanding of the culture of celebrity, the programme, as well as the ways in which this is made manifest. However, Ferguson only proffers a partial means with which to explore the show. Firstly, his appraisal denies the ambiguities highlighted by Masciarotte, and secondly he is mistaken to look at a single show for an overall meaning when the sign 'Oprah' has acquired a cultural resonance over time and through the serial presentation of a variety of subjectivities. The value of Ferguson's work lies in pointing up the limits of *Oprah's* potential to address overt and contentious political issues. Not having seen this particular show myself, I am not in a position to offer a critique of the programme over all. But clips from this show have formed a part of subsequent *Oprah* programmes – and these I *have* seen. From this it is clear that although the tensions may have been inadequately handled on the original programme, the fact that Winfrey has chosen to revisit this site suggests that the issues continue to be aired and, to some extent, interrogated, over time. It may be that even after an evaluation of the ways in which the LA riots have been discussed on *Oprah* since the original programme was broadcast, Ferguson's position remains unaltered. It does have to be recognised however, that the excess of emotions displayed on this particular show shine a spotlight on the management strategies employed by Winfrey to contain the conflicts and contradictions that are inherent within the show itself, and their recuperative effect.

Janice Peck is also interested in the *Oprah* shows broadcast in response to the Rodney King riots and represents and advances on Ferguson's position. The two shows taped on location in Los Angeles in direct response to the riots (one of which is used by Ferguson) form part of a thirteen-part series entitled 'Racism in 1992'. Although the two shows are atypical of talk show fare, Peck (1994) argues that they share features evident across the series on racism as a whole and are an expression of 'a popular discourse about "race" '.[101] Like Ferguson, Peck acknowledges Winfrey's apparent ambivalence in relation to 'race' suggesting that it is a strategy necessary to remain advertiser friendly and to maintain the large number of white viewers; thus at times she minimises her blackness, while at other times she foregrounds it. Peck's central premise is that the racism series 'constructs an understanding of 'race' and racism formulated within a liberal politics, a therapeutic view of human relations, and a generic civil religiosity'.[102] This, of course, could be applied to *Oprah* more generally. However, Peck argues that within the racism series, these discourses, operating as 'regimes of truth' in the Foucauldian sense, contain 'utopian sentiments in their quest to find a meaningful bridge across social difference'.[103] Thus, these discourses in defining what may be said, by whom and what subject positions the speaker may occupy, legitimate the social order whilst at the same time manifesting dissatisfaction within it. As I have been reiterating, it is this series of conflicting and contradictory positions that I find most interesting about *Oprah* and which needs to be explored more fully rather than obliterated in the quest to condemn or condone the programme. Ultimately, Peck concludes that talk of racism on *Oprah* is circumscribed by the dominant discourses that enshrine the code of the individual. To attempt to do more than change individual perceptions of 'race' would be to call into question the entire 'sociohistorical edifice'[104] that sanctions the dominant discourses as well as the television industry itself.

This is close to a position surprisingly adopted by Squire who, it will be remembered, had argued in 'Empowering Women?' that *Oprah* employed black feminist principles for the empowerment of women in general. However, in her later work we have evidence of the slippage between the unproblematic, rather utopian, view of the silence that surrounds 'race' difference on talk shows enunciated in 'Empowering Women?' towards that which Peck exemplifies and which addresses the polysemic nature of the texts. Squire (1997) examines a broad range of daytime talk shows which, she argues, in taking their prompt from *Donahue*, are formed around a white, liberal model in which psychological discourse positions white as the dominant and unmarked term. The white, liberal, male paradigm works to co-opt 'representations of African Americans and Hispanics . . . either whiting them out or reducing them to stereotypes of oversexed Latinos, loud black women, and infantile black men'.[105] Even where the talk show host is a black woman – Oprah Winfrey – difference remains verbally unmarked. Although this was seen as a positive in her earlier work, Squire's position has shifted. Now, the silence around a different skin colour ensures that 'every American becomes honorarily white'.[106] However, this is not a gleaming white but a 'trailer park trash'[107] white marked by low socio-economic class and by familial dysfunction. So, this system of representation compromises the whiteness inherent in talk shows: representations of blackness, visually present in non-white hosts, guests and experts, allows for their own use of talk show traditions in which to 'talk back' in mainstream culture. Consequently, non-white participants inflect the white liberal frame through a process of appropriation just as the unmarked term of white dominance works to white out, or reduce to stereotypes the black and Hispanic identity. Thus, Squire describes a process of cultural miscegenation by which 'race', visually present but verbally unmentioned, becomes conflated with 'trailer trash', blurring the black–white boundary resulting in an 'unnamed but significant color that is rarely visible else-where, a less than sparkling white'.[108]

As is clear from the above, with the singular exception of Squire, the writers who focus on the representation of 'race' focus on *The Oprah Winfrey Show* for their analysis, and so it can be assumed that the skin colour of the show's host is recognised as a meaningful sign. However, only Masciarotte fully engages with a black culture and a black feminism to examine the ways in which it impacts on the subjectivity produced within the shows. Although the show is not overtly a black feminist project, Winfrey's frequent foregrounding of her racial identity and the fact that the show speaks to millions of women signal points of reference which are underexplored in the majority of critiques. As stated earlier, this tends to obscure influences that are fundamental to the construction of the show, the ways in which it addresses its audience, and how Oprah operates within it all. Although those commentators who focus on 'race' open up the debate on talk shows in addressing the complexities inherent in the production of popular texts for a mass audience, by themselves, 'race' issues cannot form the sole point of reference in an analysis of the shows. The question that emerges, then, is: how does black feminism sit alongside the confessional and therapeutic practice of talk shows? On the one hand, speaking openly and freely about private, hidden subjects – confessing – has the appearance of liberation, offering the means of meaningful communication (Gamson, 1995; Priest, 1997; Illouz, 1999). On the other, a Foucauldian perspective posits the normative function of therapeutic talk (Alcott and Gray-Rosendale, 1996; Landman, 1996; Epstein and Steinberg, 1998). And, given that black feminism provides a powerful tradition of thought evident in the show that positively inscribes the individual (Masciarotte, 1991; Squire, 1994), how do/can we make sense of the obliteration of colour when 'race' is represented (Peck, 1994; Squire, 1994; Ferguson, 1998) on commercial television?

Further, there is the possibility that talk shows operate as a new democratic public space (Livingstone and Lunt, 1994; Carpignano *et al.*, 1990), but also one in which common sensibilities articulated by the 'ordinary' person are actually formed through a discourse of bourgeois expertise (McLaughlin, 1993). Linked with this is the possibility of creating a virtual community in which social bonds are forged in the meeting of individuals through the articulation of an American identity (Fogel, 1986; Carbaugh, 1989; Munson, 1993). But this community is also a product of the corporate interests of the television industry that profits from the displays of emotional distress and excess. The resulting dissolution of the public/private split is liberating (Munson, 1993; Squire, 1994; Gamson, 1995; Illouz, 1999) or, conversely, threatens the fabric of social life and cultural values through the commodification of therapy and bourgeois expertise (Himmelstein, 1984; Abt and Seesholtz, 1998).

In varying degrees, each of these positions has some merit and points up the constellation of cultural practices and critical thought that construct both talk shows and the meanings generated by them. At this juncture the ambivalence that marks the cultural phenomenon that is *The Oprah Winfrey Show* is recognised (Peck, 1994; Alcott and Gray-Rosendale, 1996; Landman, 1996; Epstein and Steinberg, 1998; Shattuc, 1998) but underexplored.

An exploration of this ambivalence presents, I believe, an opportunity to get below the surface and closer to the dynamics that produce Oprah and *Oprah*. Bakhtin's formulation of carnival and the related notion of the grotesque facilitates an understanding of how the 'body' of Oprah operates as a conduit for the processes that are evident in her show and that can be described as carnivalesque.

An example of the way that this will work is Mellencamp's discussion (1992) of gossip – one way in which she characterises talk on these programmes – as a grotesque body of excessive bad taste. Conceptualising talk show discourse as grotesque mobilises a discussion that encompasses 'race', gender and class issues in a way that differs from the accounts delineated in the debate on talk shows to date. In her formulation, gossip is situated as a scorned or trivial pursuit linked with women, standing in contradistinction to 'big' issues of national and international policy, corporate interests, the province of masculinity:

> Gossip's grotesque body of excessive bad taste is a lower-class body, frequently a female body, while the upper-class body of the news (and its scandals) is sleek, refined, tasteful, discreet, often a male. Women as excess, one version of which is affect...belong to the tabloids – the place of the body and the emotions. Men belong in the legitimate newspapers and magazines – the domain of intellectual and rational thought...The accepted difference between news and gossip...is also the difference between men and women.[109]

So, here are the beginnings of a formulation that enables the discussion of multiple discourse – heteroglossia in Bakhtin's terms – that begins to make coherent sense out of the disparate influences found in *Oprah*. Carpignano *et al.* argue that talk shows operate as the site of a struggle of discourses, in part because the women's movements have challenged the social agenda 'in this country' over the past twenty years, redefining the relationship between the public and private and what constitutes the political.[110] In part, but it is also the gendered inflection of talk shows together with emotional excess that works to draw disparagement and condemnation. Mellencamp's Bakhtinian framing makes this more transparent, and suggests a way in which the debate can be opened up that moves us away from the either/or issue that marks the existing structure.

As stated in the Introduction, the aim of this book is to develop an understanding of the programme and Oprah as a cultural icon through an investigation of the self that is constructed through the programme. The means will be an exploration of selfhood expressed in conflicting discourses that are made evident in the literature surveyed here. The following chapter will address the contemporary cultural climate in which Oprah has risen to prominence. The chapter discuses the history of the *Oprah* show, and the broader cultural traditions in which the show is produced and consumed. Anxiety, consumption, hope and renewal are themes that emerge from two key traditions of thought in American culture. The constructions of self evident within these traditions are made manifest on the programme and, therefore, offer a readily available means through which *Oprah* may be understood by audiences and which also offer frameworks for critics of the genre. Throughout, we will see how, in *Oprah*, *both* versions of self are articulated on the show, and that these key formations of self combine and converge in the programme. This enables an understanding of *Oprah* as a carnivalesque play of disparate voices and discursive formations that combine to produce *something new*. The chapter will, then, place the history of *Oprah* within the cultural conditions in which it is formed.

2
Anxiety and Agency: *Oprah* and Constructions of Self

As the biography page on the official Oprah Winfrey website (oprah.com) states, 'Oprah Winfrey has left an indelible mark on the face of television...Her legacy has established her as one of the most important figures in popular culture' [accessed on 10.1.03]. The biography continues with a list of the areas in which Winfrey's influence has extended: publishing, music, philanthropy, education, health and fitness, social awareness. Whether or not we see her through the same lens, it can be of no doubt that Winfrey is a cultural icon of some considerable stature. In 1998 *Time* magazine voted her one of the 100 most important people of the 20th Century. She has won seven Emmy's for 'Outstanding Talk Show Host' and nine Emmy Awards for 'Outstanding Talk Show'.

Winfrey's rise to this position of prominence began when, at the age of 19, she became the first African American woman to anchor the news at Nashville's WTVF-TV. From here she moved on to co-host their local talk show *People Are Talking* before moving to Chicago in 1984 to host the morning TV programme *AM Chicago* which, within one month, became the number one television talk show. In 1986 *AM Chicago* was renamed *The Oprah Winfrey Show* and was syndicated nationally. In this same year Winfrey was nominated for an Academy Award and a Golden Globe for her role as Sophia in Steven Spielberg's film version of *The Color Purple* (1985). These markers of success in film and on television undoubtedly combine to reinforce Winfrey's status as celebrity and, at the same time, work to define the nature of her celebrity persona. Although Winfrey's film performances and public activities, as her biography web page tells us, transcends that of her TV talk show, it is this forum that constructed the celebrity persona that remains consistent across media and genres. Having looked, in the previous chapter, at what a range of commentators argue that TV talk shows *do*, in this chapter I want to look at the cultural context within which *The Oprah Winfrey Show* emerged. In doing this, we can see the range of social and cultural influences that are made manifest in the show, and which offer a means to recognise the processes at play. This, then, paves the way for an examination of the ways in which Winfrey's performance as talk show host contains a range of conflicting discourses while she simultaneously embodies them.

Of course, *Oprah* is not the first TV talk show, or even the first of what Jane Shattuc calls the 'issue orientated'[1] talk shows that emerged in the 1980s (see Chapter 1). Commonly cited as the first TV confessional talk show, the *Phil Donahue Show* appeared, in 1967 and, according to Shattuc, fulfilled a need for the airing of socio-psychological issues and thereby creating a broad appeal. Although Shattuc makes a direct link between the emergence of *Donahue* with the rise of identity politics and the civil rights movement of the 1960s and 1970s, this show 'represents a genre born in [the] 1950s and 1960s that investigated the private or personal side of the news'.[2]

As Shattuc (1997) demonstrates, there is a link to be made between the rise of daytime talk shows and the political movements in America during the 1960s and 1970s; and that their ' "can-do" logic [arises] from the American revisions of Freud's psychoanalysis'.[3] However, I want to take a sustained look at some of the cultural/historical conditions that explain the genesis – and rise in popularity – of the confessional talk show. Elements of these are apparent in both *Oprah* and in the commentary upon the shows, especially that which subscribes to the social harm critical position. Keller (1993), Abt and Seesholtz (1994, 1998) voice concerns with technological advance, consumerism and corporate interests and their relationship with the therapeutic.[4] *Oprah* emerges from this set of cultural characteristics; in fact, the show would not exist without them. Equally, Oprah's celebrity persona is a product of corporate interests, consumption and the popularisation of Freud's talking cure. Technological advance generates a wide range of responses to it in order to attempt an explanation of its impact on subjectivity. The relationship between the two – technology and the self – is key when considering what is taking place on *Oprah* and how Oprah, as a celebrity, is constructed. Oprah's relationship with her guests and audiences is produced through formations of intimacy which lie at the heart of the meanings generated by the programme. The stories articulated on *The Oprah Winfrey Show* reveal ways in which selfhood is a discursive formation premised on pre-existing ideas of self, and the self's relationship with the contemporary cultural landscape. The nature of this sense of self, and the importance of it becomes apparent if we look in detail at two key traditions of thought within American culture. That which is articulated by 'elite' cultural critics represent a history of ideas on selfhood that is reflected in the wider debate on the social harm of mass and popular culture and which is manifest in some of the literature on talk shows. The work of critics such as Herbert Marcuse, Christopher Lasch and Fredric is interesting because of the anxiety expressed in relation to the formation of selfhood in post-industrial society. The spectacle of the serial presentation of stories of distress and dysfunction on *Oprah* is an articulation of the cultural anxiety evident in this 'elite' tradition. The mediation of these stories is through the technological means precisely delineated as causing social and personal fragmentation. Thus, the set of ideas that constitute 'elite' cultural criticism provide a con-struction of self that is recognisable on *Oprah* as well as providing the frame of reference through which the programme has been understood critically. In addition, an exploration of this tradition reveals the ways in which selfhood is seen to emerge from processes of commodification which is tied so closely to the system of celebrity.

But, crucially, this does not constitute the totality of the programme. A position formed within black American feminism that posits self-recovery and self-esteem emerges from a subordinated social and class position which is the legacy of slavery and the struggle to establish civil rights for black Americans. The right to selfhood is therefore central to this tradition of thought. This is made manifest in the programme through the mediation of the guests' voices and the structure of their narratives. Further, Oprah embodies this discourse in both her performance and through her references to prominent black feminists such as Maya Angelou, Toni Morrison and Alice Walker. These references occur within the show itself and outside of the programme through Winfrey's film roles in Walker's *The Color Purple* (1986) and Morrison's *Beloved* (1999) and in TV films such as Gloria Naylor's *Women of Brewster Place* (1989) and *Before Women Had Wings* (1997). In the previous chapter, I pointed to a work by Gloria Jean Masciarotte and Corinne Squire that examines the centrality of a black feminist discourse in *Oprah*. My aim is to expand on this and then to examine the ways in which this is simultaneously articulated *with* discourses of the therapeutic, consumption and corporate interests.[5]

This chapter will explore these two key traditions of thought, and the ways in which self is constructed through them. The most striking difference between them is the locus of selfhood. The former posits a self that is constructed through forces external to the individual – technological advance and the mass media – with the effect of producing a free-floating anxiety made manifest in descriptions of emptiness, depthlessness, and a lack of agency. In this tradition, it is this sense of meaninglessness that drives the cultural acceptance of, and the (neurotic) turn to, the therapeutic for a cure. The latter, black feminist, position posits a self that is located from within the individual's lived experience and his/her relation to important significant others – family and friends. Selfhood in this model develops through inner forces such as emotional experiences and attachment to community, which generate possibilities of agency and empowerment.

'Our fear is enormous': anxiety and a sense of loss of agency

Broadly, the 'elite' cultural criticism both analyses, and is an expression of, a sense of hopelessness in the face of social disturbance, and in the response to this which is seen as the turn to therapeutic language and practices. In the preceding chapter, we saw how this is linked with the argument that talk shows lack an address to the larger political climate. The literature to be discussed in this chapter presents a view of American culture in which the combination of therapeutic discourse, with all its connotations here of bourgeois angst, meets with a concern over the absence of a reliable political framework within which to position oneself. This is extrapolated to suggest that there is no alternative to the paralysing acceptance of a media dominated, apolitical, consumption-driven and corporate-managed space – America – in which individuals are units of commodification, measured by an ability to display and be displayed. The anxiety and the therapeutic tendency identified by 'elite' critics is evident in *Oprah* which, it could be argued, is a manifestation of this cultural malaise.[6] This is the case both in the strategies employed on the show and by its being very much a part of the technological landscape that is argued to promote fragmentation and dislocation. Not only does the discourse of cultural anxiety, with its focus on the therapeutic, offer a recognisable way of understanding the processes at work on *Oprah*, it also informs the theoretical/critical positions taken in the debate *about* the show.

In his Foreword to *Amusing Ourselves to Death* Postman (1985) writes: 'In short, Orwell feared that what we hate will ruin us. Huxley feared that what we love will ruin us. This book is about the possibility that Huxley, not Orwell was right.'[7] Because 'the average shot on network TV is 3.5 seconds...the eye never rests, always has something new to see ... Therefore, how television stages the world becomes the model for how the world is properly to be staged'.[8] According to Postman, television informs by disinforming, by giving out misleading, fragmented, misplaced, superficial and irrelevant information which is itself driven by the imperative to entertain. 'The result of all this is that Americans are the best entertained and quite likely the least well-informed people in the Western world.'[9] The danger inherent in a wholesale public acceptance of incoherent and fragmented dissemination of information is that it not only defines the ways in which information must be delivered, it structures our responses to it. This view of the impact of television on public discourse mirrors the debate on talk shows which sees them not just as a degraded form of television, but as a threat to the fabric of society as a whole.

So, the central concern for some post-war cultural critics is the condition of the human self in relation to technological advances and the mass production of images made possible – desirable even – by and through technology in the post-industrial age. Barthes (1993) observed that:

> One of the marks of our world is ... [that] we live according to a gener-alized image-repertoire. Consider the United States, where every-thing is transformed into images: only images exist and are produced and consumed ... when generalized [the image] completely de-realizes the human world of conflicts and desires, under cover of illustrating it. What characterizes the so-called advanced societies is that they today consume images and no longer, like those of the past, beliefs; they are therefore more liberal, less fanatical, but also more 'false' (less authentic) – something we translate...by the avowal of nauseated boredom, as if the universalized image were produ-cing a world that is without difference...'[10]

Clearly, it is not the case that 'only images exist', but Barthes' concern is more rooted in his notion of a 'world without difference', a world in which 'belief' has become displaced by an easy acceptance of an 'image' of that belief. Barthes' statement typifies a theme which preoccupies many post-war American critics. Much of this concern hinges on the notion of identity. Ferguson (1998) cites Bauman to demonstrate how the issue of identity is linked with insecurity. 'One thinks of identity whenever one is not sure of where one belongs; that is, one is not sure how to place oneself among the evident variety of behavioural styles and patterns...'Identity' is a name given to the escape sought from that uncertainty.'[11] Uncertainty is a key word for all the writers discussed in the first part of this chapter. It is an uncertainty fostered by the ever changing cultural landscape wrought by the advance of capitalism, the attendant increase of the use of technology, both in the home and in industry, and the apparent collapse of any meaningful metanarrative.

This sense of anxiety is evident in the talk show debate and helps to position the social harm argument within a broader cultural context. The discourse of 'elite' cultural criticism appears in response to mass production and mass consumption, linking these developments with an emptying out of self and recourse to therapy. As stated earlier, *Oprah* is a product of the cultural acceptance of the therapeutic as well as the corporate interests of the television industry. Thus, the therapeutic and commercial television combine to provide a structure for the show – along with all its participants – in which the self is inscribed as a commodity. However, my argument for the carnivalesque nature of the text depends on an acceptance of this as *one* constitutive element, so I am interested in analysing in more detail, the nexus of concerns that forms the relationship between the therapeutic, commercialism and commodification, and technology in order to understand what it is that we see at work on the programme and the ways in which selfhood is mediated in the process.

The therapeutic, consumer culture and the self

The idea of a 'one-dimensional' or 'other-directed' self is characterised by Lears (1988) as a 'weightlessness' that he identifies as a predominant cultural concern from as early as the turn of the 20th century.[12] What differentiates the 20th from earlier centuries, he argues, is the rise of capitalism and the technological advances which simultaneously enhanced the living standards of many (but by no means all) and eroded conceptions of selfhood that were premised on a grand narrative based on religious principles. Lears makes the historical claim that, in the period from 1890 to 1920, the emergence of corporate capitalism gave rise to the discourse of the advertising industry, which in turn became enmeshed with therapeutic discourse, which was becoming popularised just at the time when faith in a transcendent Being had been undermined by Darwinism.[13] In this account, the quest for an ideal nationhood and an American selfhood, made emblematic by the Frontier, becomes an apparently ever more anxious pursuit as industrialisation advances. At times, this anxiety is attributable to specific fears in relation to the threat of nuclear annihilation during the height of the Cold War. Later, the anxiety just becomes more diffuse, as in Christopher Lasch's work, which identifies the plethora of images that stand in for the 'real' displacing 'authenticity' – as suggested by Barthes, cited earlier. Whatever the cause, Lears argues, the idea of identity has always been precarious for certain groups within American culture, and no less at the turn of the last century than at the turn of this.

Lears is helpful here because he explores the historical relationship between a sense of individual self and social practices of consumption and advertising – discourses which are central to *Oprah*. Others add to these observations, explaining the roots of American psychoanalytic culture which helps to explain the popularisation of therapeutic discourse. According to Sherry Turkle, for instance, Freud was amazed at America's acceptance of psychoanalysis which he felt was endorsed too easily, and which he took as a sure sign that they were 'misunderstanding it, watering it down, and sweetening it to their taste'.[14] However, as Turkle points out, while psychoanalysis was resisted in France, psycho-analytic theory – shaped to what would be found most helpful – spoke to the 'special mix' of American optimism and individualism in which the individual is considered a 'virtuoso or entrepreneur of his or her own self',[15] capable of success if there is a willingness to change. This, she argues, brought Freudian ideas into line with American ideals of work and work on the self without having to call social structures into question. Such observations may help to explain some of the characteristics of talk shows identified by their critics, especially what Peck, Postman, Gamson, McLaughlin, Epstein and Steinberg identify as a lack of attention to larger political debate. But lack of recourse to the political is not simply the province of talk shows: Turkle, along with Lasch, points to the disillusionment with, and abandonment of, politics that often accompany a turn to psychoanalysis.[16] Rootlessness, geographic and social mobility all compounded by a lack of a coherent national culture, provided fertile ground for the development of Freud's ideas. 'Many Americans shared an insecurity about their *parvenu* status that encouraged continual self examination and the strong desire for self improve-ment.'[17] Turkle characterises the search for meaning and the adoption of the therapeutic thus: 'psychiatry, like literature, is a medium on to which social values can be projected as themes and preoccupation'.[18] She argues that, according to Nathan Hale, by the time Freud visited in 1909, America was in the midst of two crises: a crisis in the morality of social life in which:

> religious and cultural conservatives complained of a crumbling of moral codes, a new mass society bent on business and pleasure ... Darwinism, relativism and pragmatism were 'blasting the Rock of Ages' and

destroying a reverence for moral truths once believed to be eternal. A few Americans asked whether their country were progressing or degenerating.[19]

The second crisis was in the practice of grounding psychological disorders within a somatic base: it was becoming apparent that the major 'varieties of insanity'[20] could not be explained in terms of physical dysfunction.

Turkle's work (1979) provides a context for understanding the popular acceptance of the therapeutic in American culture, as well as lending support to Lears' claims concerning the disintegration of a unifying moral code. Like Turkle, Lears documents the erosion of ethical and religious frameworks in late 19th-century America in which the search for health was becoming a secular and self-referential project.

> The coming of the therapeutic ethos was a modern historical development, shaped by the turmoil of the century. And the longings behind the ethos – the fretful preoccupation with preserving secular well being, the anxious concern with regenerating selfhood – these provided fertile ground for the growth of national advertising and for the spread of a new way of life.[21]

Lears argues that the emerging consumer and therapeutic culture provided the context in which advertisers spoke of the same concerns articulated by many liberal religious leaders and therapeutic ideologues. 'A dialectic developed between Americans' new emotional needs and advertisers' strategies; each continually reshaped and intensified the other.'[22] According to Lears, the shift towards urbanisation resulted in feelings of anonymity; and lives of increasing comfort were accompanied by a sense of weightlessness precipitated by both technological innovation and the national market economy which separated individuals from 'primary experience'.[23] The therapeutic ethos was underpinned and energised by an increasing dread of unreality and a 'yearning to experience intense real life; in all its forms', feelings that provided the 'psychological impetus for the rise of the consumer culture'.[24]

Therapeutic ideas held the promise of salvation, the hope of self-realisation, the language of which became inextricably bound with that of advertising through the tying of material products to psychic states of well-being, vitality and worth. The therapeutic ethos, therefore, reinforced the process of industrial rationalisation by promoting a new set of controls over the inner life of the individual. Advertisers strengthened this process in their claims to secure identity through abundance and through consumption. Advertising companies institutionalised therapeutic strategies through their employment of psychological consultants: 'the most potent manipulation was the therapeutic: the promise that the product would contribute to the buyer's physical, psychic, or social well-being would be undermined if he [sic] failed to buy it'.[25]

Even though many products did not easily lend themselves to therapeutic appeal, by 1920 the symbolic world of advertising, with its promise of relief from unreality, had, according to Lears, acquired an Alice-in-Wonderland quality achieved through the collapse of meaning traditionally attached to visual and verbal signs external to the self. This collapse of meaning, leaving, in Rieff's words (cited in Lears, 1988), 'nothing at stake beyond a manipulative sense of well being',[26] is central to the process of the consumer culture in the joining of the therapeutic ethic with the advertising industry.

The linking of advertising with the therapeutic in this way is important if we are to understand the processes at work on *Oprah*. It offers a way of understanding the relation between the advertising industry and ideas of the therapeutic, and the ways in which this manifests on the show. The programme is constructed around (usually) five segments between which are advertising breaks. Even when the show is broadcast in Britain on BBC – and therefore has no commercial breaks – we are aware that they occur as Oprah informs the audience of what is coming up next 'after the break' and/or what conversations have been taking place during it. This then sutures individuals into a process of consumption within which their narratives become inextricably bound. In addition, the conventions employed in the commercials inform, in part, the construction and display of the narratives on the show. As with the displays of commodities, a guest's spoken story is often accompanied by visual images, both moving and still, that support the narrative articulated. Frequently, a series of images is deployed to reflect a process of therapeutic change that is recounted in the spoken narrative. This visual display of self validates the spoken word at the same time as appearing as the means through which self is advertised. This will be developed in the following chapter.

The psychopathology of American culture and the turn to the therapeutic

Lears convincingly demonstrates the interrelatedness of advertising and the consumer culture, the sense of a self characterised by weightlessness and divorced from 'real' experience and the therapeutic sensibility. Rieff

(1966) chooses to focus more on the ethos of the therapeutic itself, calling it 'the unreligion' of an age in which, as cited above, there is 'nothing at stake beyond a manipulative sense of well being'.[27] *The Triumph of the Therapeutic*, published some half a century after the time which Lears investigates, argues that contemporary American (and Western) culture has undergone a process of 'deconversion' from the traditional belief systems and symbols that supplied meaning to a community. Our 'devastating illusions of individuality and freedom'[28] are the compensation of intellectuals' abdication of faith. Individuality and yet the desire for community combine in a 'schizoid existence... vacillating between dead purposes and deadly devices to escape boredom'.[29]

Rieff's formulation of a debilitating boredom is similar to Lears' discussion (1988) of the loss of inner-direction which is drawn from the work of David Riesman, who argues that the successful man or woman has no 'clear core self', just a set of social masks.[30] Riesman (1961) in turn acknowledges his intellectual debt to the Neo-Freudians, and especially to Erich Fromm who was influential in the 'application of a socially orientated psychoanalysis' in specific reference to characterising 'problems of historical change'.[31]

Riesman's influential *The Lonely Crowd* (1950) follows in the tradition of work linking culture and personality established by Fromm, Margaret Mead, Geoffrey Gorer and Karen Horney which drew on anthropological practices and psychoanalysis to argue that character formation in early childhood is inseparable from social structures that inform parental practices. As Riesman concedes in his preface to the 1962 edition, his (Riesman's) approach is rather sweeping and overgeneralised. What is of interest here, however, is the way in which selfhood in American culture is conceptualised. Riesman's thinking forms a part of the discourse which deplores mass consumption and the mass media for their corrupting effects on human agency. This has links with the trash TV critical position as well as the processes of mass consumption through the mass media.

Riesman uses the term 'Other Directed' in order to categorise and define what he sees as the dominant personality type in American society. Identified as middle-class, the Other Directed type arose from the post-war increase in material abundance in which society became served by an increasingly efficient machine industry. The corollary to this is the decline in blue-collar workers in traditional industries such as agriculture and heavy industry. Riesman's focus on the emergent middle-classes is justified by arguing that, faced with a growing affluence, 'it is the malaise of the privileged rather than the underprivileged that becomes increasingly relevant'.[32]

According to Riesman, the peer group has usurped traditional parental responsibilities in socialising their young, engendering an extreme need to feel popular. This pressure is fed and reinforced by the mass media which increasingly mediates relations between the outer world and oneself. Desire for recognition from one's contemporaries has fostered an 'insatiable psychological need for approval' both from peers and a 'higher' circle, the 'anonymous voices of the mass media'.[33] Continually looking for external sources of validation, the Other Directed type is extremely sensitive to the opinions and perceptions of others. 'One prime psychological lever of the Other Directed type is a diffuse anxiety. This control equipment...is like a radar.'[34] As with Lears, Riesman looks to an earlier age for the origins of this sensibility; the observations of the 19th-century writers Alexis de Tocqueville (*Democracy in America*, 1835) and Thorstein Veblen (*The Theory of the Leisure Class*, 1899), recognised a competitive aspect in the American nature evident in the race for and display of possessions even before the advent of advertising. Riesman argues that 'Americans were ready for the mass media even before the mass media were ready for them'.[35]

We can see that elements of this argument have informed the social harm position in the talk show debate, and we can also recognise aspects of *Oprah* that support this view. An individual who is often a stranger to the other guests, the audience and to Oprah reveals intimate aspects of their selves for public display. This is a gesture through which an individual seeks, and frequently gains, affirmation from the company of strangers. This promotes the atmosphere of intimacy and inclusion that marks the show: like the guests, Riesman's Other Directed type is capable of rapid 'if superficial intimacy'.[36] However, our point of departure with Riesman's position arrives when he argues that other directedness has dire consequences for the political and philosophical worlds of Americans: men and women may not actively conspire with their alienation, but currently lack the conviction to see more positive alternatives.[37]

Implicitly stated here is the idea that a sense of self is forged through the acceptance – or refusal – of images perpetuated through the mass media; that from the earliest age, the anonymous voices of the mass media shape, define and control an individual's sense of selfhood. Yet, as will become more evident through my analysis of *Oprah* narratives in Chapter 4, it is important to recognise that on *Oprah*, although guests may situate themselves within the sea of images that constitute the cultural landscape, their stories are anchored in everyday, lived experience; they commonly recount personal histories of survival.

The perception amongst dominant social groups of the decline of agency is anchored in the conception of an American technocracy defined by Roszak (1970) as:

> that social form in which industrial society reaches the peak of organizational integration ... Drawing upon such unquestionable imperatives as the demand for efficiency, for social security, for large scale co-ordination of men and resources, for ever higher levels of affluence ... the technocracy works to knit together the anachronistic gaps and fissures of industrial society.[38]

Further, all elements of culture as a whole – politics, education, leisure, unconscious drives – become subjects of 'purely technical manipulation', in the face of which 'there can be no human autonomy'.[39] This definition offers the context for Riesman's thesis, and later that of Christopher Lasch.

The concern with a lack of agency arises from the argument that the mass media works to flatten critical faculties leading to a debilitation of political life. This in turn can be linked to the tendency for writers within the 'elite' critical position to make universalising statements that in fact are class based – Riesman's Other Directed types represent the 'malaise of the privileged'. Whole groups of marginalised peoples, for whom the political structures may have already failed, are not represented in this formulation. For example, in his preface to *The Culture of Narcissism* (1979) Lasch argues that:

> modern bureaucracy has undermined earlier traditions of local action, the revival and extension of which holds out the only hope that a decent society will emerge from the wreckage of capitalism. *The inadequacy of solutions dictated from above now forces people to invent solutions from below* ... Much could be written about the signs of new life in the United States. [This book] however, describes a way of life that is dying – the culture of competitive individualism, which in its decadence has carried the logic of individualism to the extreme of a war against all, the pursuit of happiness to the dead end of a narcissistic preoccupation with the self[40] (my emphasis).

That the 'inadequacy of solutions dictated from above now forces people to invent solutions from below' could be framed in a positive way and could speak to the sensibilities articulated by frustrated and angry individuals who feel disenfranchised by the wider political structure. This option is closed down however, as Lasch proffers his diagnosis of cultural narcissism. 'Economic man himself has given way to the psychological man of our times – the final product of bourgeois individualism. [Haunted by anxiety] he seeks...to find a meaning in life. Liberated from the superstitions of the past, he doubts even the reality of his own existence.'[41] The devaluation of the past has, according to Lasch (1985), 'become one of the most important symptoms of the cultural crisis...A denial of the past...proves on closer analysis to embody the despair of a society that cannot face the future'.[42] 'Selfhood implies a personal history, friends, family, a sense of place. Under siege, the self contracts to a defensive core, armed against diversity.'[43] Concern for the self in the post-industrial age manifests in a concern for psychic survival, with holding the self together and 'surviving the general wreckage'.[44]

What is interesting in this account of post-war American cultural life is the totality with which it is perceived and what is excluded from its field of vision. Firstly, and as stated earlier, it is this discourse which informs the social harm/trash TV position within a media studies account of television, and which represents its limitation. Secondly, we can see that discourses of consumption, technological advance and the therapeutic represent an American vernacular that is articulated on *Oprah*. In addition, the stories spoken by the guest frequently speak of individual distress in the face of some social disorder, exemplifying the discourse of cultural fragmentation and personal fracture that marks the view of the 'elite' cultural critics. However, this series of interrelated issues are not the only ones articulated through the programme. There is a black feminist model of self that I will be delineating in the second part of this chapter and which underlines the centrality of history, family and community in the construction of selfhood. This is repeatedly rehearsed in the narratives offered by the guests on *Oprah* where significant others are cited as central to self-recovery and self-realisation. By contrast, Lasch's account is of a self characterised by *loss* of 'personal history, friends, family, a sense of place' and one that is concerned with 'surviving the general wreckage'. However, these two constructions of self do not cancel each other out; rather, they converge on *Oprah* to produce a text that is characterised by a carnivalesque ambivalence.

Consumption, family and interpersonal relations

As stated earlier, Riesman's speculations arose from a body of work which established the tradition of psycho-cultural analysis with Gorer and Mead cited as influential in the methodology employed in *The Lonely Crowd*. Slightly earlier, Gorer states that psychoanalytic theory and practice became more widespread and accepted in the United States than in any other country.[45] Explaining his own methodology, he states that his work is informed by the training he received from Mead and Ruth Benedict. This provided an understanding of 'anthropology, behaviourist psychology and psychoanalysis' in an attempt to isolate 'consistent themes underlying and informing American actions by examining... a number of typical relationships: child to father, child to mother'.

Gorer's thesis (1948) is that the father rejected, it falls to the mother to shape the psychological form of the American character. Gorer's examination of the mother's impact on the socialisation of her offspring reveals ambivalence towards the mother – and by extension, women in general. His argument proceeds thus: American ethical well-being is dependent on the (presumed female) teacher who is the source of moral guidance for children after six years of age, and as such has an immensely important role. She is 'the guide and emblem of proper American conduct'.[46] This female conscience gives rise to 'idealism: the proclaiming of moral rules of conduct other people should follow'.[47] However, a significant proportion of women are possessive, clinging too long to their sons thereby posing 'a great emotional menace in American psychological life... and psychiatrists have written books to prove that [the mother] is the main, and sufficient cause for nervous breakdowns or psychoneurosis among recruits to the American army'.[48] If not misogynistic, then certainly ambivalent, Gorer positions women in an impossible double bind: despite being the chief cause of neurosis 'they are our chief bulwark against chaos'.[49]

Popular culture becomes the antidote to a restless mobility, boredom and loneliness as individuals engage in a perpetual search for an escape from a debilitating ennui of contemporary life. Of particular concern to Gorer are the popular radio quiz shows which present a grave political danger: intellectual passivity. The psychological effects of commercial radio, with its constant 'switching of attention'[50] to various advertisements, are damaging in the extreme.

This focus on radio quiz shows seems quaint some fifty years later. However, the core of Gorer's concerns is the spiritual impoverishment of American society in the face of material abundance that has provided the fertile ground for the adoption of a psychoanalytic culture as identified by Lears and Turkle. Gorer's formulations of familial relations foreshadows that of Lasch; both present the family as a constellation of dysfunctional relationships, the aetiology of which lies within the consumer-driven ethos of contemporary society.

The mass production of images is at the heart of Lasch's concern; the boundaries between self and not self become unclear, eroding difference. The technology of mass culture 'embodies by design ... a one way system of management of communication', impeding the circulation of ideas by and through the concentration of economic, political and cultural control in 'a small elite of corporate planners ...'.[51] Mass culture is the tool and method of social control: 'The social arrangements that support a system of mass production and mass consumption tend to discourage initiative and self reliance and to promote dependence, passivity, and a spectatorial state of mind both at work and at play ... [T]he state of mind promoted by consumption is better described as a state of uneasiness and chronic anxiety.'[52]

Narcissism appears then to be the best way of coping with the tensions and anxieties of modern life.

> Narcissism is more associated with self hatred than self admiration ... Men have always been selfish, and groups have always been ethnocentric ... [but] the emergence of character disorders as the most prominent form of psychiatric pathology, however, together with the change in personality structure this development reflects, derives from quite specific changes in our society and culture – from bureaucracy, the proliferation of images, therapeutic ideologies, the rationalization of the inner life, the cult of consumption, and in the last analysis from changes in family life ...[53]

Changes within family life, Lasch argues, determine in turn a wider set of social relations and contemporary social patterns and institutions. This, he argues, works against the creation of a rich inner life through which individuals find substance and meaning in their beliefs and in their relations with others. 'The cult of personal relations, which becomes particularly intense as the hope of political solutions recedes, conceals a thoroughgoing disenchantment with personal relations ... The ideology of personal growth, superficially optimistic, radiates a profound despair and resignation. It is the faith of those without faith.'[54]

The guests who appear on *Oprah* embody the social malaise/relationships in crisis, to which their stories stand as testimony. A common theme in the programme is that of disintegrating family life and estrangement among family members. The guests' desire to repair this damage is a frequently cited reason for appearing on the show either by presenting themselves as a group to discuss their difficulties or to make an appeal to a missing family member. For example, 'Estranged Families' (BBC2, 8.4.96) includes three sisters who have not spoken to each other for years, Kevin who has been estranged from his brother for 10 years, Lucille who has not seen her father for 40 years, Jackie who has not had contact with her father for 20 years, and Dawn who was reunited with her brother after a 15-year separation. In 'Letters from Children' (BBC2, 19.1.96), 14-year-old Chakka writes to Oprah as 'the only person who could listen' to her story of loss – her mother is dead, her father in jail – and rejection by her family. Other children on this show also present a catalogue of missing fathers, friends and family members (apart from in Chakka's story, absent mothers do not figure in this particular programme).

The narratives of loss and fragmentation on these programmes exemplify the cultural conditions recounted above and in two ways. One is that these individuals represent a larger social pattern: [Oprah] 'I get lots of letters from people who always want to be reunited' ('Estranged Families'). This suggests not only untold number of stories of estrangement, but also a yearning for re-connection. The second is that this process is constructed through a series of images and played out within the context of a popular television show. The therapeutic ideal is articulated through the expert guests who appear to flag a recent publication and to offer advice. The self is thereby constructed through a series of testimonials of loss and loneliness (Oprah is 'the only person who could listen'), and requires therapeutic intervention.

However, this is not the only model available. As indicated earlier, my structural analysis of the guests stories reveals a repeating pattern that positions family and friendship networks as central to the formation of well-being and self-esteem (see Chapter 4). The stories of loss and separation referred to above are positioned within the overarching narrative that articulates the importance of cohesive family and social relations for the formation of self-identity and realisation. As Oprah says on 'Estranged Families', 'We figured that if we could get this family together, then there is hope for you at home.' The possibility of self-recovery through connection with family and friendship communities is a leitmotif within the body of black feminist literature that I will be examining shortly.

Thus far, I have presented the ways in which selfhood is constructed within a limited body of work that exemplifies a larger discourse dominant in American cultural criticism.[55] This account of self is inextricably enmeshed with technological advance made manifest through the mass production of images and the omnipresence of the mass media, with a neurotic dependence on therapeutic process and characterised by disconnection. The claims of depthlessness and weightlessness are placed within a context of fractured family and social relations, and lack of agency that point to a deficit of a reliable political frame. Popular culture, in this discourse, operates as a distraction from the debilitating boredom that pervades contemporary life.

The feeling of well-being engendered through the mass media – characterised by Herbert Marcuse as the 'mind controllers' – is not only false but also works to erase difference and evacuate the self of any inner life. The ability to consume, in Marcuse's view (1964), precludes the possibility of envisioning alternatives, cancelling a political and philosophical engagement with the world.

> Now it is precisely this . . . 'space within' . . . which is being barred by a society in which subjects as well as objects constitute instrumentalities in a whole that has its *raison d'être* in the accomplishments of its over powering productivity. Its supreme promise is an ever-more comfortable life for an ever-growing number of people who, in the strict sense cannot imagine a qualitatively different universe of discourse or action.[56]

The media – the chief mediator for the expression and perpetuation of 'one-dimensionality' – promotes ideas of unification, of positive thinking and doing. The language of politics becomes that of advertising, closing the gap between two historically different realms. 'This universe of discourse closes itself against any other discourse which is not on its own terms . . . [By assimilating] all other terms to its own, it offers the prospect of combining the greatest tolerance with the greatest possible unity.'[57] In Marcuse's terms, it is this total unity that precludes any individuality in all areas of society.

This tendency to universalise a cultural condition characterises a part of the problem with the trash TV/social harm position discussed in the previous chapter and represents a denial of other processes at work. As Riesman himself points out, his concerns lie with the 'the privileged', but this tells us little of the less privileged and/or marginalised groups. Lasch's culture of narcissism is, in his formulation, more accurately described as the province of white middle-classes. This is most evident when he argues that:

> in some ways middle-class society has become a pale copy of the black ghetto, as the appropriation of its language would have us

believe. We do not need to minimise the poverty of the ghetto . . . in order to see that the increasingly dangerous and unpredictable conditions of middle-class life have given rise to similar strategies for survival. Indeed the attraction of black culture for disaffected whites suggests that black culture now speaks to a general condition, the most important feature of which is a loss of faith in the future.[58]

This argument raises the question of cultural stereotypes. In the context of Lasch's work here, black experience and black culture = despair, uncertainty, poverty, crime and struggle, and is translated into a language of ritualised 'aggression and abuse' reminding us that exploitation is the general rule for the users of such language. What we see here is a world-view in which white America = middle class and black America = poverty, struggle and violence. Where does the black middle class sit in this paradigm? This equation works to efface black American voices through the appropriation of that voice in order to make a claim about a group that has historically occupied the position of dominance. The African American voice is filtered through the convention of employing a stereo-type which reinforces the Otherness of that group in the sole aim of furthering an understanding of the cultural crisis that appears to beset the white classes.[59]

This preoccupation with the crisis within the white middle classes is interesting in that it perpetuates the inability to accommodate the Otherness of Others in a cultural narrative of self that has been developing since the arrival of the first European settlers. This is a narrative con-struction that positions indigenous peoples, African slaves, and later Asian and South American immigrants, as the Other through which white settlers defined themselves, rendering those Others invisible. Pluralism itself becomes subsumed within this discourse, representing the manifestation of postmodernism, the 'strange new landscape',[60] in which depth, according to Fredric Jameson, is replaced by surface or a multiplicity of surfaces.

The new (postmodern) person inhabits a landscape that is free of the (elitist) rituals of modernist culture and in which cultural production is open to all that wish to indulge. However, postmodernism's populist rhetoric is:

> notoriously unreliable, since people will always be found out there who decline the characterization and deny any implication in the matter. Thus microgroups and 'minorities', women as well as the internal Third World, and segments of the external one as well,

frequently repudiate the very concept of postmodernism as the universalizing cover story for what is essentially a much narrower class-cultural operation serving white and male-dominated elites of the advanced countries.[61]

Whilst Jameson recognises the truth of this argument, he at the same time cancels out that truth by arguing that the very evidence of these 'microgroups' – a whole range of small-groups practising non-class politics – is in itself a postmodern phenomenon: the dissolution of social class and political activism through technological advances.[62] The all-pervading sense of anxiety and its associations with annihilation of self through technology that I have delineated here is not confined to academic literature but also evident in post-war American fiction exemplified in Delillo's novel *White Noise* (1984) in which Jack Gladney, an academic heading the department of Hitler Studies, is afraid of death. His department is admired by Murray Jay Siskind, his new Jewish colleague who lectures on living icons, for its sense of achievement, identity and purpose. Discussing Jack's morbid fears and anxieties, Murray advises Jack to:

> put your faith in technology. It got you here, it can get you out. This is the whole point of technology. It creates an appetite for immortality on the one hand. It threatens universal extinction on the other. Technology is lust removed from nature...It's what we invented to conceal the terrible secret of our decaying bodies.[63]

Jack's wife, Babette, also fears death and teaches keep-fit classes to groups of old people as her way of denying the same terrible secret. She and Jack discuss one another's demise: 'She claims my death would leave a bigger hole in her life than her death would leave in mine. *This is the level of our discourse. The relative size of holes, abysses and gaps*' (my emphasis). Jack and his children watch Babette's class on television:

> with the sound turned down low so we couldn't hear what she was saying. But no one bothered to adjust the volume. It was the picture that mattered, the face in black and white, animated but also flat, distanced, sealed off, timeless. It was but wasn't her... Waves and radiation. Something leaked through the mesh... We were being shot through with Babette. Her image was projected onto our bodies,

swam in us and through us . . . The kids were flushed with excitement but I felt a certain disquiet. I tried to tell myself it was only television . . .[64]

Jack's all-encompassing disquiet and fear of death is given a focus during The Airborne Toxic Event, 'a horrifying thing' in which the community is driven into quarantine. But to the outrage of all those gathered, the media is absent. 'Our fear is enormous. Even if there hasn't been a great loss of life, don't we deserve some attention for our suffering, our human worry, our terror? Isn't fear news? Applause.'[65]

The lack of centre, the absence of agency and meaning, the all-pervading emptiness of human experience save a fear of death that is evident in *White Noise* – and in other of Delillo's works along with many other American post-War writers such as Richard Braughtigan, Joseph Heller, Bret Easton Ellis – circulates, but never fixes on, a fear of technology which simultaneously threatens to annihilate (as much through boredom as through a material impact) as it saves. This is underlined by Jack Gladney's academic interest in Hitler, which despite Murray's observations to the contrary, does not offer Jack the locus on which his fears coalesce; his is a futile attempt at therapy for his morbid fears. The 'white' in Delillo's title may be an indication of a white male identity in crisis.[66]

The narratives on *Oprah*, referred to above, are situated within the discourse of identity in crisis in which the turn to the therapeutic is indicative of fracture and dislocation, hallmarks of contemporary American culture.The position held by the 'elite' cultural critics posits anxiety as a universal condition, but this existential angst is perhaps more meaningful to this group of intellectuals than to Jameson's 'microgroups' practising identity politics. Docker (1994) certainly sees Jameson's *Postmodernism* (1991) as a form of therapy to assure frightened or angry modernists 'who can now take comfort that one of their own has masterfully shown that postmodernism lacks what they still possess, a sense of genuine historicity'. The search for a centre, a 'fundamental ground,' betrays an anxiety and desire for a 'reassuring certitude'.[67]

In Oprah however, this, as I have stated, is tempered by a discourse that emerges from an African American intellectual tradition and that contributes to an aspect of black feminism embodied by Oprah. The values embodied by the host provide a significant contribution to the production of meaning in *Oprah*.[68]

'There's hope for you at home': African American and black feminist thought, self and agency

In February 1998, Oprah Winfrey emerged the victor in a libel case brought against her by Texas cattlemen. Their claim was that her declared intention never to eat another hamburger had caused beef sales to plummet, ruining their livelihoods. Winfrey's statement had been made on one of her shows that discussed the prevalence of 'mad cow disease' affecting individuals who had consumed infected meat. Following the jury's judgement, journalist Kettle (1998) wrote: 'Ms Winfrey said that the verdict was a victory not just for her and not just for free speech but for Afro-American civil rights... "I have come from a people who have struggled and died in order to have a voice in this country and I refuse to be muzzled" she said.'[69] In an interview with Duncan (1999) a year later, Winfrey discusses her preparation for her role of Sethe in the film adaptation of Toni Morrison's *Beloved*. Attempting to experience the 'physicality' of a runaway slave, Winfrey was left alone in a wood with the aim of finding a house some miles away. 'I was able to touch the psychic space of slavery inside myself. Hollow. Dark.... I began to weep and became hysterical... The next day I wrote in my diary, "How dare I think of quitting? I've come from a people who had no voice, money or shoes to run – but they ran anyway." '[70]

In addition to Winfrey's explicit identification with 'a people who have struggled and died to have a voice in this country' is her growing role as a public intellectual-in-performance.[71] By this I am referring to her mediation of African American cultural material through the promotion of black women writers in her book club, her key perform-ances in the film versions of Alice Walker's *The Color Purple* and Toni Morrison's *Beloved*, Harpo's TV production of Gloria Naylor's *Women of Brewster Place* and her relationship with Maya Angelou who has referred to Winfrey as her 'prodigy'.[72]

The incidents described by Winfrey in press interviews offer examples of the way in which she foregrounds her 'racial' identity. She places her own sense of selfhood within a tradition located in the historical context of slavery and the civil rights movement, but which is also inextricably linked with contemporary social conditions. Winfrey's statements provide us with evidence of an alternative to the debilitating effects of the postmodern (historyless) landscape and of the possibility for self to be constructed as an active agent. As Winfrey's remarks suggest, this is a self that is realised through a recognition of the ways in which the past impacts on the present, and of an empowerment that arises though connection to a wider community of individuals – especially when that community shares a similar history. By turning to this body of work, I aim to illuminate some of the discursive processes at work in *The Oprah Winfrey Show* that fix identity in a manner that stands in contradiction to the 'elite' tradition explored earlier. I want to reiterate that I do not see the two discourses as a simple either/or binary, however, by separating out the work of some African American writers and black feminists, a way of viewing selfhood emerges that goes unrecognised by the 'elite' critics discussed above. This will enable me to expand on one of the most significant strands within my arguement: that *Oprah* presents a paradigm of selfhood that has its origins in black American culture rather than in (white) feminist or white male models of the self. The construction of self that emerges from this history of ideas combines with the version produced within the 'cultural anxiety' to produce a cultural form that is 'something new'.

This strategy is complicated. For example, the work of Collins (1991) offers a useful contribution to my map of the black feminist discourse that I draw on because much of her academic writing articulates the same concerns – the enrichment of a self – and through similar means as that displayed on *Oprah*. Further, the themes that provide the focus of her material are already familiar when one is acquainted with the work of writers such as Alice Walker and Toni Morrison. Collins argues that 'literature by black women provides the most comprehensive view of black women's struggles to form positive self-definitions'.[73]

The problem with Collins' position arises in her discussion of who can be considered a black feminist. On the one hand she warns against an essentialism that masks the role of politics and ideology in the construction of 'race' and gender categories. On the other hand, Collins suggests that 'black feminist thought encompasses theoretical interpretations of black women's reality by those who live it'.[74] Although she recognises that not all black women generate that thought and that it is possible that other groups may play a critical role in its production, Gilroy (1993) claims that 'another version of essentialism is smuggled in through the black porch'.[75] His criticism of Collins is one that could be made of my own approach here. Placing self and lived experience always first is to perpetuate intellectual thought that makes claims about the world based on ideal and stable subjects. 'Experience-centred knowledge claims ... simply end up substituting the standpoint of black women for its forerunner rooted in the lives of white men.'[76] This might be useful in the short term, Gilroy argues, but is an approach that ultimately lacks a radical edge, prohibiting movement beyond this limitation.

Although black women's experiences and their attitudes to the meanings of motherhood are central to Morrison's *Beloved*, Gilroy argues that the novel has a wider political reach. '[*Beloved*] encapsulates the confrontation between two opposed yet interdependent cultural and ideological systems and their attendant conceptions of reason, history, property and kinship'.[77] Thus the novel can be placed within the diasporic web that Gilroy calls the Black Atlantic.[78] Clearly this formulation of Morrison's work is one that positions it as sophisticated and more politically complex than Collins' approach. I recognise Gilroy's argument and should state that my own use of the material selected for this chapter is modest, and limited to that which explores black women's experiences and the self in relation to motherhood, and community in the formation of self-recognition. I am mapping a struggle for a positive self-definition that marks Oprah's autobiographical narrative as well as that of her guests. But most of the participants on *Oprah* are not black, and we can assume that the same is true of the audience; therefore, I am not suggesting that the views represented here apply to *only* and/or *all* black Americans, but that the black feminist and African American literature that I draw on represents a way in which selfhood is constructed through the formation of self-definition. This formation of self-definition represents a political gesture through which an individual mounts a challenge to existing definitions constructed by others in the maintenance of unequal power relations. Collins foregrounds her own position in the preface to *Black Feminist Thought*. 'This book reflects one stage in my ongoing struggle to regain my voice.'[79]

Despair, self-recovery and community

I have previously referred to David Riesman's view that America is comprised of mainly 'other directed' personality types who are marked by an anxiety that revolves around the need for recognition and acceptance. In fact, the condition of anxiety is strikingly absent from much African American discourse on selfhood. The state of mind more frequently evoked is that of despair. The *OED* defines anxiety as 'concern about an immanent or future difficulty' whereas despair signals 'the complete absence of hope'; the two terms are qualitatively different. However, what is also evident in black American literature is that despair is frequently the starting point from which recovery is posited as a possibility. This stands in contradistinction to the nihilism that denies the possibility of agency manifest in the view of selfhood examined earlier. What is interesting about the African American perspective explored here is that this process shares some of the concerns of the writers in the 'elite' tradition in which self is defined within a sense of crisis. This is not surprising; discourses are not self-contained units of meaning but overlap with others and change over time. But the overlap discussed here exists only up to a point.

A dialogue between bell hooks and Cornel West held at Yale University's African-American Center underlines my point. As intellectuals trained within 'white' cultural and philosophical traditions, this dialogue articulates some of the concerns delineated in the 'elite' cultural discourse. hooks and West begin by recognising the:

> existentialist chaos that exists in our own lives and our own inability to overcome the sense of alienation and frustration we experience when we try to create bonds of intimacy and solidarity with one another. Now part of this frustration is to be understood again in relation to structures and institutions. In the way in which our culture of consumption has promoted an addiction to stimulation...[T]he effect of this addiction to stimulation is an undermining, a waning of our ability for qualitatively rich relationships.[80]

What follows is recognition of the despair experienced by many black Americans, and a critical examination of the social, cultural and historical conditions that have combined to create that despair. However, hooks and West advocate mutual affirmation and support as the means of transcending the degradation signalled in the above quotation. West argues that when the crisis in western civilisation is talked about, it needs to be remembered that black people are a part of that civilisation:

> even though we have been beneath it, our backs serving as the foundation...and we need to understand how it affects us so that we may remain attuned to each other's humanity...We need to affirm one another, support one another, help, equip and empower one another to deal with the present crisis....[81]

While West frames his formulation within contemporary conceptualisations of postmodern sensibilities, commercialism and corporate ideologies, hooks reminds the audience that experiences of alienation and estrangement are tied to an 'historical memory' that engenders black peoples' thinking about the past in order to understand and come to terms with it. These are:

the conditions which enable a work like Toni Morrison's *Beloved* to receive so much attention. To look back, not just to describe slavery but to try and reconstruct a psycho-social history of its impact has only recently been fully understood as a necessary stage in the process of collective self recovery'.[82]

West argues that spiritual crisis manifests in the pursuit for therapeutic release. Here, in addition to 'existential chaos' we are reminded of the debilitation that the turn to the therapeutic both signals and engenders. West says that:

> you can get very thin, flat, and uni-dimensional forms of spirituality that are simply an attempt to sustain the well-to-do black folks as they engage in consumerism and privatism...In this syndrome, me-ness, selfishness, and egocentricity become more and more prominent, creating a spiritual crisis where you need more psychic opium to get you over.[83]

However, despite the occupation of common ground in describing the experience of a psychic/social malaise, the pathways then diverge; it is this divergence which marks the two discourses as qualitatively different. The West–hook dialogue calls for a move beyond the paralysis of pessimism that marks the cultural critiques of the dominant discourses and that also threatens to ensnare black Americans. They argue that this mobilisation depends on breaching the divide between the privileged and the underclass, and that the former needs to forego its 'bourgeois dream of liberal individualistic success'; that an ethic of service needs to be fostered; a realisation that rich human relations on a personal and communal level provide support and affirmation, acting as an antidote to the fracture evident in black communities (whether they be privileged or disadvantaged). The inevitability of struggle is integral to this process. hooks (1991) reminds the audience that:

> When we sang together 'We shall overcome' there was a sense of victory, *a sense of power that comes when we strive to be self determining*...In our liberatory pedagogy we must teach young black folks to understand that struggle is process, that one moves from circumstances of difficulty and pain to awareness, joy, fulfilment[84] (my emphasis).

In this dialogue, fracture, dislocation and a reductive sense of 'nothingness' are evoked through the metaphor of homelessness. West states

'We confront regularly the question: "Where can I find a sense of home?" '[85] 'Home' here stands in for that place that signifies the end of one's journey, of belonging, of self-realisation and of completion. This deployment of 'home' as a metaphor stands at odds with the way in which it is employed by Michael Wood and neatly illuminates the disparity between the view of the self – or, potential for self – articulated by hooks and West and the pathological self discussed earlier. Wood says 'America is not so much a home for everyone as a universal dream of a home, a wish whose attraction depends upon its level of remaining at the level of a wish.'[86] Contrast this ethereal depiction of a space with West's formulation:

> a sense of home can only be found in our construction of those communities of resistance bell talks about and the solidarity we can experience within them. Renewal comes through participating in community...That sense of home we are talking about and searching for is a place where we can find compassion, recognition of difference, of the importance of diversity, of our individual uniqueness.[87]

Wood's definition (1989) suggests the impossibility of self-realisation that is located within an ideal that is predicated on its being an ever-unobtainable wish or dream. Conversely, West suggests the possibility of self-realisation through active (political) participation in the construction of community. Furthering this, hooks argues for 'politicized mental care' seeing it as the new revolutionary frontier for black people, a frontier first opened up by Frantz Fanon in *Black Skin White Masks* (1952). This 'message of politicized self-recovery' could be presented to a mass black audience through the 'production of self-help literature...through the spreading of the word through the churches, community centers, houses etc.'.[88] hooks' idea of a political self-recovery remains undeveloped. Nonetheless, it is noteworthy that the spatial locations for the process of enlightenment that she envisions move beyond the confines of the university and the therapist's room and is located instead in institutions that comprise aspects of daily communal and family life.

The work of hooks that I have thus far drawn on comes from her book *Yearning*[89] in which the four epigraphs that face the opening page underscore the central concerns of her thinking. Two of these epigraphs read: 'Women yearn for change and will make great sacrifices for it.' (Lydia); and 'In this world-weary period of pervasive cynicisms, nihilisms, terrorisms, and possible extermination, there is a longing for norms and values that can make a difference, a yearning for principled resistance and struggle that can change our desperate plight.' (Cornel West) The work already cited is taken from the three essays which come at the end of the book, one of which is the dialogue with West; the final two are dialogues with Gloria Watkins (bell hooks' given name) and represent an interior conversation. The positioning of these essays marks their affinity with the epigraphs at the beginning, framing the discourse of the text as a whole. Further, the subject matter of these final essays is self-recovery – on both an individual and collective level – inflecting the earlier parts of the text with a particular meaning that works to construct a subjective identity insinuated within a larger political and historical frame. In 'An Interview With bell hooks' Gloria Watkins asks: 'let's return to the issue of self-recovery ... I know you are interested in spirituality. How do you reconcile that concern with radical politics?'

> bh: Well that's difficult isn't it ... Spiritual life has much to do with self-realization, the coming into greater awareness not only of who we are but our relationship within community that is so profoundly political.
> GW: And this is connected to self-recovery?
> bh: Very much so.[90]

In this formulation, ideas of a self that has integrity and agency are inextricably linked to self-recovery and self-realisation achievable by means of challenging apathy, ignorance and feelings of powerlessness engendered by:

> concrete circumstances of exploitation. But much more dangerously, [powerlessness] is also learned through the media, through television, because it is through watching TV that many black people learn to adopt the values and ideology of the ruling class even as they live in circumstances of oppression and deprivation.[91]

Self-recovery in this schema is linked with education, the raising of a critical consciousness and the will to protest.

Here, hooks is providing an example of cultural commentary that is enunciated by Winfrey and which, arguably, appropriates the 'elite' tradition of intellectual reflection, adapting it for political and cultural practice. hooks' repeated use of the term 'self-recovery' here presupposes a self that is always already damaged but recoupable. This is a narrative that constitutes Winfrey's public biography, that is rehearsed frequently on her shows and that is central to her persona. This is exemplified in a show cited at the beginning of the Introduction ('Teachers' Salute', BBC2, 17.10.95). In this show the audience is introduced to Winfrey's 4th grade teacher, Mrs Duncan. This woman had rescued the young Winfrey at a time of huge emotional distress – when her best friend had killed herself – and had inspired a love of learning. The teacher's interest in and compassion for her pupil is celebrated years later on *Oprah*. The reunion of Mrs Duncan and Winfrey is staged for the show and forms the frame within which the subsequent guests take their cue.

Another key characteristic of the presentation of a guest's story is their introduction through reading a piece of writing authored by the guest and taking the form of either a letter or a diary extract. In 'Girl Power' (BBC2, 15.11.95) – which is analysed in detail in Chapter 4 – the guest expert discusses 'the healing power of writing', arguing that in the face of powerlessness, self-expression through writing can foster feelings of empowerment. This position is endorsed by Winfrey who reminds us of her past sense of powerlessness, and of the transformative qualities inherent in self-authorship in both the written and spoken word. The public display of a private communication – a letter or diary – signals control through ownership of the narrative which, in turn works to validate the speaker's position. This is a form of testimony that recurs throughout *Oprah* shows; the practice of speaking out that which is personal and individual is a means of talking back in the face of oppressive forces. This act connotes the agency that provides the locus for hope rather than despair, standing in diametric opposition to the passive, one-dimensional model of self in which inner-directed agency is annihilated that is constructed by the 'elite' cultural tradition.

Hope, writing and self-definition

Speaking out and talking back are two strategies advocated by hooks (cited in Ferguson, 1990) as acts of political resistance, acts that are inextricably bound with writing. 'For [writers from oppressed and colonised groups] true speaking is not solely an expression of creative power, it is an act of resistance, a political gesture that challenges the politics of domination that would render us nameless and voiceless.'[92] Linking the act of writing with resistance has a powerful resonance in the discourse I am delineating here, and which is in itself an act of resistance within which resides hope and possibility.

Alice Walker has argued that while black and white authors are writing, for the most part, the same story, they come at it from multiple perspectives. 'The gloom of defeat is thick' in the writing of white Americans.

By comparison, black writers seem always involved in a moral/physical struggle, the result of which is expected to be some kind of larger freedom. Perhaps this is because our literary tradition is based on the slave narratives, where escape for the body and freedom for the soul went together, or perhaps this is because black people have never felt themselves guilty of global, cosmic sins.[93]

Walker (1983) draws too simplistic a separation between the work of black and white writers but is useful in that she underlines several key issues in the difference that she perceives between these groups. She demonstrates this by contrasting Kate Chopin's *The Awakening* (1899) and Zora Neale Hurston's *Their Eyes were Watching God* (1937). Both novels deal with the desire of the central female character to elude the restrictive confines of marriage to a society-conscious man and dull propriety-conscious community. However, the former novel concludes with Mme Pontellier's suicide, an option seen as preferable to the defiance of husband and community, whereas in the latter novel, Janie Crawford 'refuses to allow society to dictate her behaviour, enjoys the love of a much younger, freedom-loving man, and lives to tell others of her experience'.[94] The refusal to accede to powerful external social forces is that which marks the difference between the inner life of Hurston's female protagonist and that of Chopin's.

I have stated that Walker's is too simplistic a distinction between black and white writing. By this I mean that not *all* black writers produce optimistic accounts any more than *all* white writers create works of pessimism. For example, Ralph Ellison's *Invisible Man* (1952), Richard Wright's *Native Son* (1940) and Nella Larson's *Passing* (1939) could all be proffered as examples of pessimistic texts – whereas, apart from the celebrated *Yellow Wallpaper* (1898), most of Charlotte Perkins Gilman's fiction is very optimistic (and less critically acclaimed). My interest here however is in the political potential of writing. To take *Invisible Man* as an example; although Ellison's protagonist remains invisible, nameless, and underground throughout his narrative, his journey illuminates institutional practices and processes that produce his subjugated position. The act of writing itself is a potentially political act, and *Invisible Man* is a highly politicised text in which a history is excavated in order, as Craig Werner states, to repudiate 'the concept of history and the vocabulary in which history is written'.[95] So, there is an alternative reading to the pessimistic portrayal of black American experience. Rather, the 'burrow' of 'Ellison's *Invisible Man* [is] the ritual ground where the individual can examine his/her relationship with history in all its textual manifestations and strive for control of the text of his/her experience'. Excavation derives from the need for 'the power to force others to recognise your presence, your right to be there'.[96] This then is the intention behind the invisible man's narrative and is evident in concluding the excavation of his history by announcing the end of his hibernation. 'I must shake off the old skin and come up for breath. There's a stench in the air, which, from this distance underground, might be either of death or of spring – I hope of spring.'[97]

Werner (1983) presents a powerful argument for the empowering act of excavation in *Invisible Man* in particular but also in (re)writing one's own history in general. Looked at from this perspective, Kate Chopin's *Awakening* can be seen as a refusal of social and cultural practices that subjugate women in the same way that Ellison's novel is a disavowal of the history that subjugates black people in America. And Kate Chopin did not commit suicide any more than Ralph Ellison lived underground (he was a prolific essayist): the producers of these texts are not the texts themselves but exemplars of the ways in which challenges to existing order can be made through writing.

The notion of refusal is key within the black feminist discourse that I am interested in here and in its relation to *Oprah*. Appearing on the show is a means of denying marginalised and/or victim status through, firstly, simply *being* on the programme and secondly, through the rehearsal of lived experiences, the excavation of a personal history. This is as equally true of Winfrey as it is of her guests – and here it is useful to recall Masciarotte's (1991) claim that Winfrey refuses the 'essentialist algebra of hegemonic acceptance: black + woman = Mammy = m/Other = the absolutely Othered = the Other to us all'.[98]

This idea of disavowal through the reclamation of a history is one that stands at odds with the ways in which contemporary American culture is constructed within the 'elite' cultural tradition. For Lasch and Jameson it is the erosion of historicity that both represents and recreates depthlessness in the cultural psyche. However, mining the past in order to make sense of the present is, to repeat bell hooks, 'to try to reconstruct [the] psycho-social history' in order to understand the impact of institutions such as slavery. Walker remarks that black writers seem to be engaged in a moral and/or physical struggle that is possibly located within the tradition of the slave narrative which refutes the subjugated positioning of the enslaved. For contemporary black American writers, a refusal to be silent is contingent upon recalling the voices of the past, situating them in the context of the now. Walker recounts writing a short story 'The Revenge of Hannah Kemhuff' that was based on her

(Walker's) mother's experiences and on Hurston's collection of black folklore:

> In that story I gathered up the historical and psychological threads of the life my ancestors lived, and in the writing of it I felt joy and strength and my own continuity. I had that wonderful feeling...of being *with* a great many people, ancient spirits, all very happy to see me consulting and acknowledging them, and eager to let me know...that, indeed, I am not alone[99] (emphasis in original).

Memory, excavated and reconstructed histories

Writing has provided a potent means through which the subjugated voice may be heard, co-existing with the vitality of oral address by those speaking publicly in the crusade against slavery and for civil rights, and in stories passed down. There is a way in which the two modes of communication are inseparable here. Walker uses the voices of her mother and grandmother as the basis of her writing *In Search of Our Mother's Gardens* in a way that is related to Morrison's articulation of unspeakable and unspoken stories that combine to create *Beloved*. Walker writes of the stifled creative potential of her forebears, an act which both stands as a challenge to the controlling images that marked those women's existence and provides the frame for her own sense of self.

> Our mothers and grandmothers, some of them: moving to music not yet written. And they waited. They waited for the day when the unknown thing that was in them would be made known...For these grandmothers and mothers of ours were...Artists; driven to a numb and bleeding madness by the springs of creativity in them for which there was no release.[100]

The act of uncovering a past by drawing on the spoken as well as written word is one part of the process which culminates in Walker's sense of strength and continuity; the act of *writing* the story in which past and present cohere, is the means through which Walker achieves this. The community evoked in this writing is codified by a distinctive temporality through the inclusion of voices from the past as they impact on those in the present. The act of writing as instrumental in escaping the confines of a dislocated or solitary existence becomes conflated with my final observation here and that is the role of authorship in the process of self-recovery. 'It is, in the end, the saving of lives that we writers are about.

Whether we are "minority" writers or "majority". It is simply in our power to do this... [and] *the life we save is our own*[101] (emphasis in original). Throughout Walker's fictive and non-fictive writing, issues of historical memory, spirituality, political activism, artistic production and selfhood converge.

The idea of self-respect and recovery emerging in the wake of self-definition is played out on *Oprah* when individuals appear to present their own construction of a self that has been vilified in the larger social context: those who are overweight, underweight, advocate same-sex marriage, single parents, mothers of overactive children... The empowering possibility afforded to participants of speaking from the margins is a point taken up by some talk show commentators and discussed in the previous chapter. Joshua Gamson, for example, argues that shameful though the spectacle of freakishness is, the *most* shameful aspect of the display is that this represents the only public arena in which 'freaks' can talk back. Similarly, Patricia Joyner Priest's study of *Donahue* participants demonstrates the empowerment experienced in public declaration. Rehearsing one's own story is both a means of excavation and the process through which ownership can be claimed. Further, an important sense of community is engendered in reaching others who hold similar positions. This is particularly potent when the individual occupies a marginal social space.[102]

Marginality, remembering and the self

Ferguson (1990) raises an interesting question: when we think of issues relating to marginality, 'we must always ask, marginal to what?' The question is difficult to answer because 'the place from which power is exercised is often a hidden place. When we try and pin it down, the center always seems to be somewhere else. Yet we know that this phantom center, elusive though it is, exerts a real, undeniable power over the whole social framework of our culture, and over the way we think about it'. This 'centre' carries 'tacit standards' that serve the interests of the powerful and which can be internalised by those oppressed by it – indeed, I would argue that the internalisation of these standards by oppressed groups is *fundamental* to dominant interests. However, Ferguson's question introduces a volume of work by writers who refuse 'this unspoken structure,' who 'don't allow themselves to be defined only in relation to something else. They stand their own ground...'.[103] In this volume, bell hooks develops the issue of 'Marginality as site of Resistance' where she argues that as well as a site of deprivation, the margin is a potentially powerful space to occupy: it affords the possibility of mounting a counter hegemonic discourse through the imagining of alternative worldviews. Quoting from her earlier work *Feminist Theory: From Margin to Center*, hooks says 'To be in the margin is to be part of the whole but outside the mainbody', enabling a view of both centre and margin. 'This sense of wholeness... [provides] a mode of seeing unknown to our oppressors that sustained us [in segregated Kentucky], aided us in our struggle to transcend poverty and despair, strengthened our sense of self and our solidarity.'[104] The margin here is refigured as a positive space in which the capacity to resist is nurtured, is a site of radical possibility, and is therefore a place to hold on to.

Memory is necessarily that which facilitates the process of excavating the past of which *Invisible Man* is an example. The act of remembering provides a means to challenge oppressive structural regimes. Here, recalling a spiritual life, customs and practices offer a grounding for selfhood that is both connected to the past and to others within a community. We have already seen how hooks and Walker explicitly draw on the voices of ancestral women to articulate a sense of selfhood which stands counter to the hegemonic discourse that would position them otherwise. The reclamation of a history that is both personal and collective marks the discourse of the African American writers explored here. Willis (1994) writes that:

> When memory is conceptualised as form rather than content, it suggests a structure of meanings more fundamental than commonly attached to theories of resistance that focus on the content of meaning making. Memory as form also provides access to a continuum of cultural forms – some older than capitalism – whose influence on social relationships may continue into the present as an alternative to alienation and abstraction.[105]

Memory as form provides the meaning to Morrison's novel *Beloved* (1987) in which the eponymous ghost represents the buried memories of slave experience reaching back further than the personal narrative of Sethe, the novel's central character and mother of the dead baby girl, Beloved. Beloved, murdered by her mother in an act of refusal to be recaptured by slave catchers, returns in physical form once Sethe's burial of the past is disturbed by the reappearance of Paul D., a fellow slave from Sweet Home and not seen for some twenty years. Paul D.'s appearance acts as the catalyst for the excavation of Sethe's memories, hitherto locked away in her inert existence within a timeless present in which the future consists of holding the past at bay. However, the story to come to the surface as Sethe and Paul D. each confront fragments of their past is not theirs alone, but becomes a chorus as the various other voices combine to add their version of the same fragments. Ultimately, freedom – or the faint possibility of freedom – comes when the past has been hunted down and can no longer hold the memory-owner hostage. As the narrator of Sethe's inner world says, 'Freeing yourself is one thing; claiming ownership of the freed self was another'.[106] Ultimately, Sethe's recovery is dependent on the others with whom she shares her story. What we are left with at *Beloved*'s conclusion is the possibility of a tomorrow freed from the shackles of the past but also a past that needs to be remembered, recognised.

Beloved represents an important moment in American literary history in which, as Gilroy argues, the interest in, and exploration of, slavery is openly political, is a means to 'restage confrontations between rational, scientific, and enlightened Euro-American thought and the supposedly primitive outlook of prehistorical, cultureless, and bestial African slaves'.[107] The desire to articulate the confrontation between two opposed but interdependent cultural and ideological systems arises from 'present conditions'. Morrison states that:

> Modern life begins with slavery . . . from a women's point of view, in terms of confronting the problems of where the world is now, black women had to deal with the post-modern problems in the nineteenth century and earlier. These things had to be addressed by black people a long time ago: certain kinds of dissolution, the loss of and the need to reconstruct certain kinds of stability.[108]

The narratives spoken on *Oprah* are not an equivalent to *Beloved*, but their political work lies in the importance of acknowledging a history to better understand the present. This is a recurring feature of the stories told on the programme. The guests' narratives are also marked by a repeated assertion of the centrality of family and social relationships, of community and lived experience in the construction of a stable identity. The following section delineates the ways in which these aspects of daily life are articulated within a black feminist discourse.

Community, lived experience and black feminist thought

I have argued that the act of remembering provides a means through which structures of domination may be challenged and we have seen how this operates through the medium of the novel. But the message that Morrison articulates in *Beloved* in many ways echoes that which is argued by some black women scholars; the importance of the past, of one's community, of the experiences of everyday life. Hooks (1981) underlines the particular issues faced by black women in America by pointing to the double marginality and invisibility of their experience. 'No other group in America has had their identity socialised out of existence as have black women. We are a barely recognised group separate and distinct from black men, or as a present part of the larger group "women" in this culture.'[109]

Collins sees her project (in *Black Feminist Thought*) as one in which, given the fact that many African American women are silenced, 'the voice that I now seek is both individual and collective, personal and political'.[110] As with hooks, who sees the marginal site as a space in which to develop alternative ways of viewing the world, Collins argues the importance of everyday, non-scholarly activities in the formulation of a knowledge that may sit uncomfortably with the dominant group.

We can make a comparison here with Winfrey, who in her various roles of intellectual-in-performance, activist, media producer and popular entertainer mobilises a discourse that is also located in Collins' political project. Analytically, black women intellectuals have developed the foundation 'for a distinctive standpoint on self, community and society and, in doing so, have created a black woman's intellectual tradition' that is striking in its thematic consistency.[111] These themes are: (1) the interlocking nature of 'race', gender and class oppression; (2) the replacement of denigrating images of black women with self-defined images; (3) the belief in black women's activism as mothers, teachers and community leaders; (4) the sensitivity to sexual politics. I would argue that this tradition extends beyond the academy to include works of fiction such as those of Gloria Naylor, Alice Walker, Toni Morrison as well as the autobiographical material of Maya Angelou which broadens the reach of the audience. The blurring of the boundaries between works that are in circulation for popular consumption and those that are written with an academic audience in mind occurs because the subject matter is consistent, as is often the language employed within the texts. The erosion of these boundaries is furthered when these novels are transposed to the television and film screen.

Taking up hooks' argument that black women have historically been effaced by discourses of 'race' and of feminism, Collins argues that this black women's tradition has been relatively unknown until now for reasons that are neither accidental nor benign. The invisibility of black women empowers the oppressor pervading 'the entire social structure'. In Collins' view, the politics of black feminist thought is marked by the 'dialectic of oppression and activism, the tension between the suppression of black women's ideas and our activism'.[112] Resistance and empowerment begins with self-definition from which it is possible to develop an autonomous group identity that can then be deployed to create a dialogue with other groups. Clearly, in this schema, the sense of an individual self is the fundamental basis enabling political activism; the self and the group are explicitly and inextricably enmeshed. Drawing on the work of bell hooks, Collins argues that resistance to oppression is to be found in the process of self-identification, of telling one's own story.

This formulation of individual selfhood – achieved through reclaiming one's history and telling one's story – stands at variance with the American ideal of individualism which posits the possibility of self-realisation through individual endeavour and success which are Oprah's hallmarks. The difference lies in the formulation of self that is positioned within a communal context, within a series of interdependent relationships. It is Collins' view that 'the primary guiding principle of black feminism is a recurring humanist vision' so that the right to 'life, liberty and the pursuit of happiness' enshrined in the Declaration of Independence becomes inalienable to all. Walker's term 'womanist' is evoked to speak of the desire to aim for the 'survival and wholeness of an entire people'. Therefore, the black feminist project is 'a process of self-conscious struggle that empowers men and women to actualize a humanist vision of community'.[113]

The self-conscious struggle that Collins points to must begin by recognising that '[t]he commonplace, taken-for-granted knowledge shared by African-American women growing from everyday thoughts and actions constitutes a first and most fundamental level of knowledge'.[114] Referring again to writers such as Walker, Naylor and Morrison, Collins suggests that these women have succeeded in producing a new community that, rather than acting as consciousness raising, 'affirms and rearticulates a consciousness that already exists'.[115] Non-traditional sources of knowledge – black churches, black communities, the ideas shared by mothers and 'othermothers', teachers and the children of the community – represent the experiences of African Americans which form the standpoint of black women, a fellowship that includes artists, musicians and writers. The process of self-definition and affirmation facilitates contestation of oppressive structures that have sought to define the black body as (degraded) other. The legacy of struggle, dating from the days of slavery, is that which has stimulated the black women's capacity for self-reliance and interdependencies.

This posits a worldview in which selfhood is formed through the direct engagement with a series of significant relationships so that, in this discourse, the model of self is premised on an inner locus of control. This stands in contradistinction to the 'elite' cultural critics whose concept is of a self formed by the external forces of a technologically advanced, consumer-driven culture in which a turn to the therapeutic signals attempts to counter feelings of emptiness. At the heart of this black feminist discourse is the mother and 'othermother' who is key in the facilitation of a positive formation of self. The assertion is that mothers, 'othermothers', teachers and sisters 'were central to the retention and transformation of [the] Afro-centric world view'.[116] This offers an alternative explanation of slavery and continues to be used to challenge negative evaluations of black womanhood. There is link to be made between the model of the mother/othermother of the black feminist discourse and Oprah's performance on her show; this will be discussed below. In the meantime, it is helpful to delineate the role of the other-mother figure here.

Standing in contrast to the formulation of mothering offered by Geoffrey Gorer and Christopher Lasch – who see the mother as central to the development of psychoneurosis – discussed above, the mother in this discourse is an empowering and empowered figure. The role of the mother in the formation of self-reliance and in stressing the importance of community and roots is taken up by Stanlie M. James who says that:

> [w]hile western conceptualizations of mothering have often been limited to the activities of females with their biological offspring, mothering within the Afro-American community and throughout the black diaspora can be viewed as a form of cultural work or what Bernice Johnson Reagon calls "the entire way a community organizes to nurture itself and future generations".[117]

It is James's contention that the African American tradition of mothering has its roots in traditional African culture and that it holds the possibility of 'new models for social transformation in the twenty-first century'.[118] This tradition draws on the concept of 'othermothers' who, while not being the biological parent of the child[ren] in their care, take on the responsibilities of childcare both in the long and the short term and is a method of nurture traceable to the days of slavery. Enslaved families were fragile and unstable units due to the possibility of death or of being sold; other slave women would often take care of children left without parents. This pattern of mothering has in turn stimulated what

Collins refers to as a 'more generalized ethic of care where Black women feel accountable to all the Black community's children'.[119]

James (1993) argues that this ethic of care, or, othermothering, has empowered the women that practice it and those who benefit from it. Lack of access to traditional sources of power, especially within institutions such as the armed forces, political systems, economic systems and the mass media, has impacted on the African American community in ways that necessitated the development of non-traditional sources of empowerment. As the source of sustenance, othermothering has 'been critical to the survival of Black communities'.[120] The othermother is not located solely within the realm of the domestic however; her reach extends to the wider, public arena to encompass political activism. For example, James offers Ella Baker – a prominent activist in the National Association for the Advancement of Colored People (NAACP) during the late 1930s – as an example of a community othermother who 'served as a kind of political midwife at the births of the Southern Christian Leadership Conference (SCLC) and the Student Nonviolent Co-ordinating Committee (SNCC) in the 1950s and 1960s'.[121]

The uncovering and celebration of the activities of many black women, and their role in empowering a disempowered community has been the work of an increasing number of black women writers. 'Black women have been talking quite a lot since 1970 attempting to resist masculine bias in black social and political thought.'[122] Work has been carried out to reveal the activities not only of those involved in large scale political movements, but also of those on the ground, engaged in the everyday lives of the people with whom they lived. Historian Darlene Clark Hine declares that her own mission in compiling such a history is 'the transformation of American history', to reveal the ways in which women formed large networks creating 'vast new communities', and to empower and 'make visible the lives and deeds of ordinary folk'. As Hine argues, even traditional historians know that 'history is a construct that reflects systems of power relations'.[123] Hine's work (1994) unveils the networks of enslaved women that operated a system of support and care, fostering a self-reliance. Kim Marie Vaz, in the preface to her edited volume *Black Women in America* (1995) says: 'Within the content of the material [that comprises *Black Women*] are pragmatic strategies for changing one's own life conditions. Hence, the nature of the subject matter acts as a personal and group organizer.'[124] *Black Women* delineates the history of black women's participation in social and political activity that has gone previously unrecognised by a larger audience but nonetheless has been influential in the shaping of their respective communities.

The concept of individualism is not one that is foregrounded in the essays, but rather the interdependence of group members and the positive sense of agency that this engenders.

My purpose in referring to these writers here is not to rehearse the historical findings of the authors, but to underline the theme that connects them: the role of women in the formation of a sense of community, continuity and self-respect that is derived from these various activities. Their mode of operation forms systematic and alternative ways of being which have stood counter to the dominant systems that excluded and undermined a body of people. The work of black historians not only uncovers stories absent from the traditional historical canon, but is of itself part of the process of self-reclamation carried out by mothers/othermothers, church leaders, schoolteachers and black political activists.

It is the case that on *Oprah* as each guest speaks their narrative, they are claiming ownership of that story. But the process, mediated by confession and testimony, is mobilised by Oprah whose own persona provides the filter through which the stories are understood and acquire meaning. As we will see in Chapter 4, *Oprah's* overarching narrative is one of self-realisation achieved through overcoming disabling circumstance and a subsequent transformation of self-identity. The self that is realised in this metanarrative is one that is premised on self-respect and on meaningful, intimate relations with significant others. Oprah's performance in facilitating this process is underpinned by her film roles of Sophia in *The Color Purple* and Sethe in *Beloved*. As such, comparisons can then be made between the relationship between Oprah and her guests and, by extension, her audience and the figure of the mother/othermother in this black feminist discourse. However, there are also differences. The influence of the mother/othermother of black feminism is situated within a specifically delineated group – black American women – and represents an actual relationship that arises from daily life. Oprah, by contrast, is a construct formed through the system of celebrity, inextricably linked with processes of commodification and commercialism, and deployed in a TV show with a mass and variegated audience. Intimacy formed through encounters in daily life is not the same as the appearance of intimacy engendered for the television screen. These represent significant differences. However, in her performance as talk show host, Oprah facilitates expressions of selfhood that are grounded in self-esteem and self-identity, thereby reproducing some of the qualities ascribed to the othermother in black feminist literature.

The processes of excavation and self-reclamation provide the structural model for the narratives spoken on *Oprah* and which frequently provide the means of countering definitions imposed externally and by others. So, we often see an individual replacing a status of victim with that of victor, reinscribing their sense of self as active social agent in control of their own narratives as well as the representation of those narratives. This process of self-definition is also one that occurs within the black feminist literature I have been discussing here.

A challenge to controlling and oppressive images is mounted in both the *activity* of excavating a past and the *results* of that excavation. Collins argues that images have operated as a part of the systematic control of black women and exist as an exercise in power 'by elite white males and their representatives'.[125] These images are reinforced by a dichotomous either/or mode of thinking embedded in western societies. Among the most frequently evoked images are Mammy, the faithful domestic servant, the Matriarch, the mother deemed 'bad' because she fails to execute her womanly duties within the home, the Welfare Mother who operates as the updated version of the woman breeder of slaves, and the Jezebel, deemed sexually aggressive and a whore. These controlling images are, in Collins' view, central to the 'nexus of white male images of black womanhood because efforts to control black women's sexuality lie at the heart of black women's exploitation'.[126]

For Collins, self-definition lies in resisting the mammy and matriarch stereotypes, the resistance to which resides at the core of black women's consciousness. Safe spaces in which dialogue can occur are prerequisite for finding a voice and the articulation of a self. Identifying the same spaces as those advocated by hooks as arenas for politicised mental health, Collins points to extended families, churches and African American community organisations, schools, in literature, through the media and in popular culture. 'Afro-centric communication maintains the integrity of the individual and his or her personal voice, but does so in the context of group activity.'[127] The means through which autonomy, self-identity and group cohesion is made possible are those offered in close relationships with one another – between daughters and mothers, friends and sisters – through writing and through blues music.

Winfrey's continual reiteration of her roots, and her relationship with prominent black writers enables her to endorse their work, offering a platform from which to address a mass audience. In an interview with Toni Morrison on the publication of her novel *Paradise* (1998), Katherine Viner remarks that the book's instant popular success is due in part to its sanction on Oprah's book club. Morrison states that 'Oprah has made it all right to turn off the television and read a book in the middle of the day...Spreading the readership of my own book is one thing, but spreading the idea of not being unwilling to pick up a fairly challenging book via somebody on television is quite extraordinary.'[128] This overlap, articulated by Morrison, points to the way in which Oprah Winfrey moves beyond the discursive structures of television to articulate and underpin a self-identity that is then reinforced through the ways in which she represents herself on her show. In the process, she moves her mass audience/potential readers with her, while simultaneously remaining connected to her own community. This connection is signalled not just through an affiliation with black spokespersons but also through her relationship with her partner Stedman and her best friend Gail, both of whom are black, and her use of black vernacular. Winfrey presents a voice that is both a part of, and apart from, the television industry, the organisation of which is largely dominated by white men, and which speaks to a mass audience in a 'race' conscious society that has historically positioned the black body as the undesirable – but absolutely necessary – other (this is developed in Chapter 5). The vehicle for this voice, and therefore that which shapes the voices that combine to create any one *Oprah*, is also rooted in the tradition of Gospel and orality and mobilised through call and response, an 'African derived...*process* of communication'[129] (emphasis in original).

Speaking out and talking back: call and response, and *Oprah*

Geneva Smitherman states that in black street vernacular:

> 'gittin ovuh' has to do with surviving...In Black America, the oral tradition has served as a fundamental vehicle for gittin ovuh. The tradition preserves the Afro-American heritage and reflects the collective spirit of the 'race'. Through song, folk sayings and rich verbal interplay among everyday people, lessons and precepts about life are handed down from generation to generation.[130]

However, Smitherman also argues that to write one's own story rather than to have one's story written by an other can also be the means of empowerment. This is evident not just through the literature discussed in the second part of this chapter but we will also see that on *The Oprah Winfrey Show* guests frequently support their testimonies or confessions with written statements in the form of diaries or letters. These pieces of writing underscore that which is verbalised, confirming ownership of the narrative.

Written or spoken, the words uttered on the show form part of a pattern that can be described as call and response, 'a black mode of discourse', that is defined thus: 'spontaneous verbal and non-verbal interaction between speaker and listener in which all of the speaker's statements ("calls") are punctuated by expressions ("responses") from the listener. In the traditional black church, call–response is often referred to as "talking back" to the preacher'.[131] Smitherman argues that call and response acts as an organising principle through which balance and harmony in the community of men and women are unified in line with the traditional African world view. Most carefully preserved in the black church, call and response enables the mobilisation of the 'emotion packed blend of sacred and secular concerns' that characterise the church service. 'Since the church is a social as well as religious unit, the preacher's job is to make churchgoers feel at home and to deal with problems and realities confronting his people as they cope with the demands and stresses of daily living.'[132]

As well as being an important social unit that offers support for the needy, the church functions as a buffer 'and source of release against white oppression'.[133] Of call and response, Smitherman (1977) writes:

> This interactive system embodies community rather than individuality. Emphasis is on group cohesiveness, co-operation, and the collective common good. In the traditional black church, we find that spiritual regeneration depends on the visitation of the Spirit, but the efforts of the total group are needed to bring this about.[134]

The call and response paradigm suggests a redistribution of power that is evoked in the service of 'gittin ovuh', and is the product of an interdependent collection of individuals who combine to create and define the whole. Individual testimony underpins and is underpinned by the leadership of the preacher to produce a communal whole in which the possibility of empowerment emerges. My argument is that the dynamics of the large majority of *Oprah* shows mirror those of the black church with its call and response patterning, its dependence on participants – the congregation – under the steerage of the host/minister. Typically, what we have is a pattern in which:

> Oprah calls by introducing the topic and the guests.
> First guest responds by telling their story.
> Oprah calls by contextualising and introducing another guest.

Second guest responds by adding to the narrative.
Oprah calls by endorsing the act of bringing the issue to the public arena.
Expert responds by offering a frame of reference for the topic.
Oprah calls to the studio audience inviting participation.
Audience responds by offering experiences of their own or by calling to the guests in the form of a question.
Further guests respond by adding their voices.
Oprah adds a response to that of the guests and so on.

Frequently, calls are responded to by the display of a video clip from an earlier show, a series of images that support the spoken word and through the reading out of diary extracts. However, on *Oprah* there is divergence also in the introduction of non-verbal material that facilitates the flow of information produced. Oprah not only calls but responds also, sometimes to her own call and sometimes in response to a call by a participant. This constitutes a part of a communicative process in which positions of authority and power migrate. This will become more apparent in the following chapters.

In this chapter, I have delineated two separate – but at times overlapping – traditions of thought that are at play in the programme. Firstly, the 'elite' cultural critics describe and perform a self fragmenting under the pervasive influences of technological advance, consumerism and commodification. It represents a discursive practice in which ideas of the therapeutic are inextricably enmeshed both in its methodological framing and in the ways in which recourse to therapy constructs a pathological self. Here, the fracture of intimate family and social relations is the consequence of the omnipresence of the mass media, which offers flat, one-dimensional models of self within which there is no possibility of political agency. This is made evident on the programme through the serial presentation of fractured and fragmented individuals whose inclinations towards therapy and televisual display seem to offer the best chance for recovery.

The second tradition traceable in *Oprah* is one that arises within black feminism and African American thought in which self is constructed in relation to community and significant others. Here, agency is possible through opposition to oppressive and debilitating circumstance, and through the excavation of a history that is both personal and collective. I have discussed how this offers the paradigm for the stories articulated by the guests on *Oprah* (and which will be analysed in more detail in subsequent chapters). In addition, the call and response dynamic of the black church that operates in service to 'gittin ovuh' is similar to the testimonial and confessional dynamic of *Oprah*.

The chapter that follows offers a detailed examination of a single *Oprah* show. This analysis reveals how the voices on the programme are managed, and how relations are formed through confessional and testimonial practice. It is only through a detailed textual analysis that it is possible to draw out the particular dynamics and the relations of power that are produced in the process.

3
Confessional Discourse on *Oprah*

In the preceding chapter, I pinpointed two divergent cultural commentaries on the formation of selfhood. Both of these modes of thought present available means for understanding the construction of selfhood, and both are evident in *The Oprah Winfrey Show*. In addition, each of these positions offers recognisable frameworks for the critical responses to the talk show genre in general and *Oprah* in particular. It is this that explains the either/or dichotomy that characterises – and limits – current critical debate on the cultural role and political effects of the talk show.

The purpose of this chapter is to look at the deployment of voices that are heard on *Oprah*, and the relationship of those voices to one another. Further, I will explore the relationship of Winfrey to her guests by considering the way in which she positions herself within the nexus of the stories articulated. I have chosen to examine a single show in order that the paradigmatic dynamic of confessional practice may become clear through an analysis of the discursive practices employed within *Oprah*. Confession is one of the key discursive strategies at play in the presentation of self through the medium of the show; and I will be adapting Michel Foucault's analysis of confessional practice as a means to examine the ways in which relations of power are produced on *Oprah*. I need to point out that there is a danger inherent in looking at an isolated example of a show that, over time, handles a variety of subject matters in numerous ways; the regular viewer will gain a broader perspective.[1] This being the case, to isolate one programme from the rest can work to limit understanding of a programme, the analysis of which lies in the consideration of a broad spectrum of shows broadcast. So, the show investigated here needs to be read within the context of the wider analysis that will be offered in subsequent chapters exploring the narrative structure of the stories told (Chapter 4), the construction of the Oprah persona and the relationship with guests and viewers (Chapter 5).

The dynamics of confessing

Confessional discourse is central to *Oprah*. Mimi White has examined Michel Foucault's discussion of confession as an 'agency of truth and power in Western society' revising Foucault's theorisations in relation to contemporary American media culture. White argues that 'confession and therapeutic discourse centrally figure as narrative and narrational strategies in television in the United States ... Problems and their solutions are narrativized in terms of confessional relations ... Self-identity and social recognition ... hinge on participation in the process of mediated confession'.[2]

In *The Will to Knowledge: The History of Sexuality*, Vol. I (1978), Foucault's premise is that confession is the means through which networks of power and knowledge converge and circulate. Standing at the heart of a nexus of disciplinary discourses – of the church, the army, educational institutions, and as White argues, the media – confession is the mode by which disciplinary power is exerted on the bodies of individual men and women. Because of its perceived path to truthfulness, the cleansing power of confession has, Foucault argues, taken on a therapeutic hue in western societies – the truth heals – a notion underpinned by the scientific requirement for observation and classification. The act of confessing itself displays the power relations inherent in a process which operates to make visible, define, codify, normalise and exclude.

> The confession is a ritual of discourse in which the speaking subject is also the subject of the statement; it is also a ritual that unfolds within a power relationship, for one does not confess without the presence (or virtual presence) of a partner who is not simply interlocutor but the authority who requires the confession, prescribes and appreciates it, and intervenes in order to judge, punish, forgive, console and reconcile; a ritual in which the truth is corroborated by the obstacles and resistances it has had to surmount in order to be formulated; and finally, a ritual in which the expression alone, independently of its external consequences, produces intrinsic modifications in the person who articulates it: it exonerates, redeems, and purifies him; it unburdens him of his wrongs, liberates him, and promises salvation.[3]

This formulation is the paradigm with which I will examine the management of voices on the *Oprah* show analysed in this chapter.[4]

An *Oprah* show broadcast in Britain in December 1995[5] examines the repercussions of losing weight. In this programme, a number of women guests are invited to speak about their weight loss and how this has affected their self-image. But the stress of the show is on the way in which the move from a negative to a positive sense of self – signified by and through weight reduction – has adversely affected these women's relationships with those family and friends closest to them. During the course of the show Oprah Winfrey places herself in a variety of positions, locating herself as host and star of *Oprah*, interlocutor, friend, interpreter and fellow confessor. As each guest discloses her own experience relating to weight gain and/or loss and self-perception, Oprah frequently interjects with examples of her own experience in this area. In this instance, all the guests are female; no male guest appears on this show other than as silent members of the studio audience. As we look, we can see Oprah moving from one position to another, drawing the disparate threads together and uniting the various voices of the invited guests and the studio audience creating the sense of one community facing and experiencing a shared problem.

The structure of the show 'Lose Weight, Lose Friends'

Segment one: Introduction – today's topic and guests who are to appear.
Segment two: First guests – Oprah interviews two cousins, Lisa and Sheila.
Segment three: Correspondence from viewers – viewers' letters are read; some of the authors are interviewed.
Segment four – Oprah interviews Rosemary and her daughter Jennifer; followed by audience participation through asking questions and directing observations.
Segment five: The expert voice – the guest therapist makes an intervention.
Segment six: Audience participation – a debate that takes place within the audience while the guests remain seated on the stage.

The show opens with Oprah standing on a raised platform, the camera and studio audience in front of her whilst a series of still photographs of large women are shown on a screen behind her. Those of us watching at home see Oprah standing to the left of, and dwarfed by, the video screen displaying the images of large women. Oprah is addressing the camera in front of her so that the studio audience is out of shot, placing us, the viewers, in the position of those present in the studio. A brief biography of each woman is offered as her image appears. 'This woman lost 150 lbs in one year. She has also lost her dearest friend in the world ... And this woman said her life would never be the same again.' These images and biographies serve as an introduction to the theme of the show: loss of weight and the subsequent loss of friendship. We are promised that 'Later, you're going to hear first time confessions ... and share shame also from the daughter of this suburban mother. Feelings too tender to share until today.' Oprah tells us, that 'It's really unbelievable.' The images behind Oprah are now those of the 'suburban mother' in her obese form and as her new, slim self. The video footage is accompanied by an extract of a letter, written and read by the daughter, Jennifer, who is expressing shame and embarrassment now that she is fatter than her mother. But this story is for later.

Throughout this introduction, the studio audience remains silent as Oprah introduces us to the first guests, Lisa and Sheila, two women who have been friends for 30 years (they are in fact cousins also). 'Now there is one thing now too big for them to overcome.' The women have made a video tape which is narrated by them and is played on a giant screen at the far end of the studio. Their voices are heard off screen whilst images, both still and moving, are played against a background of soft music. The music, images and quiet tone of their voices bear testimony to that relationship. The video narrates the lifelong friendship that has existed between the two women. Lisa has always been overweight, but after childbirth, Sheila found that her own weight also increased beyond her control. To her (Sheila's) dismay, Lisa, after a long diet, became the thin one. The film narrates Sheila's growing concern and consternation about her friend's new attractive body shape and her own negative self-image in relation to this. The video ends and is left without comment by Oprah, who now positions herself on the stage sitting opposite Lisa and Sheila who are seated together. All three sit on comfortable-looking chairs at a side angle to the audience. The camera angle remains straight on, so that for the moment, we remain positioned as the studio audience.

Leaning towards the two women slightly, Oprah encourages them to talk further about the difficulty facing them now that they see that their friendship has altered, become problematic. Feelings of jealousy and guilt are expressed over the change that has occurred to the detriment of the friendship. That the two women still feel warm towards each other is evident from the frankness of their testimony, the tone of their voices – which are calm and sad sounding – and the occasional physical contact such as a hand placed momentarily on the other's knee. Although the main problem discussed is one of not feeling comfortable with one another any more, the staging and the behaviour of the women belie this. Oprah adopts a stance similar to Lisa and Sheila in her interview/ conversation with them. In doing this, Oprah is immediately aligning herself with her guests in the way that she mirrors their seating arrangements and behaviour, in her positioning of herself with them on the stage and not among the studio audience, and in her method of questioning. Her opening words following the video are, 'Wow. When you lose 150 lbs, do you feel differently?' The word 'wow' denotes her appreciation of Lisa's verbal testimony given in the film. It also connotes that theirs is a friendship deserving of some sort of positive affirmation as well as offering the possibility that Sheila's may be seen as an astonishing confession coming from someone who, by the definition of friendship, should be more supportive of another's success.[6] However, the ambiguity of the word 'wow' is not left any space in which to be considered as Oprah straight away launches into her first question. However, before Lisa can respond, Oprah foregrounds herself as subject by answering her own question, relaying information relating to her own experiences of weight loss. She tells the women (and studio and home audiences) that having lost 80 lbs herself – 'half a person' – she felt completely different physically. As Oprah speaks, Lisa nods her head in agreement.

Interjection is frequently practised by Oprah; not only does this signal her control over that which is being spoken, it also works to mark the shift in subject relations as she becomes the confessor. This movement identifies a key aspect of her persona as well as a reconfiguration of power relations that is produced through the confessional discourse and becomes more evident in the following segment of the programme.

During the brief conversation that follows, we see Oprah adopting a number of positions almost simultaneously. She is interviewer, putting questions to the two women about the way in which the nature of their relationship has altered; she is confidant and interlocutor to whom private thoughts and feelings are given; she is subject as she too confesses her own private difficulties; and she is friend and equal aligning her own problems with those of her invited guests. The sense of intimacy is further enhanced by Oprah's attention being given entirely to the women in front of her. The camera and studio audience are apparently not present as we are focused on the faces of the three women in turn. All we see of the background is what is immediately behind the chairs occupied by the guests; the screen bearing the *Oprah* signature which is usually present is absent at this moment. The notion that we are eavesdropping on a private meeting is breached on occasions when close-ups of one of the two guests include a view of the studio audience in the background, but the audience is silent and slightly out of focus. While Oprah effaces her role as show host and star during this stage of the programme, she simultaneously privileges her status by frequently interjecting before and during a response by Lisa or Sheila, foregrounding not only her own experiences, but the fact that she is in control of the proceedings and able to direct audience attention. (We learn later that she is also in control of her own weight problem.) Her own voice, in whatever guise, is heard over and above those of her guests. Only once during this part of the show are we reminded that this is a performance when Oprah, following a confession from Sheila relating to her initial wish that Lisa would fail to lose weight, says 'This is so interesting. The dynamics of this is so fascinating.' Although this observation is offered to the two women, the camera angle places us in front of Oprah as she speaks. From the direction of her look, we can see that it is Lisa and Sheila who are addressed, but there is a brief flicker of attention which moves her gaze away from the guests and towards the camera implicating the home audience in her address. The observation momentarily changes the status of Lisa and Sheila from friends and fellow confidants to that of subjects appraised from the distance of the clinically therapeutic; in addition, it turns them into a spectacle for the audience. That Lisa and Sheila seem unperturbed by this serves to further remind us that this is a public confessional show and that scrutinies of this sort are expected, indeed are integral to the genre. The guests know this and so do we the viewers.

From these exchanges it is clear that a complex arrangement of voices and relationships emerges as a result of the strategies employed by Oprah and that what we have here is not simply a host interviewing a guest/ guests about an issue.

In her examination of therapeutic discourse in American television, Mimi White[7] argues that the deployment of therapeutic and confessional strategies allows for a more direct participation in the production of programmes than in other forms of popular culture.

They speak in their own voices to help produce the texts of our multiply mediated, information/therapeutic culture. The audience is given the opportunity to speak – as expert, as authority, and as celebrity – even as their voices are channelled and contained to a great extent. Yet this channelling does not resemble forms of power and domination at stake in a dialogic interpersonal exchange. Instead, all voices are dispersed through and across contemporary technologies, information and financial exchanges, and conventions of entertainment in contemporary consumer culture. The voices of individuals are mobilised in the process. Indeed none of these systems would work properly without these confessional voices, whether they are fictional or not.[8]

White's argument is that audiences are already caught up in the therapeutic and confessional mode along with the consumer culture that is overtly supported through the advertising appeals that intersperse television programmes. Thus the therapeutic mode ensures the commercial viability of a programme while it at the same time re-articulates a cultural ideal projected through the class and lifestyle images displayed in the programmes and in the advertisements.

> The flexibility of the therapeutic ethos is particularly striking, insofar as it is deployed to engage, even recruit, viewers for (and from) a wide range of class/lifestyle images within contemporary consumer culture. Like television itself, therapy offers something for everyone, or can be tailored to fulfil a variety of needs and fantasies.[9]

The system of contemporary technologies – financial exchange, entertainment codes, information – are dependent on the deployment of confessional and therapeutic discourse which act to shore up instability and uncertainty; at the same time, however, these technologies' appropriation of therapeutic discourse 'supports a dispersion of subjectivity and meaning that has been seen to characterise the postmodern condition'.[10] Family and social relations are overdetermined by traditional gender roles and inscribed within consumer culture that is itself inextricably linked with what White refers to as the 'telecommunications culture'.[11]

This appropriation of the therapeutic by dominant discursive regimes in contemporary culture is a recognisable aspect of *Oprah*. In the chapter that follows, we will see how traditional social and family structures are inscribed throughout the narratives: sexual relationships are overwhelmingly discussed within a heterosexual frame whilst family units are comprised of father/mother, husband/wife, son/daughter. Thus far, White's formulation does offer a recognisable framework within which to view the discursive practices that constitute *Oprah*. A deeply embedded social acceptance of the therapeutic reinforces normative sexual and social practices while standing in service to the interests of consumerism. The voices that speak on the show are mobilised through the system of celebrity – embodied by Oprah – that itself acts as an avowal of the cultural ideals of individualism and success that are in turn enmeshed with notions of commodity and consumption.

The exchanges between Lisa, Sheila and Winfrey indicate that this 'ritual of discourse' is familiar to participants and audience alike – through therapy and images of it. As White says, 'All [television] viewers are always already inexorably caught up in the confessional mode . . .'.[12] Winfrey is the authority within the 'power relationship' to whom the confession is offered. The confession, far from destabilising the friendship between Sheila and Lisa, seeks to cement it; Sheila, in confessing to feelings of guilt and envy of her friend, is being redeemed, exonerated and purified. Lisa validates the process by her acceptance of Sheila's difficulty and her own counter-confession: 'I feel as if it is all my own fault.' Winfrey's own relationship to the two women is more problematic. Primarily, she is 'the authority who requires the confession', but she also moves from this position to that of the one who confesses. Although her speech is directed towards the women immediately in front of her, she is also addressing a studio audience and an audience at home. In doing this, she appears to be investing the average person with the same power that she herself possesses. By putting herself in this one down position – the means by which an individual can be seen to be placing themselves in a position of less, rather than more, power – she effaces her star persona, conveying a sense of equality. Although both she and her audiences are aware that this is a fictitious state of relationship, it contributes to the sense of intimacy engendered during the exchange and validates Oprah's claim of being Every Woman – a declaration she makes of herself in this and other shows and which is her theme tune for this season.

In addition, this shift endows Oprah with another form of power and authority, one that derives from personal experience: I know because I have been there too. This authority based on experience is enhanced through its relationship with the expert voice, which is only fleetingly heard in this show. As we saw in Chapter 1, the voice of expertise is seen by some to be an indication of the degree to which an individual's appearance on talk shows is an act of transgression or recuperation. In this programme, the voice of experience is that which carries authority rather than that of bourgeois expertise. I will comment further on the expert in this show later.

While the subject matter – weight loss and the attendant disruption of important relationships – is the focus, the principal concern of this show is the narrative of confessional relations facilitated by the articulation of personal experience. Even if the difficulty between Lisa and Sheila had resulted say from drug misuse, child abuse, a disagreement over an item of clothing, the structure and pattern of the exchange, and the power relations within it, would remain the same. What makes this particular example fertile ground for exploration is the audience's knowledge of Oprah's own series of weight gains and losses. These, as regular viewers will know, have been the topic of many shows. Indeed, as this particular programme proceeds, it appears as if Lisa and Sheila are used as a frame for Winfrey to explore her own relationship with her audience, a relationship that is defined through and by the fluctuations in her weight.

If the shifting nature of Winfrey's relationship with her guests and audience is recognisable in her interview with Lisa and Sheila, it becomes increasingly evident in the next part of the show. Foucault's theorisation on confessional discourse continues to offer the paradigm with which to frame an analysis, but we see how increasingly unstable the positioning becomes. It is my proposition that it is this instability which distinguishes Winfrey's relationship with her audiences. In Foucault's framework, confession is the enactment of a power relation that endorses the authority of the interlocutor and the subjugated position of the confessor. '[T]he agency of domination does not reside in the one who speaks (for he is constrained), but in the one who listens, and says nothing... And this discourse of truth finally takes effect, not in the one who receives it, but the one from whom it is wrested.'[13] Winfrey's insertion of her own confessional narrative reconfigures (and mobilises) the locus of power and authority. Foucault's formulation here is a response, in part, to the predominance of psychoanalytic analyses of politics and power. His, then, is a historical counter-narrative. The question for us here is how far is this applicable to a television production? Clearly, the confessional dynamic located in the (private) practices of the Catholic church and the therapeutic relationship, and which are delineated by Foucault, is not the same as that emerging between Oprah, Lisa and Sheila. Rather, Oprah appropriates the confessional mode to facilitate dialogue which is presented for public display. Oprah's own confessions operate to (appear to) close the gap between her celebrity persona and her 'ordinary' guests. This act is central to the Oprah persona and will be explored in detail in Chapter 5.

Winfrey as confessing subject

At one point during the interview with Lisa and Sheila, Oprah interprets Lisa's new problem: 'Outsiders like you more, but your friends like you less.' These words foreshadow the change of focus of the show. In introducing a number of letters 'from people who think I have, quote, changed [after weight loss]', Oprah seeks to demonstrate that she too has known the troubles faced by her first two guests. A sequence of letters is shown on the screen with sections highlighted. The texts are privileged with a picture of the writer shown in the bottom left corner. Extracts are read out loud in the voices which presumably belong to the authors. All correspondents are female, and all are white. 'Please don't say negative things about yourself when you were heavy. I feel like you are saying them about me too.' Another woman accuses Oprah of being 'more like an interrogator than a friend' now that she has lost weight. A Judy Marcum writes, 'I'm sick of hearing about your wonderful weight loss [aided by a specialist diet chef and a weight trainer] ... You do not live our lives, so quit pretending that you are just ordinary folk.' This is the final letter to be shown and is followed by Oprah announcing 'And this is Judy who wrote that letter friends!' The word 'friends' immediately places the audience on an intimate footing with the show's host, but at the same time emphasises the fact that this is what Winfrey actually is, star and host. None of the correspondence is from personal friends, and the fact that viewers have been sufficiently moved to write to her in such familiar terms supports her status rather than detracts from it. Paradoxically, the more Oprah attempts to show she is just 'ordinary folk', the more her celebrity position is confirmed.

Unlike Lisa and Sheila, Judy is positioned in the front row of the audience; Oprah joins her in order to discuss further the intention and meaning behind Judy's letter. Judy and Winfrey are now a part of and apart from the rest of the studio audience. It is in the exchanges between these two women that we see the complex dynamics more clearly: each in turn becomes confessor, judge, authority and redeemer. Judy explains that she was very angry when she wrote that letter, that it followed a conversation Judy had had with her hairdresser concerning the change in Oprah's relationship with her viewers since her weight loss. This is the reason that neither watched the show any more. 'We were talking about you, the way we always do ... I just don't feel comfortable with you any more. You don't come across as the same person. When you were on TV you were just like down home folks to me before.' Judy continues to evaluate the difference in Winfrey by locating an inner change which is attributed to a greater self-confidence; that before this shift, Oprah was someone that Judy would have invited into her home 'and offered a doughnut' to. Now she 'doesn't come across as that same person'. Oprah replies that she *feels* like the same person but 'lighter'. Judy refuses this evaluation: 'You're a different person, not like us any more.' Again Oprah attempts to refute any significant difference between her self when fat and her self when slim. She uses the phrase 'in my heart' twice to impress the essence of her persona which remains stable despite outward appearances to the contrary.

What is clear from this exchange is that Judy, who may be typical of a number of female viewers, had a definite idea of what Oprah represented in the past, and that was the preferred version. That body weight, as the consequence of excessive consumption, is the issue here represents one of the contradictions embedded in *Oprah*. The fat Oprah who appeared on the television screen is the Winfrey with whom they can identify, and who is perceived as the real – and, therefore, more desirable – Winfrey. Pertinently, it is the *way* in which Winfrey seems to have achieved her goals: with the help and support of a chef and trainer. These are props that are beyond the scope of ordinary viewers, whereas the numerous diets that had been used in the past were those that all had access to. The Oprah who is met now is a usurper. Judy explains her reasons for coming onto the show:

> Judy: 'I wanted to come here and see if you were the same person.'
> Oprah: 'But you didn't know me before.'
> Judy: 'But I saw you on TV all the time and I felt like you could come to my home. Like you were my cousin. Now I think 'she's forgot about us'. I feel this in my heart, like you forgot about all us people.'

As Judy confesses her discomfort with Oprah, Oprah seeks to reassure that she still feels 'like down home folks. If anything I feel even more downer homer [sic]'. She is the authority to whom the confession is made, but she does not punish, judge or exclude. Rather, she uses Judy's confession as the platform from which to make her own disclosure. She explains that this apparent shift is due to a change she had experienced within herself, that she came to recognise that her weight problem was due to unresolved psychic conflicts of her own. That, once she began to see and address the problems in this light, she was able to deal with the physical manifestation of them. In response to the criticism that she too often refers to her weight loss, Oprah states that she will in future check this, but that she used the weight gain/loss as a 'metaphor for all the other stuff that I was carrying...pain, non-confrontation, not dealing with fears'. The specificity of this pain and fear is not referred to but have themselves been disclosed in other shows and will be well known to regular viewers of *Oprah*. They include sexual abuse, teenage sexual promiscuity and poor self-image. Winfrey reiterates her claim that 'I feel like I'm Every Woman; I've had almost every problem!' At this point we get a glimpse of the rest of the (mixed 'race'and gender) studio audience as they respond to this declaration with knowing laughter.

In this section of the show we have a confessor – Judy – articulating feelings of anger, betrayal and loss towards the figure of power and authority – Oprah – who consoles and reconciles by becoming the confessional subject herself. The patterning of the relationship here mirrors the relationship conveyed earlier by Lisa and Sheila. The familiarity that appears to exist between the latter couple is replicated between Oprah and her guest. What is particularly noteworthy is the fact that although Winfrey, through her own confessions, is denoting intimacy with Judy, she (Judy) disavows this by insisting on her preference for the down home Oprah of the past who she has come to know through television. Oprah's power, it would seem, comes from her 'ordinariness', from her appearing to be like everyone else. It is not her power of authority in the discourse of confession which builds trust and a loyal following. Rather, it is her own acts of confession that validate her role of authority. The irony of the flesh and blood version of Oprah being insufficient to seduce Judy from her preference for the earlier television version is left unexplored.

Interestingly, from this exchange and the others that follow, the issue of wealth is declared not to be of concern to the women who had written letters similar to that of Judy's. This is somewhat contradictory as wealth is the means through which Winfrey achieved weight loss this time, and that has worked to alienate these particular viewers. What this implies is that so long as wealth is not foregrounded, the myth that Oprah is like 'down home folks' can be sustained. Once this appearance is violated viewers' perception of the screen persona, and their relation to it, changes. Differences based on 'race' are effaced here.

Judy's disaffection, echoed by other guests, sets up a paradox: this series of confessions register a fragmentation, a splitting of relations, specifically conveying a sense of betrayal and a disappointment in Winfrey's perceived abdication of her 'down home' self. But what is implied is the reverse: that the act of articulation actually evokes the notion of a system of interdependency and one that does not privilege any one individual over another. The ritual is located in Winfrey and Judy, but moves beyond that which is immediately visible on the television screen to include a much wider audience. Oprah turns to address the studio audience behind her, asking questions that begin, 'Do you all believe that?' or 'Is that what you all think?' And on one occasion the whole of America is included: in response to Susan's demands that Winfrey act with more humility and acknowledge her position of wealth,

Oprah's reply is 'OK, I'm humbled. I'm humbled America!' The whole nation is seen as participating in the ritualistic process, is offered the authority and power of interlocutor and is mediator facilitating exoneration and redemption.

The sense of community that is generated is fundamental to the meaning of the show. The studio audience participates through asking questions, making observations and offering similar confessional articulations. The audience at home is included even when the programme is off air during the commercial breaks. On three occasions Oprah informs viewers at home that during the commercial break, dialogue has continued, gives a synopsis of that conversation and whom it has been conducted with. The discourse of confession is thus linked to commodity and consumption, while at the same time the ellipsis created by the intrusion of advertisements is, in part, obliterated. It is worth recalling White's argument that 'problems and their solutions are narrativized in terms of confessional relations...Self-identity and social recognition within familial and consumer networks hinge on participation in the process of mediated confession'.[14] Oprah colludes with the audience's perception of her as a friend or family member (a significant other). Her management of voices, her concession in allowing the confessor to also be interlocutor, her incorporation of home viewers, studio audience and commercial breaks conveys a sense of totality, inclusion and recognition. Private experience and confessional exchange are played out in the public arena, becoming a communal event replicating the intimate relations that form the basis of individual lives and social units. The therapeutic function of this particular *Oprah* show lies in the recognition of the social self in relation to friend and family networks through the confessional discourse of the subjects. In presenting her own experience as an example of the show's main issue, Oprah is using her authority based on knowledge of that issue in a way that works to recognise a shared group identity with women who struggle with their weight, reinforcing what they have in common. This notion of equality signals the starting point for the empowerment of individuals. Thus, the dynamic between Oprah and her guests evokes the network of relationships fostered by othermothers discussed by Patricia Hill Collins and Stanlie M. James and which I argue is akin to (one of) Oprah's performances as host.

The boundaries between notions of friendship and family ties are continually blurred. We have seen how Lisa and Sheila, who are cousins, relate to each other as friends, how Judy regards Winfrey as a friend who might also be a cousin. Winfrey further seeks to efface differences between herself and the audience by addressing them as 'friends', and by not suggesting to Judy that they are unlikely to be related since one is white, the other black. This raises questions about what the word 'friend' signifies here. From the dialogues of Judy, Lisa and Sheila, it would seem to refer to a person who is not likely to judge negatively, and a person who might be another family member. Concepts of friend and family overlap here. Winfrey's own discourse suggests the same points of reference. However, these relationships are problematised by and through their construction in an economic production: we know that Lisa and Sheila, Judy and the other letter writers/readers are viewers who represent ratings and the commercial viability of the *Oprah* show. While the obliteration of the commercial breaks in the show is in part a denial that this is a commercial enterprise, a commodity for consumption, the presence of these women – and their relationship with the show's host – represents the commodification of familial networks and bonds of friendship which is articulated through confessional discourse and mediated by the means of commercial television. There exists a mutual dependency between the confessional subjects and the television industry (represented by and through Oprah): the existence of one relies on the existence of the other and forms the position from which speculations about selfhood are voiced.

The section of the *Oprah* show which deals with Judy and the other viewers' correspondence ends with Winfrey's self-affirmation. She states that she recalls a time when letters of such anger and criticism would have reduced her feelings of worth, inducing her 'to go straight to the refrigerator. And I would have felt the need to apologise inside myself... I no longer feel the need to apologise' (Loud applause from the audience). So far, this show has established the fundamental premise that close human relationships can be (are) fraught with contradictions and conflict. Oprah's personification of the therapeutic dynamic establishes and validates the confessional process, and, importantly, makes it safe. Through her engagement with her guests, her continual interjections, confessions and self-disclosure, the process can be seen to be working, and working towards the realisation of selfhood. This frame provides the context for the guests who are to follow.

The confessing family

Representative of the family is the mother and daughter who appeared briefly at the beginning of the programme in the teasers. This is the section in which we were earlier promised confessions of 'feelings too tender to share until today'. The words 'tender' and 'share' dictate the tone and spirit in which we are to experience the forthcoming narrative. 'Tender' tells us that whilst the women's stories may convey a conflict, it is a conflict which is to be seen in the context of affection and warmth; this is not to be an aggressive, gladiatorial spectacle. In 'sharing' these tender feelings, the audience is being honoured with an intimate glimpse into the lives of others, but we too are expected to share the feelings of tenderness expressed by the mother and daughter. This will be important: the mother and daughter relationship is often characterised as one of conflict and opposition, but in the context of this show we are not being encouraged to view this mother and daughter as two individuals separated from one another or to take sides. Rather, the perception of this pair of guests will be as of the others: an indivisible unit. Division and conflict can be made safe and repairable if articulated through confession, especially if that confession is dependent on, and spoken by, the two voices that make up that story. Unity and cohesion rather than disunity and partition is the underlying narrative which is played out in the context of the private social unit of the family, but which also speaks to broader social groups of friendship networks in general and female friendships in particular.

'Weighing in at 180 lbs, sent this woman on a 12 year soul-searching journey.' Rosemary Green 'has chronicled her battles in *Diary of a Fat Housewife*...A story of joy for herself, but shame from someone closest to her.[15] Take a look at this'. As with Lisa and Sheila, a video is used to introduce Rosemary and her daughter, Jennifer. Like the earlier video, we see a series of moving images, which are both contemporary, and from an earlier time showing Rosemary alone and with her family. We see how the 180 lbs Rosemary looked, and how the new slimmer Rosemary is now. Still photographs display the relationship between the mother and her adult daughter. These images show smiling, confident women who are unafraid of the camera they gaze at. The similarity of their faces and their physical closeness convey an impression of familial intimacy while their smiles signify a sense of pleasure in one another's company. As with the Lisa and Sheila video, soft music accompanies the narrative which this time is spoken in one voice, Rosemary's, who reads an extract from *A Diary*.

This time, the confession is initially mediated through the written word. 'Dear diary. I want to share my feelings with my best friend, my daughter Jennifer. But I cannot do that; it hurts too much.' We then hear of Rosemary's sense of shame that her own weight loss has provoked feelings of anger and jealousy in her daughter who has a weight struggle of her own. Other than instilling bad eating habits into her daughter, the cause of Rosemary's shame is unclear. What is evident and reiterated throughout the brief narrative is that Rosemary's sense of accomplishment is tempered by Jennifer's anger and jealousy now that she (Jennifer) is heavier than her mother. But again, the tone of voice, the accompanying music and the images work against the idea that these women are in conflict. The unity of their relationship is signalled in much the same way as in the Lisa and Sheila video. Once the tape ends, we see a tearful Rosemary and Jennifer seated side by side and holding hands on the platform alongside the two cousins, occupying the comfortable-looking armchairs. Oprah is seated on the platform facing them. No applause marks the end of the tape, rather, a respectful silence is held. 'This is the first time Jennifer and Rosemary have talked about her weight loss.' We learn that Jennifer has written her feelings towards her mother in a letter, which Oprah had read that day. Encouraging Jennifer to read the letter, Oprah states 'I cried this morning when I read the letter.' As the daughter begins to read the letter – 'Dear Mom' – Winfrey interjects with 'Let's establish this before.' Turning to Rosemary, the history of weight loss is reiterated. For a moment, the subject, Jennifer, and the matter of her confession – pain and anger – becomes displaced while the mother is allowed to articulate her triumphant control of her weight problem. The swift shift from the daughter to the mother blurs the distinction between them but it also separates them as Rosemary's triumphalism eclipses Jennifer's shaky confessional start. The mother's successful management of a problem that she had battled with for so long foregrounds the fact that this story is one of personal struggle and personal triumph. This mirrors Oprah's own story which had been the confessional subject a few moments earlier; the mother equates her own success with that of Oprah's, drawing parallels between them. In addition, wittingly or not, the joyful expression of Rosemary's success acts out that which has separated mother and daughter in the first place – Rosemary has lost weight and is happy, Jennifer has not lost weight, is unhappy and feels herself to be in her mother's shadow.

The tone of the show changes as Jennifer is finally allowed to read her letter. She is the subject confessing to feelings of anger and jealousy now that her mother is slimmer than she. 'Dear Mom. All my life you have been fat. Very fat. I have been teased at school...Now you are thin, thinner than me.' As Jennifer falters Winfrey encourages her to continue: 'Hold on. You can do it.' The camera gives us close shots of the mother and daughter individually – both in tears – and then, of them together. This follows with a shot of the two with Oprah. All three become encapsulated in the drama of the one confession. We know that Lisa and Sheila are close by and that an audience is present, but for the time we are given the impression that this is a private and intimate situation. Jennifer's confession continues, detailing how ashamed she feels now that it is she and not Rosemary Green who is the fattest in the family, and speaks of her anger towards her mother who can no longer be 'relied upon' to be the biggest person. Here, it is the act of confessing which is acknowledged to be the difficult and courageous task – 'Hold on. You can do it.' Winfrey can suggest a solidarity and equal footing as much with Jennifer as with her mother, she too knows the sheer hard work involved in the struggle. Winfrey has been Jennifer as much as she has been Rosemary and it is Jennifer's 'courage' that is applauded once the letter has been read, not Rosemary's successful diet. By offering what is perceived to be a communal experience a sense of cohesion is evoked, working against the feeling of fragmentation expressed by the confessors. This is reinforced through the actual structuring of the show. By placing Rosemary after Lisa and Sheila, and after Winfrey and Judy, we have a context for the potentially more damaging revelations that occur between mother and daughter – which is, on this particular programme, representative of the most basic and fundamental social unit. We have seen how the dynamic of the confessional discourse works, we know that these women will use the experience in their aim to become purified, redeemed, liberated and reach salvation.

White argues that, 'Confession and therapy are engaged toward finding one's "proper place" as an individual and social subject, even as they are mediated through the apparatus of television.'[16] The confessional exchanges between Lisa and Sheila, Winfrey and Judy, Rosemary and Jennifer represent a paradigm of social and interpersonal relations. The processes of the therapeutic and the confessional are validated by Winfrey's own active participation. During the segment of the show which deals with viewers' criticism of her, Oprah continually reiterates that her loss of weight was only possible once it 'finally clicked that it [overeating] was not about food' but about inner turmoil and that maintaining her new self involves 'pain and effort' on a daily basis. The pain and effort in this context refers explicitly to the control of weight. Implicit is the message that pain and effort are integral to the management and control of personal positive self-identity, interpersonal relations and the construction of the social self. This is acted out through mediated confession. The self-identity of women who believe themselves to be overweight is a complex issue and one that I will turn to when I discuss Oprah's persona in Chapter 5.

As is typical of any *Oprah* show, a guest therapist is present and, on this show, is introduced as someone that 'I am anxious to talk to'. The expert witness on this occasion is a psychotherapist who has had 'first hand experiences' of dramatic weight reduction. Photographic images are shown to support the claim that this woman has conquered her own obesity. However, despite Oprah's 'anxiety' to talk to this woman, the therapist is given 30 seconds of air time in which to explain the mental mechanisms involved in overeating and includes an interjection from Oprah. This stands in contrast to the 45 seconds it takes for Oprah to introduce her to the audience. Essentially, the expert here is not given a prominent place in the show. The brevity of her allocated time and her seating position – among the studio audience – places her on an equal footing with the majority of other participants, leaving Oprah's own significance intact while reinforcing the communal activity which is therapy and confession.

Again, the structure of the show emphasises the communal and egalitarian nature of confession in the context of popular television. Once the expert has been introduced and swiftly dispensed with, the remainder of the show is taken up with comments, observations and some confessions from studio audience members. We occasionally are shown glimpses of the guest therapist, but she no longer has a voice. It becomes clear that large numbers of the audience know one another, some describing how weight loss in one has affected the friendship with another, others offering interpretations of the behaviour of the guests on the platform. Frequently, the comments are directed towards Winfrey and the exchanges between herself, her guests and the letter writers. The hitherto largely silent audience members now become vocal participants in the communal confessional process that acknowledges Oprah as the central reference point.

Writing, power and selfhood

It is noteworthy that the majority of confessions articulated in this show – and very commonly in other *Oprah* Programmes – stem from a piece of writing. In the case of Rosemary, the writing is published material which is her *Diary*, or their confessions originate from letters written to Winfrey or, in the case of Jennifer, (it would seem) for the express purpose of appearing on the show. Letters are written to be read in private by the addressee. That they are read by the author to the addressee in a very public domain instigates the move from the personal and private to the social and public signalling the move from inner to outer that typifies the confessional process. It is an outward display of that which is to come and it intensifies the privileged nature of that which is about to be uttered.

The telling of one's own story – autobiography – has a long and complex history in which gender represents a complex issue. Nancy K. Miller points out that while the male autobiographer is understood as autonomous, in the female Western tradition of autobiography, the self is always positioned in relation to significant others.[17] Further, Miller (1994) points to a work which demonstrates that the female autobiographical self is located 'not only in relation to a singular, chosen other, but also – and simultaneously – to the *collective* experience of women as gendered subjects'[18] (emphasis in original). Exploring canonical, male-authored texts, Miller acknowledges crucial differences between the experiences and identities of male and female autobiographers, but argues that patterns found in female-authored texts are also evident in male-authored texts. 'In many important ways, the project of autobiography is *always* tied to [the] intergenerational, historical and fantasmatic matrix'[19] (emphasis in original). Thus, the autobiographical subject is always defined in relation to others.

Without wishing to make sweeping generalisations, autobiography in black America has a political impulse that is rooted in the desire to challenge existing positions of subjugation, and the need for the power to self-definition. In this way, positioning of the autobiographical subject in relation to others is an explicit project in that it is used to present a self that stands counter to the socially ascribed shape and definition of that self.

In the previous chapter, I argued that the process of excavating a history and rewriting that history represents a political activity in which the subject's voice is privileged over controlling hegemonic forces. With specific reference to autobiography, Andrews (1993) writes:

> Autobiography holds a position of priority, indeed many would say pre-eminence, among the narrative traditions of black America... The number of important twentieth-century African American novels that read like or are presented as autobiographies confirms a recent black critic's contention that "ours is an extraordinarily self-reflexive tradition".[20]

The critics referred to here are Robert B. Steptoe, who claims that the African American narrative tradition is based on a call and response patterning, and Henry Louis Gates, who emphasises the self-reflexivity in black American literature.[21] The autobiographical form, with all its self-reflexivity, continues to have a powerful force within contemporary black American culture. Stone (1993) argues that 'As readers have known since 1945, autobiography is one of the richest, and most revealing modes of black expression in present day America' and represents 'a powerful force and characteristic in contemporary culture'.[22] The black writer's words – '"I was there. This happened to me", and "This is me – in my own words, thoughts, feelings"' – make a claim that it is at once individual and collective.[23]

Considering the slave narrative, Steptoe (1993) argues that the collection of letters, tales, guarantees and prefaces that constitute Fredrick Douglass' *Narrative* (1845) forms a unified narrative that he calls 'integrated': 'a figurative account of action, landscape and heroic transformation'.[24] Within the slave narrative, the appeal of self-authorship is obvious. In exerting control over the text the writer is asserting his/her authority, autonomy and order over their lives.

Time and again, guests on *Oprah* introduce their stories by reading a letter or diary extract as a public declaration of a private self. I would argue that the collection of letters and diary extracts that are read aloud on *Oprah*, together with the series of video images that underpin a story, combine to produce an integrated narrative within which the author has control over the ways in which their story is represented. It would be naive to suggest that writing or speaking one's own story represents a total liberation from discourse that orders, judges and categorises. Each act of speech or writing is carried out with the larger social configurations as a reference point. It is true that these manuscripts will be mediated by and through the apparatus of television, the commercial interests of the production company, the generic conventions of 'letter' and 'diary', the English language that embodies hierarchies of power in its form, and the cultural boundaries determining limits of taste and decency. However, it is also the case that for many of the guests – including the ones described in this chapter – the act of uttering that which has been privately hidden becomes a tool for empowerment, a means through which taboo subjects may be broached. Acting as a testimony of a self rather than a confession through which self is constructed, the autobiographical nature of the material validates and underscores the integrated narrative.

Processes of 'raced' identification

'Race', as stated earlier, is eclipsed from the discourses in this show. Time and again contributions from the studio audience emphasise the degree to which viewers identify with the programme's host. This identification can be summed up by one (white) woman who says 'We think you are one of us...It's because we call you Oprah that we think you are really down home.' 'Oprah' clearly signifies a relationship that is warm, non-threatening and safe. That individuals are willing to bear testimony to private aspects of their lives and to reveal feelings for the first time on a television chat show displays not only a cultural accept-ance of the genre itself, but the medium through which it is deployed. As the locus of control in *Oprah*, Oprah represents an ideal in which the figure of friend/family member/interlocutor all merge. What is not openly articulated, but is implicit in these exchanges is how Winfrey is perceived as a black woman. Although she does not do so in this show, Winfrey has often foregrounded her blackness, at times seeking alle-giances from other black members of the audience in support of specific claims. Towards the end of this programme, a black woman from the audience who has been 'overweight for 40 years' offers the formulation that 'America has a love/hate relationship with obese people, particu-larly women. There are things associated with being obese which are positive: warmth, nurturing...'. Oprah: 'They called me aunt Jemima when I started!' The woman nods.

According to Bogle (1994), aunt Jemimas 'are toms blessed with religion or mammies who wedge themselves into the dominant white culture. Generally, they are sweet, jolly and good tempered – a bit more polite than mammy and certainly never as headstrong'.[25] The recognition of the aunt Jemima figure embeds racial representation firmly in the text and correlates closely with the phrase 'down home' which has been used on five occasions in this show. On each occurrence it is applied to the perception of Oprah, both as the way in which the audience sees her and as the way in which she describes herself. Clarence Major's dictionary of *Black Slang* (1971) says: 'Down Home: (1950s) An honest, unpretentious life style or personality; in Jazz an earthy way of playing.'[26] Major's definition sits comfortably with the usage of the term in the context of this show. The focus of interest for the letter writers (and a number of the studio audience) is a perceived shift in Oprah's persona now that she triumphantly celebrates her weight loss. More, it was the means through which this was enabled that particularly incensed some viewers: a special chef and weight trainer. These means, as articulated by a number of people, are beyond most 'ordinary folk'. The extreme response of these women viewers to Oprah's conspicuous display of wealth points to an indignation over the 'uppity nigger' who has reached beyond their station in life.[27] This is never openly articulated but there is, of course, an overt contradiction here; although Oprah's con-spicuous display of wealth signals a move away from an unpretentious and earthy life style, the audience continues to relate to her, through their discourse, as if this were not the case. And she was a wealthy celebrity even before she used a diet chef and trainer. More significantly, the white audience uses and adopts a phrase that has its origins in black cultural life. In his introduction to *Black Slang*, Major writes:

> This so-called private vocabulary of black people serves the users as a powerful medium of self defence against a world demanding participation while at the same time laying a boobytrap-network of rejection and exploitation . . . It is a language unconsciously designed to prove a way toward positive self images.[28]

In using a term that originates in black talk to positively describe Oprah, a way that she chooses to describe herself, 'down home' is a means of identifying her racial identity in a world in which she fully participates. As an erstwhile attribute it is a means of rejection also.

Cultural stereotypes are evoked through Oprah's recollection of the aunt Jemima label – triggered by the contribution from the one other black woman to speak throughout the show – and by the frequent use and acceptance of 'down home'. The use of this term by the white audience members in attempting to align themselves with Oprah, in equating her 'down home' quality with being 'one of us', also marks a slippage, a crossover of cultural reference points and positions. Through the selection of white only guests on the show, Oprah is seen to be wedged into the dominant white culture, while that culture demonstrates that it has absorbed, integrated, appropriated and identified with parts of the black experience. Throughout the whole of this one show, issues of gender and 'race' are not explicitly addressed but are nonetheless present through the all-female guest list and through the adoption of black vernacular by both Oprah and the guests. Class is more evidently a problem. Winfrey's sleek new body and, crucially, the means through which this was achieved is a problem for the guests on this programme. Oprah's use of a diet chef and personal trainer represents a conspicuous display of wealth (and paradoxically, consumption) not available to the majority of her viewers who in turn, feel alienated from the down home Oprah that they believe they have come to know.

Private stories, public display

So far, I have been arguing that Oprah's authority resides in her experiences that she then shares with the guests; that this disperses the locus of power amongst the show's participants who in turn become figures of authority. As such then, the confessional strategies displayed during the programme represent a reconfiguration of relations of power formed within confessional relations described by Foucault. However, yet to be addressed is the public nature of a process (confession) that historically has operated within the private realm. It is the insertion of private issues within the public domain that is the source of concern for writers such as Vicki Abt and Mel Seesholtz, which is discussed in the Chapter 1. For them, the exuberant display of intimacies, 'abnormalities' and indiscretions signals an alarming collapse of boundaries constructed in the name of 'good taste'. For Abt and Seesholtz, those who appear on talk shows are, by definition, codified as abnormal, judged as representing the seedier side of American society, categorised as trashy, and should have no place in the public sphere. On the other hand, we have the views of those represented by Joshua Gamson – also discussed in Chapter 1 – who argues that this is the only space available through which these hierarchies may be challenged. Clearly the public spectacle that is *Oprah* alters the meaning of the confessional talk on which the show hinges. I have already argued that while Winfrey appears to efface the line of separation between herself and her guests through the dispersal of authority, she also remains in control over that which is spoken, a privilege that foregrounds her star status. However, the question here is: what impact does the rendering of the guests into public spectacle have on the presentation of self on the show?

Frank Lentricchia writing about Delillo's novel *Americana* (1975) states:

> In the dialogue from *Americana* the genius of television emerges as nothing more than the desire for the universal third person...the person we dream about from our armchairs in front of the television, originally dreamt by the first immigrants, the pilgrims on the way over [on the *Mayflower*], the object of the dream being the persons those pilgrims would become...a new self because a new world. Sitting in front of the TV in our armchairs is like a perpetual Atlantic crossing...[I]t is not the consummation of desire but the foreplay of desire that is TV advertising's object. To buy is merely an effect, but to dream is a cause – the motor principle, in fact, of consumer capitalism. TV advertising taps into and manipulates the American Dream; it is the mechanism which triggers our move...from the self we are to the self we would become...To be real in America is to be in the position of the 'I' who would be 'he' or 'she', the I who must negate I, leave I behind...[29]

Lentricchia's formulation (1990) of Delillo's novel – which is about a television executive – returns us to the concerns raised in Chapter 2 and the idea of a negated I that persists in postmodern theory, elements of which are evident in this *Oprah* show. The use of video footage to introduce the main guests is a display of the I who has left I behind to become she. Whilst the reading aloud of letters, the means of private communication, signals the transition from the (valid) personal to the public, the introductory videos are a visual representation of selfhood advertising the desirability of the reconstructed self. As stated earlier, this form of self (re)presentation offers a parallel narrative that speaks to and supports the voices that accompany it. We are offered proof of the words spoken; but the videos also ground the discourse in a dream of leaving the self behind for the self we would become. Pleasure (entertainment) is located in the expertly compiled tapes which juxtapose images of the past with the present, fat with thin, still with moving. As the images fade into one another, we are given a synopsis of the individuals' lives and their relationships with significant others. This sense of pleasure, of being entertained, is enmeshed with the notion of the reconstructed self. As we watch, we see Lisa and Sheila as children turning into teenage girls becoming transformed into women and mothers. Jennifer moves from dependant toddler to young woman. We witness Lisa and Rosemary achieving their goal, their metamorphosis into a socially desirable self. The documentation of movement and change underpins the verbal discourses; the seamless presentation of this change denotes a certain ease (and naturalness) with which alteration is achieved. The desire to be entertained is met with the invitation to watch, to look at the desirable achieved and at a self transformed. The wish for a metamorphosis into a third person is made actual and material.

The videos in this show not only advertise the reconstructed self, they foreground a perceived need for perpetual change and development. Nirvana has not been reached because the new self has brought along with it a new set of difficulties located in the relationship between self and others. The process of renewal is ongoing and dynamic and is facilitated through confessional practices. The videos are a dream of what a self may become; the verbal discourse that the dream intersects is a display of the means through which the dream is realised. The series of conflicts aired on this show represent the new challenge, the next site of desired change, and as such, function as fuel for the economic engine through the provision of new material for another programme.

As host/facilitator/interlocutor, Oprah's authority resides in her own experience of being self-reconstructed. More importantly, for the purposes of display it is the audiences' knowledge of Winfrey's biography and her own acknowledged daily 'pain and effort' that enable her to stand as the personification of the dream and is the foundation of her claim to be Every Woman.

This chapter has, then, examined the ways in which Oprah uses the confessional, with all its connotations of therapy, in her engagement with guests and audience. Each guest is participating on *Oprah* because they have a story to tell, and whether or not this hinges on the confession of emotional difficulties – and not all stories do this as we will see in the following chapter – the show offers a space in which to display a representation of self. It is clear, through this example of a single show that discourses of fracture/dislocation/anxiety interplay with narratives of self-actualisation through the articulation of one's own story. It is also evident how central to the process of self-definition is Oprah's confessional performance. This binds the disparate narratives lending cohesion to the show over all. It also presents the guest/viewer with a point of identification, one that appears to eclipse Oprah's star status. It is my argument that the way in which confessional discourse is deployed on the show, and the narrative structures of the stories told by the guests facilitated by and through the Oprah persona, combine to form a platform for a representation of self. The chapter that follows is an analysis of that narrative structure and the meanings generated by it.

4
Oprah and Narrating the Self

The previous chapter focused on the interaction between the host and guest/s that is facilitated by a series of confessional disclosures. I explored the ways in which confessional discourse is deployed on *Oprah*, and how consumerism, expressions of anxiety and fragmentation, and therapy all coexist with the pronouncements of self-reclamation and self-realisation that emerge from narrating one's own story. I argued that Oprah operates through an interplay of the 'ordinariness' which is her mark as well as that of the guests, and extra-ordinariness confirmed by her celebrity status. The celebrity system, and Oprah's construction through it, will be discussed in the following chapter.

In this chapter, I will look at the stories themselves, and examine the emergent patterning that generates the meaning attached to *Oprah*. In particular, I am interested in the ways in which selfhood is constructed, and in the development of agency. It is my argument that the commercial interests of *Oprah*, together with the normative ideology of 'official' discourse, combine to create a legitimate space that allows for individuals to collect and to rehearse their life experiences. In being the author of their own narratives, participants become active agents. This process can be more clearly understood if we think of *Oprah* in terms of heteroglossia which Bakhtin describes as 'the conflict between... "official" and "unofficial" discourses' and as a 'process that creates the possibility of free consciousness'.[1] Bakhtin's notion of 'official' discourse is that which is in accord with fully formed values of social morality, class and worldview, whereas 'unofficial' discourse is socially and historically determined but is incompletely formed.

The value in using Bakhtin's ideas at this juncture lies in the ways in which they allow us to think about the creative potential of popular culture *in conjunction with* the processes of commercialism. Rather than seeing the commercial as that which empties out meaning, reducing the participants to commodities, it is, in the case of *Oprah*, the commercial that allows for the 'unofficial' and the creative to take place. In Bakhtin's formulations (1968), the social force of 'unofficial' discourse is characterised as the language of the market place. He argues that the market place in the Middle Ages 'was the center of all that is unofficial; it enjoyed a certain extra-territoriality in a world of official order and official ideology, it always remained with the people'.[2] Liberated from the fixed norms and hierarchies that ground the official sphere, the market place and its language became 'a peculiar argot' forming a 'special collectivity'[3] which was especially expressed during carnival, 'the borderline between art and life'.[4]

The creativity that is the result of social interaction informs Bakhtin's concept of dialogism which posits human communication as creative, social, ideological and, crucially for my purpose, historically specific. Morris (1994) writes that Bakhtin's argument is that 'Subjectivity is ... produced on the *"borderline"* where inner experience and social world meet ... This borderzone of continuous interaction between individual consciousness ... is the location of all creative activity'[5] (emphasis in original).

If we take this dialogic model and broaden its application to incorporate a system that includes the non-verbal, it becomes possible to apply it to *The Oprah Winfrey Show*. The programme is a result of a dialogic engagement between the conflicting cultural practices and discourses that shape the show: the television industry, entertainment conventions, the celebrity system, the therapeutic sensibility, bourgeois expertise, and the individual everyday experiences of those who speak on the show and who watch from a distance at home. The resultant heteroglossia, the 'clash of antagonistic forces',[6] is that which denies the possibility of any unitary meaning. Hence the ambivalence in *Oprah* is reflected in the divergent evaluations and readings that are evident within talk show commentary.

So, *Oprah* operates as the borderzone in which the dialectical relation between the multiple official and unofficial discourses is played out. As a borderzone, the show offers a space of interaction between the outer social world with its norms, laws and values and the inner world of private experience. The discourses of the dominant culture meet and combine with those of the folk, the everyday, to produce the (carnivalesque) process through which new forms of subjectivity are created that are in part informed by hegemonic forces but which are also separate from them.

The narratives explored in this chapter are performed within the context of the processes discussed above. I have taken a small sample of six shows that were chosen at random and broadcast in Britain during October and November 1995. This sample of shows present what is perhaps a self-evident feature of the talk show, which is the central role of storytelling. Clearly, a television show that relies on talk for its very existence is going to demonstrate the validity of talk. What I am looking at is the nature of that talk, which in the case of *The Oprah Winfrey Show* is largely the presentation of a series of stories rather than simply a discussion of this or that topic. The stories themselves are articulations of a journey that has either been taken, representing completion (success/ completion narratives), is in the process of being taken (ongoing narratives) and those journeys just about to start (commencement narratives). For the sake of clarity, I am considering chiefly those narratives articulated by the invited guests rather than those offered by members of the studio audience.

I began this analysis with no conscious preconceptions; I watched the shows two or three times during which I became aware of a number of recurring themes – the reference points offered by social and family structures; the call to God or other transcendent being; and the issue of control. The repeating structure of the narrative shape did not become evident until I began to formulate my findings. I am familiar with Vladimir Propp's structural analysis of the folktale in which the action and function of the dramatis personae remain fixed and unchanging.[7] Although I did not set out with the intention of applying Propp's methodology, I believe that his approach has had some influence on my own recognition of the patterning of the stories considered here. Propp's structuralism (1928) is helpful to a point; content is revealed but without contextualisation. So, the analysis of these shows needs to be considered within the context of the cultural discourses that I have outlined in Chapter 2, and within the context of relationships and subject positions that are formed through the confessional/testimonial strategies discussed in the previous chapter. What I offer here is the examination of the structure of stories that comprise the shows in recognition of the limits of a structuralist approach, but form a part of my overall analysis.

Narration in the sample presented here is the means by which the individual articulates a sense of self through the recitation of a story that is the property of the speaker, confirming his or her status as an independent, active agent. At the same time, that story, once uttered, also becomes the property of the audience, other studio guests, the guest expert and the show's host thereby engendering a sense of communal activity. Of course, these stories are constrained and framed by the discursive boundaries of commercial television: air time, the commercial breaks, the highly structured format of the show, the parameters of acceptability. Perhaps most defining of all, the stories are heard through the filter of the host's own celebrity persona, which is predicated on her authority derived from lived experience and which shapes the relationship that she has with her guests and audience.

The shows in this sample offer a total of 29 stories spoken by individual men and women, by heterosexual couples and by families (Table 4.1). The shows can be further broken down thus: 'narratives of completion' numbered 17 of the total 29 stories in this sample; 10 of these are spoken by women – one of which is a chorus of female voices, 4 are male speakers, 2 are heterosexual couples and 1 family. Those which I have termed 'ongoing' number 7; 2 are spoken by women, 5 by men. There are 4 heterosexual couples that represent those that I call 'commencement'. There is one narrative in the sample which does not fit any category and represents the failure to embark on any such journey. This story is spoken by a family represented by the parents of a murdered girl and the letter written by their (absent) younger daughter.

The various stages of the journey narrative are framed through a series of themes which elucidate situations that are specific to those whose stories we hear, but which speak to larger concerns and the possible experience of the studio and home audiences. Generally speaking, the individual shows tend to be devoted to one or other type of narrative. Narratives of completion are seen in 'Men and Women Communicating' (Channel 4, broadcast 31.10.95) with one male central storyteller; 'Real Life Dramas' (BBC2, 4.11.95) contains 8 narratives with 3 male speakers, 3 female speakers, 1 family group and 1 couple. 'Girl Power' (BBC2, 15.11.95) presents 6 individual female narrators. The show 'Date Violence' (Channel 4, 24.10.95), presents three central stories and is the most

Table 4.1   Breakdown of narrative structures and speakers

Narrative structure	Number of stories	Spoken by
Completion	17	10 women; 4 men; 2 heterosexual couples; 1 family comprised of father, mother and son
Ongoing	7	2 women and 5 men
Commencement	4	4 heterosexual couples

complex of the sample. Here, two stories (spoken by one woman and one ex-couple) which could be classified as narratives of completion also indicate ongoing challenges as the storytellers continue to struggle with the problems and difficulties aired. The third narrative is unique to the sample as it represents a story of a failure to recognise a problem which proved life threatening, resulting in death.

'Forbidden Thoughts' (BBC2, 9.11.95) represents the ongoing narrative in which 5 women and 2 men participate. 'Sex – [or rather, (dys)functional relationships]' (Channel 4, 21.11.95) is a demonstration of commencement narratives; it is these which are articulated by 4 heterosexual couples.

The stories presented are those of a process, are the claim of selfhood through a move from difficulty to resolution, from powerlessness to empowerment and are underpinned by agency and action which ultimately prevent the individual from collapsing into fragmentation and even death. As we can see from Table 4.2, most commonly in this sample the speakers recount their experiences from the position of completion, of having already been through the process. Such a position is marked by the achievement of an inner strength, a self-awareness and often greater appreciation of their world as a result of facing and

Table 4.2 Composition of narrative structures

Narrative structure	Name of show	Broadcast date and station	Gender and grouping of storytellers
Completion	Men and Women Communicating	Channel 4, 31.10.95	1 male
	Real Life Dramas	BBC2, 4.11.95	3 male; 3 female; 1 family group; 1 heterosexual couple
	Girl Power	BBC2, 15.11.95	6 females
	Date Violence	Channel 4, 24.10.95	1 female; 1 heterosexual ex-couple; 1 family comprised of mother, father and two absent daughters
Ongoing	Forbidden Thoughts	BBC2, 9.11.95	5 females; 2 males
Commencement	Sex	Channel 4, 21.11.95	4 heterosexual couples

overcoming their – sometimes – extreme difficulties. What is striking is that individual shows tend to adhere to one or other type of narrative. It is only by looking at a number of *Oprah* shows that we obtain a sense of the overarching narrative structure, of the movement towards selfhood. This indicates that meaning is constructed from the flow of programmes rather than from any one particular show viewed in isolation. Clearly, by concentrating on one particular type of narrative – commencement, ongoing or completion – within a given programme, a necessary coherence is lent to a show which otherwise might appear fragmented and disordered. The internal structure of an individual *Oprah* show mirrors the external overarching narrative structure of the show's storytelling subjects: they are – or will become – coherent, complete selves.

During this process, it becomes evident that the majority of the narratives are testimonial and perform a different function to that of confession; testimony is the defining feature of the completion narratives signalling the end of the journeying process. Although part of the narrative may concern feelings of worthlessness, fear or shame, the expression of this is not confessional in nature as redemption and exoneration is neither sought nor offered. The *OED* defines 'testimony' as a 'declaration or statement of fact'. This stands at variance with confession, which, as we saw in the previous chapter, is a ritual within which power relations form, and is linked to the therapeutic process through the uncovering of a 'truth'. The distinction between confession and testimony in the context of *The Oprah Winfrey Show* lies in the way in which testimony is used as a mode for the articulation of self-esteem and self-realisation and which form the overarching narrative of the show; confessional speech facilitates the *process* of 'becoming'. I argue that it is the act of standing up and 'being counted' that marks the function of testimony on the programme, and is an articulation of self-identity. Common throughout is the absence of debate on wider social and political issues which is a concern for writers such as Debbie Epstein and Deborah Lynn Steinberg whose work is discussed in Chapter 1. It is useful to remind ourselves of Shattuc's observation (1997) that '[talk shows'] discursive structure involves testimonials rather than confessions... Within evangelism the act of standing up and speaking one's religious experience is a social obligation...'[8] As I have argued, *Oprah* provides a forum for standing up and talking back, a practice which is located within protestant evangelism but which is also associated with the call and response dynamic of the black church.

I am not arguing that the acts of testimony on *Oprah* cancel out confessional speech, rather, that the two modes of address coexist within the complex interplay of voices on the programme. Ahmed and Stacey (2001) argue that the proliferation of contemporary testimonial practice is bound up with notions of justice and truth. They argue that 'The position of the witness and the position of the victim are presented as the site from which justice can be delivered, and the trauma of the nation, community or individual, healed.'[9] As testimonies take different forms, requiring a variety of witnessing, the political effects are also divergent. Thus, testimony does not have a singular politics or ethics but is dependent on the context in which it is heard/used. Testimony is, they argue, a dialogic form of address that requires a listener, and creates 'the conditions for its own existence and reception by constituting different configurations of self, space and community'.[10]

Although witnessing is clearly an essential component of testimonial practice, my study does not extend to include a consideration of those who witness the testimonies of *Oprah* participants – including Oprah herself who can be described as chief witness. As Susannah Radstone states, 'the position of witness is a complex one that can exceed an empathic identification with victimhood to include identifications with other positions available in any other given scenario, including, especially, those of perpetration'.[11] Radstone's formulation (2001) of witnessing underlines the complexity of the relationship between the listener and the speaker of testimony. My own emphasis is on under-standing the 'configurations of self, space and community' that arise from *Oprah* narratives. My objective now is to look more closely at the individual shows in order to demonstrate the ways in which narratives of the self are inextricably linked to narratives of completion (or the journey towards completion) within which testimony is more frequently evoked than confession. It is through this process that self as active agent emerges.

Narratives of completion

'Girl Power' (BBC2, 15.11.95)

'Girl Power' presents six teenage girls whose stories had been collected and published in a book entitled *Girl Power*, 'a book of stories... [that] will touch your heart' [Oprah Winfrey]. All offer narratives of success, of having overcome major obstacles and express an enriched sense of self through having faced their respective trials. A developed inner strength is made evident through the display of self-confidence in who they are as individuals and what they are able and/or willing to tolerate from others. All are articulate and insightful. A mixture of home-video footage, still photographs and extracts from journals and letters are used to firstly introduce and then underpin the spoken narrative of each of the guests. The six girls sit on the stage, three on either side of Oprah, in a slightly curved line so that they are facing each other as well as the studio audience. What is noteworthy in these stories is their structure: each narrative starts at the point from which growth begins, from positions of isolation, degradation, exclusion or ridicule. But the focus of the stories is not the feelings of anger or resentment that could justifiably be articulated. Rather, it is the self which is achieved, the self which has emerged following the journey; feelings of confidence, self-worth and liberation are expressed as compared to the narrow restrictions of negative self-evaluation.

The stories are framed by Oprah's introduction to the show. To rapturous applause, she announces: 'It's fun to be on TV! It's fun to be on TV!' This upbeat opening contrasts rather oddly with her next words which are: 'I was an ugly teenager' [still photograph of a teenage Winfrey]. A brief slice of autobiography is then offered. Oprah tells us that her teenage years were 'a difficult time'. Abused since the age of nine, she became a sexually promiscuous teenager. When her mother had wanted to place her in a detention home, the two-week waiting period for an available place was considered too long and so young Winfrey was sent to live with her father. This however, says Oprah, was the making of her. And so, we can see that Oprah's own story foreshadows those of the girls which are yet to come. Speaking from the position of an immensely successful – and powerful – woman, Oprah authenticates the experiences of those we are to hear.

Although the narratives are of lone journeys, each of the guests sees themselves as vitally connected to a wider familial and social network. Sarah is the founder of Riot Grrrl, a group which is open, growing and includes 'girls from all walks of life'. Overweight and unattractive, Sarah became utterly sickened by the repeated insults from other girls and boys and decided to challenge the idea that there was only one acceptable way to be a girl: 'You don't need to be a beauty queen to get respect.' Prior to the formation of Riot Grrrl, Sarah did not feel 'proud' of who she was; now, however, she 'feels much more positive' about herself. Sarah's anger about the way in which girls and women are treated in American society is only expressed when she describes the treatment her younger sister and a group of her friends received from a number of boys just the day before she appeared on the show.

Terri, a 19-year-old black girl, was born and brought up in 'gangland', a drug infested, dangerous place where her brother was shot and no one cared about her. She describes her early years as ones full of loss, pain and isolation, and characterises her self during that time as 'closed, unresponsive'. Her 7th grade teacher who had recognised the potential in her pupil facilitated Terri's journey to self-fulfilment. This teacher – now Terri's adoptive white parent – nurtured the disturbed young girl. This 'gift of love' is what enabled Terri to cultivate her feelings of 'self-respect'. Terri's story raises the issue of interracial adoption and the subsequent responses from other members of Terri's black community. Oprah poses questions concerning 'race' conflict and the way in which it has impacted on the relationship between Terri and her mother – and there have been difficulties – however, the real focus of the discussion here is the notion that love transcends colour: 'Love has no colour' [Oprah]. And so, what could have developed into a critique of 'race' relations in contemporary America becomes instead a celebration of the possibility for the individual to overcome and rise above deeply rooted, institutionalised bigotry.

Whitney, a 17-year-old lesbian, tells of why and how she came out, the acceptance, love and support given by her parents, and of the protection her parents offer her against the worst of the small, anti-gay community where she lives. Again, what we hear is a story of triumph: Rejected by other 'kids', Whitney says: 'I decided not to degrade myself down to their level. I stayed strong.'

These narratives – along with the remaining three not recounted here – follow a similar pattern and one which mirrors Winfrey's own story at the beginning of the show: An individual faces a situation that has rendered their sense of worth and self-esteem negligible or non-existent. In all six cases, this poor self-image was the reflection of the way in which they had been perceived and/or treated by others. Someone or something acted as a catalyst for the development of a much more positive sense of self and of recovery, and the capacity to redefine who they are. Each has either accepted who and what they are with a degree of pride, or they have been able to change what they were; either way, all use their own terms of reference to define their own self, often in the face of continuing antagonism from others. Of equal importance is the role and support of close family members and friends who, while not the source of this inner strength, provide a frame of reference through which this self can be expressed. This is signalled by the inclusion of the relevant family members by way of introducing them to other members of the studio audience and to us at home, but they remain seated in the audience, apart from their daughters. The boundary between the stage and the studio floor is not breached allowing the girls to remain clearly identified as the authors of their narratives.

These stories are really narratives of completion and as such are less confessions than testimonials. These teenage girls have no need for confession as they have already been through the process of exoneration and redemption. As stated earlier, the opening of their stories provides a glimpse of their troubled beginnings – a necessary context into which their narratives are placed – but what their accounts are chiefly concerned with is the movement to self-realisation. Empowerment is the result of continuing and sustained effort on behalf of the individual. What seems to be of importance here is that the respective struggles have been driven by the desire to create a new sense of self, a drive which originates from *within* the individual being rather than through any external pressure or force. The warmth and affection expressed towards significant others indicates the fundamental importance of a well-integrated network of friends and family, but this is part of the external landscape, and not a part of their respective interior lives. These are then, implicitly, narratives of wholeness and completion. Here, the lack of address to those social forces which threatened the girls' well-being in the first place is striking; racism, sexism, poverty and abuse are factors that give rise to these stories. This implies the limits to the challenge Oprah/*Oprah* poses to 'official' ideological discourse.

'Real Life Dramas' (BBC2, 4.11.95)

'Real Life Dramas' is the one further show in the sample to concentrate on a serial presentation of success stories. There are 8 stories told, 3 by men, 3 by women, 1 family consisting of a mother, father and son, and 1 couple (with a family member in the audience). In her opening address to this show, Oprah promises us 'stories of unbelievable fortitude' and asks 'how do people cope with life after facing death?' In fact, most of what we hear on this show is not so much about how life after facing near death is experienced – although it is touched on – but how the narrators came to the decisions to act and what action they took in order to save themselves. Unlike Terri, Sarah and Whitney, whose ordeals arose from finding themselves at odds with material inequities of power, the individuals on this show found themselves in perilous circumstances through accidents and awful chance happenings. The spotlight here is on the inner strength and self-reliance that can be called on in times of acute crisis, and on the external, often spiritual, resources utilised by individuals under extreme pressure.

Mike is the guest who arguably offers the most detailed glimpse of what life is like after facing death. He, a builder, tells an apparently incredulous Oprah how he accidentally drove a nail into his heart with a nail gun while at work. The camera is fixed on Mike for the duration of his narrative which serves to focus and intensify what we are hearing. Oprah holds aloft the nail, several inches long, as she asks 'What did it feel like?' [laughter from the audience] 'Well, isn't that what you'd want to know? What did it feel like?' Of course, this *is* a question that is pertinent to the narrative, but intertwined with Mike's own telling of the tale are other questions posed by Oprah: had his family members been called, his girlfriend? What is revealed through this line of questioning is that Mike and his girlfriend – now his wife – had had a row before he set off for work that day. His wife, sitting in the audience, takes over the story, tearfully recounting being called to the hospital and seeing Mike slipping in and out of consciousness and how terrible she felt knowing that the last time they spoke, it was in anger. Both report the ways in which Mike's near-death experience has profoundly affected their relationship for the better: they state that they never fight any more and when they have a disagreement, they make certain that it is resolved and that they express their love for one another. Mike's story differs from the majority of others on this show in that he does not state that it was thoughts of family members that drove him to persevere. Nonetheless, Mike's is a drama in which others have acted and to whom he owes a great debt: his colleague present at the time, and the medical staff at the hospital. His wife's tearful, shaky testimony gives witness to the emotional component of the narrative giving voice to the power of transcendence such an experience provides. It is this which supplies meaning to the tale. In a slightly different context, Illouz (1999) argues that the emotional content of talk shows functions as a means of discussing relational difficulties between individuals – 'of entering, staying in and leaving relationships'.[12] In a complex and pluralistic society emotions supply moral points of reference offering 'powerful metaphors to discuss the content of everyday life and reconcile the contradictions that saturate liberal politics'[13] in the age of late capitalism. I would take this a step further by arguing that in this show, as in many *Oprah* shows, the expression of emotion within the narratives not only provides the means through which experience is understood, but also acts as an endorsement of that experience. This affirmation is fundamental to the meaning of the show.

All the narratives on this show are accounts calling for heroism on behalf of the storyteller but only one is a straight telling of the incident without reference to either thoughts of or the presence of significant others. The remaining seven cite their love for friends and family as a major source of their courage and determination to extricate themselves from deadly circumstances. These networks of relationships provide the context in which the action takes place. For Jim and Jean – who have been 'married for 19 years' – family ties and bonds have been strengthened since their ordeal, which took place when they were out walking and both slipped into a ravine 300 feet deep, Jean falling the furthest. Witnessed by their teenage daughter, Jessie, and her boyfriend, this is a drama in which a number of people are involved although it is only Jim and Jean who are on the stage. Both Jean and Jessie, who are seated in the audience, are tearful as they relive the experiences of that day and recount their thoughts as the drama unfolded. While all thought that they would never see one another alive again, they attempted to reassure one another as each played their part in the event. Jim assured his daughter that both he and his wife were 'alright', Jean prayed and Jessie went for help. Jim says that 'we've got a new life now, Oprah. It really brought a change'. This change is unspecified, but the suggestion is that the alteration is a positive one; the tears shed during the narration signify the terror of impending loss and the relief that this loss was never made actual. Again, the expression of emotion serves to define and to underline the relationship between the protagonists as well as working to validate the tale.

Four other tales are of lone individuals completely dependent on their self-reliance for survival – both physically and psychically. On each occasion, these people describe overwhelming feelings of terror and isolation. All state that it was thoughts of their families that gave rise to the courage that enable them to act – one man had to cut off his leg with a pocket knife after he had been crushed by a falling tree – and three of the four also called on the power of prayer in their moments of darkness; two of these are firm in their belief that the answer to their predicament came as a direct result of prayer. What is interesting about these stories is that, as is true of the other narratives, the focus is clearly on the action undertaken alongside the inner thought processes that provided the catalyst for agency but the story ends with their ultimate survival; there are no accounts of how the experience has altered their lives. They remain convinced in the belief that it was their thoughts of nearest and dearest that helped pull them through. Those who found recourse in prayer continue in their belief that spiritual guidance helped them in their predicament – the man who cut off his leg is certain that his escape from death was a miracle. Validation of these narratives comes not from the testimony of family members (who are seated in the audience) but through the production of evidence: the (blunt) pocket knife; a photograph of the plane flown by the woman who, having never piloted before, had to land the craft after her father died at the controls; a photograph of the desert in which a woman was lost and in which her husband died before reaching help. And of course, the very fact of these individuals' presence on the show, demonstrates that the most extreme of conditions can be overcome if one draws on the inner capacity to survive.

The movement to action from inaction is the overarching narrative structure of the testimonies offered on this show. Unlike the 'Girl Power' show, Oprah does not use autobiography to underpin the stories of the guests presumably because she has never had such near death encounters herself. Rather, these tales stand on their own and the interjections made by Oprah are a series of questions to promote the storytelling, along with exclamations of horror, disbelief and relief, giving voice to the facial expressions of the silent audience members.

Two further narratives are worth considering here, both foregrounding the importance of taking action. The first is one that is spoken by a chorus of women (but which I have counted as one report). In 1958, 92 children died in a fire at their school. The women on this show are survivors of the incident and were 1st grade pupils at the time. They describe briefly the horror of that day in which several of them lost their siblings. They spoke of their terror and confusion at the time of the blaze and of their knowledge that their survival was dependent on adult assistance. The aftermath of the tragedy was, for them, marked by silence. The corollary of inaction here was the burial of material which continued to exert a negative influence over the lives of these women for 35 years until the focus moved from the 92 who died to the 1300 who survived. Since then, as a group (which these women represent rather than fully constitute) they have been able to excavate their feelings of loss, grief and guilt at having been saved when others were lost. Talking has given a sense and meaning to the nightmares and flashbacks that are still commonly experienced. The experience is now being dealt with as a community rather than by a collection of isolated individuals.

This is the only story with an explicitly psychotherapeutic angle to it. It sits rather oddly with the other tales on the show which, despite the call for inner strength, are narratives of action and doing. This tale, however, is cautionary, warning of the perils of *not* taking action. As Oprah says, this was the late 1950s when ignoring issues was 'a sign of the times...[there were] no talk shows in 1958, a totally different era then'. What lies behind Oprah's statement is the conviction that talk shows are the valid – perhaps, only – arena in which meaningful, therapeutic talk can take place. This is a sentiment often rehearsed by Oprah in other *Oprah* shows (although not in this sample of six being discussed here). This flags two things quite clearly: the very act of participating as a guest is in itself an activity through which a promotion of the self can be articulated; and secondly that the talk show is the site which grounds this expression of selfhood. The guest experts represent institutional affiliation through their respective tags – of PhD, psychologist, author of this or that publication – but their points of reference come from within the show itself so that any external association becomes subsumed within the programme's narrative. In addition, this points to the com-modification of 'dysfunction' articulated by the cultural commentators discussed in Chapter 1. However, talk shows *are not* the only arena in which therapeutic engagement takes place; the implication that these shows offer a unique site for the talking cure is a self-serving statement that calls up and promotes the cultural acceptance of therapeutic discourse.[14] Nonetheless, it is also the case that the show is a site that enables the articulation of testimony, of publicly standing up and talking back, and while this may have a therapeutic effect on the individuals concerned, testifying is not a part of the therapeutic process *per se*.

The second narrative to celebrate agency is the last story in this show and so grounds the message firmly in the viewer's consciousness. What is interesting about this particular story is less the narrative but more the way in which the voices are handled. At the centre of the tale is 17-year-old Alex who was stranded in a run away hot air balloon. Alex takes the stage along with his parents, George and Linda, and Dave, the man who talked Alex through the process of landing the balloon. George and Linda recount the, by now familiar, expressions of terror and help-lessness as they realised that their son was drifting away at an altitude of 1000 feet. They state that they 'cried, screamed, prayed', believing that they had lost their son. Equipped with a CB radio, Alex – having travelled 35 miles – was able to follow Dave's guidance and successfully land the craft. This would seem to be Alex's story, but the amount of time given to the respective participants breaks down thus – introduc-tion by Oprah: 10 seconds; George: 1 minute and 50 seconds; Alex: 25 seconds; Dave: 2 minutes. Linda's voice is only briefly heard. Alex is given barely an eighth of the time allowed to Dave in which to tell his part of the tale despite his status of central character. Together, the voices make this a narrative of completion, but it is Dave who is seen as the most prominent protagonist here and that is because he is the one who took action while the others solely report their emotional response to the situation. Emotional content is insufficient in itself, as Dave's action takes on a heroic status.

Atypically, there is no guest expert or witness on this show and this signifies that these stories stand by themselves, needing no elucidation. Nor is there any attempt at using an expert to discuss with the guests and inform the audience of the sort of psychic responses commonly experienced following trauma.

'Men and Women Communicating' (Channel 4, 31.10.95)

'Men and Women Communicating' has the appearance of an advice show with information emanating from one narrator, John Gray who, as a marriage guidance counsellor, doubles as the guest expert.[15] As a married man, Gray continually uses the experiences of his own marriage to exemplify the potential pitfalls within marital relationships and the means with which to successfully negotiate difficulties and obstacles to a happy and fulfilled marriage – which he claims to have. The relationships up for examination are firmly heterosexual; as the title states, the complexities addressed here speak to those confined to male/female sexual relations. In Gray's capacity as a marriage guidance counsellor, the implicit assumption is that the target audience members are those in committed relationships: casual affairs or sexual promiscuity are not on the agenda. Validation of the counsellor's directives comes from his wife who is seated in the audience and whose nods and smiles, captured by the camera, give silent affirmation to the words spoken by her husband. The tone is relentlessly upbeat and humorous.

This show is structured in the question and answer format – the former from Oprah and the audience, the latter from the counsellor. For the greater part of the show, Oprah physically situates herself between the stage and the audience. In doing so, and in voicing her own questions, she aligns herself with the audience allowing the expert total ownership over the space which he occupies as he stands, sits and moves around at will when addressing the audience. However, by choosing this betwixt and between position, Oprah is foregrounding her status both as star – and controller – of the show. More implicitly, we can see her positioning as a signal of her own long-term relationship with Stedman Graham and a demonstration of the need/desire to learn the means of successful communication with her partner; it is an ongoing process for her. (This stands in contrast to Oprah's location on the 'Girl Power' and 'Real Life Dramas' shows where she aligns herself with the already empowered.) The counsellor's own very animated performance mirrors his insistence on the need for *active* participation on the part of those who care about sustaining enriching relationships with their partners, whilst his elevated position demonstrates his success in this area.

The dynamic between genders is set up as a universal norm and remains unchallenged for the duration of the show. The entire discourse remains grounded in the normative gender positioning of men and women in heterosexual relationships. We are told that all we need to understand one another is an awareness of differing perspectives that arise from innate, biological drives. Girls develop communication skills first, while at the same time boys 'get home, play ball'. So there is a discrepancy from the very start. When a man takes possession of the TV remote control, we are told that this is simply a manifestation of male atavism; in 'ancient times', men 'watched wild animals on the plains', in their search for food. Today this impulse is sublimated into the continual 'clicking' of the 'remote' fulfilling the need to survey (the horizon). There is however plenty of advice offered about how to surmount the intersexual conflict which arises from genetic inscription. This is where 'Men and Women Communicating' coalesces the central themes of other shows in my sample. Couples are called on to understand, tolerate and support one another. Women, we are told, *need* to hear expressions of love and so the man must respond to this need, reassure his partner through the articulation of his affection for his 'wife' even when he does not actively *feel* that love at that particular moment. Women need to understand how men desire some space sometimes, and to allow that momentary separation to occur while not feeling rejected or threatened by it. An example of a question asked: [woman] 'What do men want [from romance]?' Answer: 'To be acknowledged and appreciated' [positive response from men in the audience]. Genetic inscription programmes in men the desire to be acknowledged for their labours. Slaughtering beasts on the ancient plains for sustenance translates in modern day into 'Men do work to get paid'. So, women need to thank their men folk for tasks undertaken in the house that they (women) frequently take for granted, taking out the rubbish, washing the dishes . . .

Clearly, this show is not a debate about social gendering of roles or of the power positions that frequently have given rise to conflict on a personal as well as political level. The articulations of the women's movements over the last hundred years are effaced during this programme. The fact that here is a single – albeit married – male that is presented as the source of knowledge and the embodiment of enlightened empowerment, remains uncommented upon. There is no informed female point of view, and despite the fact that women are given as much right to expectations from their partners as are men in this narrative, this show underpins the traditional perspective of male/female heterosexual relations.

Although the question/answer format of this programme lends a more fragmentary experience of storytelling – no one complete narrative is related – the position of the guest expert as the embodiment of interpersonal success implies the same journey towards self-discovery as those narratives discussed earlier. This man has invested time and energy in examining the dynamics of his own relationship, made mistakes, made discoveries and is, consequently, the proud owner of an apparently happy union with the person most central to his life. The very fact of his own clearly demonstrated communication skills on the show underpin his overriding philosophy: listen, learn, respect and talk.

'Date Violence' (Channel 4, 24.10.95)

The show 'Date Violence' offers the final two narratives of completion found in the sample. These are more complex than those considered above because although the narrators have been victims of horrific abuse which they then sought to overcome, they remain damaged and fragmented by the experiences. We have to wait to hear these stories until a more terrible one is told and it is this one which does not fit into any one model of narrative in this sample. However, it serves to foreground the seriousness with which today's theme is to be treated and by contrast elevates those stories yet to come to ones of success. I will begin my examination of this show by discussing the atypical story first as it provides the context in which we hear the remaining narratives.

This story (spoken by a family comprised of two parents and the letter from an absent daughter) exemplifies the horrific consequences of not confronting conflict, a possibility that can – and does, as the show demonstrates – lead to death. The show opens with a sombre Oprah telling us that young girls 'expect a kiss and a slap on the first date', that this is 'common today' and is a new phenomenon signifying 'horrifying changes'. This rather dramatic way of presenting today's subject introduces a tension as Oprah tells us that she is doing this show in order to warn young girls and their parents of the dangers of ignoring vital signs of date violence and how to recognise those signs should they present themselves. Tension and expectation are heightened and sustained by the introduction of the first story, a story in which Jenny, a key protagonist, is absent. Killed by Mark, her 'first love', Oprah introduces Jenny's story: when Jenny fell in love with Mark she 'hoped and prayed that he'd call again'. The relationship did develop but she 'never recovered from her bruises' inflicted by Mark. We are then introduced to Jenny's parents,

Vicki and Greg, who are seated opposite Oprah on the stage and who, we are told, are taking the opportunity to speak to Mark directly for the first time since his trial and life imprisonment for the murder of their daughter. Mark's image is beamed from prison onto a large video screen situated between Oprah and her guests, giving each apparent equal access to him.

Greg begins his story by relating the events that took place the night he found his daughter's body in the family home. The description of his actions immediately prior to his awful discovery intimates a context that is warm, loving and secure: he had been shopping for 'baby supplies', there are younger children in the household and a normal amount of family chaos and mess in which he is placed as an active, caring father. Having finished his part of the narrative, Vicki fills in some of the detail by describing her positive impressions of Mark whilst he was dating her daughter. She also describes the kind of girl Jenny was: a 'good kid' who 'cared about her family' and who 'loved her new baby brother'. This is a quintessentially ideal American family to whom the unthinkable should never happen. But as this show attempts to demonstrate, the unthinkable can and does happen and that the best defence against such trauma is to arm oneself with knowledge – there is a list of warning signs of abusive relationships following the first story – and the self-confidence to believe that violence is *always* unacceptable, as the stories which follow this one serve to demonstrate.

Mark is then given a voice, and takes 'this opportunity' to say 'I'm truly sorry for what I did.' Vicki: 'Mark, why? Why did you do it? [Vicki in tears] You said that you loved her.' Mark: 'It's true. I had a lot of problems at home...You are not to blame. I'm the one to blame here... "Why" is a good question.' What takes place here is not so much of a storytelling, but a series of calls for testimonials with the aim of building a picture through which a story – with a degree of coherence – can be told. In fact, this exchange is a more complex arrangement of voices than is typical in this small sample of shows but serves to foreground the use of both testimonial and confession in eliciting the actuality of individual experience.

Mark, Vicki, Greg and the silent Jenny are the disparate strands that together compile this particular narrative. Many of the details that Mark is pressed to reveal – such as his thoughts at the time of the murder, of the rage that drove him to get a knife from the kitchen – must have already been heard by Jenny's parents during the courtroom trial. So the rehearsal of the events which took place on the night of the killing is largely for the benefit of the studio and home audiences.

What follows is a series of calls to Mark from Oprah to explain his actions; the evasive Mark is clearly expected to respond. On being asked what he did in the moments prior to the murder, Mark replies 'It happened.' Oprah: 'No, no, no...what was going through your mind?' Oprah reminds Mark that he had agreed to do this show and to speak to Jenny's parents implying that he had a duty to bear witness to the truth.

As we have seen, storytelling on a television confessional chat show requires an inclusion of emotional processes. Greg asks Mark if he has ever considered the 'emotion our family has to endure?', describes his feelings of helplessness and his continuing state of shock. As the voices of the dead girl's mother and father tell of their feelings of loss, grief, and betrayal, Oprah continues with her attempts to understand the killer's mind: 'What did you *think*?' Despite the sensational nature of the story that is unfolding and the spectacle of these three guests and Oprah grappling with the narrative, the tone is subdued. The studio audience participates through their silence and we are only shown occasional shots of individual audience members shaking their heads in disbelief.

A fourth voice introduced is that of Jenny's younger sister who has written a letter to Mark to be read to him on the show. The reason for her absence is not explained but this is immaterial. Regular viewers of *Oprah* will be aware that letters and diaries are often used to access the inner thoughts and feelings of the show's participants and mark the move from personal and private to the public and social. Here, the letter underlines the family's sense of continuing loss and grief and also an anger which has not been expressed by either Vicki or Greg: 'Thank you for tearing my life apart. I hope that God is as forgiving as my parents.'

The introduction of written material into the narrative at this point is interesting. The letter contains the first expression of anger, an emotion that is marked by its absence in the dialogue of either Greg or Vicki. It implies that whilst anger is understandable, natural even, in this context, it is potentially too explosive or damaging to the narrative flow to be articulated in person. It can be voiced but is safely contained on the page through which it is expressed and does not, therefore, threaten to overwhelm the voices of those actually present. As I have pointed out elsewhere, the production and reading of letters is a device commonly used on *The Oprah Winfrey Show*, signalling a move from the interior world of the individual to the exterior world of the public. The discourses of Greg and Vicki have centred on their need to *understand* Mark's motives in killing their daughter; theirs is a problem of cognition, one which needs confronting if they are to be able to 'come to terms' with Jenny's death. The letter, however, is an articulation of emotional distress separated from intellectual functioning. The problems of thinking and of feeling are made distinct through the process of articulation; the parents speak of their thoughts, the sister writes of her feelings. This speaking/writing split is made coherent through the construction of a consistent narrative as the various voices form one family unit united in their loss and incomprehension which is located in the void created by Jenny's murder. This is an unusual usage of a letter on *Oprah*.

Close-ups show individuals in the studio audience shaking their heads and crying, thereby seeming to enact the misery and incomprehension of Jenny's family; through the structure of the show, the audience becomes part of the narrative.

Greg and Vicki's story remains unresolved. We are left with Mark's reply to the letter stating that his family too are suffering, they too have lost a son: 'This is no life...I might as well be dead. That's how my family feel too.'

As stated earlier, the narrative outlined above does not cohere with any of the narrative patterns I have outlined as existing within the sample. Rather, it is presented as an (extreme) example of the dangers attendant in not taking action, of remaining inert in the face of adversity. We know that Mark's burst of violence was not the only occasion on which he had abused his girlfriend. During the interview with him, Oprah had drawn confessions from Mark to the effect that he had 'slapped her'. However, he had prefaced the recording of his actions with the word 'just', he had 'Just slapped her.' Mark's attempt at minimising his previous acts of violence had been the focus of the debate between himself and Oprah with the latter trying to determine 'at what point in an argument do you slap a person' and if it had seemed 'normal to slap her?' The reason for Oprah's persistence with this part of Mark's story becomes clear when we are introduced to the next guest, Lynn.

Lynn, looking somewhat uncomfortable, sits on the stage and listens while Oprah introduces her story. Still photographs of Lynn's badly beaten face fill the screen while Oprah's voice tells us that she (Lynn) was so injured by her boyfriend's violence that she was in need of hospitalisation. Lynn's own narrative is then contextualised through Oprah's opening address, inviting Lynn to recount her story. Oprah: 'Over the years I've spoken to lots of abused women; they express shock that this happened.' The photographs illustrating the effect of violent abuse on this woman combine with the broad brush strokes of Oprah's words to present a picture of a situation which is specific to one individual but common to many; Lynn's story stands in for the myriad that remain unmarked and unheard.

Like those stories which were heard on 'Real Life Dramas' and 'Girl Power', Lynn has successfully negotiated terrifying circumstances; her appearance on the show is testimony to the strength and courage required to overcome her ordeal. Familiar too is the source of her determination to survive: 'How would my family feel if I died?' Thinking of her two nephews, three sisters and her parents, Lynn tells us that she 'could not die and could not bring that pain to them'.

As with Jenny, Lynn hid the marks of her abuse from her family while she remained confused about the treatment suffered from her boyfriend. We hear Lynn saying 'I felt like he was my life' while further photographic evidence of her injuries – bruises and bite marks – are shown. The arrangement of pictures and words are simultaneously delivered to the audience enabling the complexity of Lynn's narrative to be conveyed. The images of brutality are juxtaposed with words that undercut a sense of that brutality, or rather, indicate the process of denial that explains Lynn's difficulty in allowing the actuality of her situation to be recognised by her family. What becomes clear is that Lynn's concern to protect her family from pain and worry, along with her desire to preserve a relationship she valued, overrode concerns of personal safety and welfare. At this point in the narrative, we can see that thoughts of significant others in this context are what *impeded* Lynn's journey to self-realisation. Here, Lynn's narrative runs parallel to Jenny's. However, Lynn did not die – although the photographs tell us how near to death she came – which is where the two narratives diverge and the point at which this story begins to mirror the accounts of success in the other shows. Clearly, there is danger attached to relationships with others, just as close ties and concern for those closest can provide the resources for recovery.

Lynn's story can be counted as one of completion as she has survived danger and is able to recount her experience. However, the narrative is problematic. The success narratives described earlier are labelled as such because there is closure; the narrators have been positively transformed through their conflicts, have enhanced self-esteem and a renewed appreciation of important friendship/familial ties. Lynn remains damaged by her ordeal. Despite the imprisonment of her erstwhile boyfriend, his figure continues to cast a shadow over Lynn's existence – he has threatened to find her once released from prison – and so she remains cowed by her experiences. This lack of satisfactory closure turns Lynn's narrative back in on itself and threatens to become a loop in which she is trapped, never fully liberated.

Nonetheless, I have included this story amongst the narratives of success for the reasons stated above and because the supportive presence of Lynn's mother, seated in the audience, points to a positive and hopeful outcome. The conclusion of Lynn's story is followed by the display of a list of warning signs, signs that might alert viewers to a situation in which young girls may be similarly trapped. Containment is the message here: symptoms of violent abuse are encapsulated on the screen, are made manageable, in the same way that it is possible to read the signs, understand their implication, and to take control of the dis-ease in everyday life.

The third narrative in this show appears as an enactment of both the successful resolution of abusive relational conflict and of the possible dangers attached to the disregard of these conflicts. The protagonists, Randy (the abuser) and Emmy (the abused), stand facing one another in the front row of the audience, each defending their respective positions within the narrative; Emmy's testimony is shaky but spoken with determination, Randy is unrepentant. Although the status of this narrative is diminished as a result of not being spoken from the elevation of the stage, we identify elements that are common to Jenny's and Lynn's narratives. A young woman so values her relationship that she (initially at least) is prepared to turn a blind eye to the damage that that relationship is inflicting on her – in terms of violent mistreatment and subsequent psychological harm and low self-esteem.

I have numbered this story among the narratives of success because Emmy has completed her journey to self-realisation and tells her story in the presence of Randy, the perpetrator of violence. Randy does not invite our sympathies as he seeks to justify his actions which are unjustifiable. Emmy had been slapped because 'she wouldn't shut up . . . she'll keep pushing the issue'. Violence, we learn, is linked to Randy's abuse of alcohol and his inability to contain his rage in the face of Emmy's provocation. Randy's voice is an echo of Mark's; the descriptions of loss of control and violent rage, the subsequent beating of the female partner are elements common to both men's narrative. And so the hostility of the audience towards Randy – marked by groans of disbelief from audience members – registers an animosity which is extended from Randy to include Mark and outward to all men whose attitude towards women results in abuse of this sort.

Emmy's narrative is only an outline, a sketch with little specific detail; we do not need to hear any more because we can identify her details with those already narrated by Lynn and by Jenny's family. We do, however, hear how desperate things became for Emmy before she took control of her situation; and here too we have echoes of what has gone before. 'He [Randy] was my world...his family and me were real close.' Emmy's sense of betrayal is palpable while she tells how very near she came to losing everything: '[I] almost had my family taken away from me...everything'.

There is a twist to this story, however, and one which explicitly inserts a moment of sensationalism: Randy is now dating a woman who is also a friend of Emmy's and who had witnessed first hand the violent manifestation of this man's rage. The girlfriend now stands to join Randy and Emmy, bringing her contribution to the narrative. This, of course, is an important element to the overarching narrative of the show. While Mark is in prison for life, Lynn's ex-boyfriend will soon be free, as Randy is now, to form other relationships with women on whom further acts of aggression can be perpetrated. How will other women deal with such men? One possible answer is provided through this third voice in the story. Oprah asks the current girlfriend 'How can you be with a man who does this to a woman...to your friend?' The – somewhat unfortunate – reply is 'I love him to death', but 'would walk away' if Randy was to hit her just once. She implies that it was Emmy's fault for being *so* argumentative, *so* provocative that Randy hit out; she believes that Randy will never do the same to her. But we have seen the effects of abusive behaviour: Jenny is dead, Lynn is scarred; Mark displaces his personal responsibility onto a difficult home life; Lynn's boyfriend continues to threaten her from prison; Randy blames Emmy for his violence – and so we do not, cannot, have faith in Randy or the testimony of Randy's girlfriend: we *know* that he is capable of such actions again.

The three separate tales are brought together by Oprah, who ties the threads of these complex and messy narratives by addressing the home and studio audience: 'I know you who are parents need to know' how to deal with this evidently growing problem. At this point the guest expert, Dr Barrie Levy, is introduced. Author of *In Love, In Danger*, Dr Levy is an authoritative witness to the testimonies given earlier. We are told that police statistics show 25 per cent of girls dating are being beaten. The enormity of these statistics perhaps is one reason why the narratives are presented as less definitively successful than those displayed in 'Girl Power', 'Real Life Dramas' and 'Men and Women Communicating'.

'Date Violence' focuses on a problem that is alive and active, the scale of which threatens to overwhelm. There is a further expert on this show who offers a more atypical analysis of the problem in that he places this specific issue within the larger social context. Eric Newberger M.D. – flagged as the Director of Family Development – offers his formulation. The 'terrible problem in our society' lies in the perception of what it means to be masculine: that boys feel that they are boys only if they are in control. Teenage girls, on the other hand, often feel 'pressure to put up with anything in order to be in a relationship'. This dynamic per- petuates its harmful cycle through a lack of communication, a failure to question expectations, and because of a reluctance to take personal responsibility for our actions. Newberger's work has led him to conclude that men and teenage boys 'often look for excuses', a way to externalise their actions, that justifies their behaviour. Mark, Randy and Lynn's boyfriend all stand testimony to this perspective of male behaviour. Newberger claims that 'we need to change the cultural script', that there needs to be a belief in 'caring and loving'. The opportunity for change lies in communication, a sentiment that is repeated several times. 'We have to keep talking, keep asking questions. Keep communication open.' Concern shifts from the inner, individual context to the outer, public arena. If this particular expert's voice had been heard at the beginning of the programme, what followed would have been an articu- lation of the ways in which *individuals* find ways to resist, act, in such circumstances. However, placing Newberger's conjecture after those of the guest speakers inverts this; the narratives become symbols of a problem that is epidemic.

What we have heard and seen in this show is the airing of a problem that threatens the physical and psychological well-being of many young women in American society. It is interesting that the summing up and contextualisation of the three narratives comes from a male expert. One can only assume that there are any number of female therapists who could have stood in place of Barrie Levy. The fact that a man was chosen for this role undercuts the premise that this is a solely feminist agenda, one requiring articulation by a female voice. The very act of Levy appearing on the show demonstrates the viability of his assertion: that men and women can – and need to – communicate openly about their respective social positions if we are to minimise the sort of trauma and pain we have heard enunciated on this show. Another way of viewing the use of a male expert is one posited earlier (in 'Men and Women Communicating'): that by offering the male voice as the authority, of holding the answers, a traditional view of masculinity is being upheld – *he* knows, *she* does not. (A noteworthy point: the 'Men and Women' show was broadcast in Britain one week after 'Date Violence'. The light-hearted tone of the former serves as a relief from the emotional trauma of the latter but it also lends coherence to the flow of the programming. Although the content of 'Men and Women' seems (is) frivolous by comparison to 'Date Violence', it nonetheless carries the theme of gendered relations forward, pointing to the possibility of harmonious union.)

In each of the success narratives I have discussed, there are elements that are common to all: (A) All the narratives begin from a position of *isolation*, of being or becoming separate(d); this is a position which threatens to undermine the physical or psychical safety of the central protagonist. (B) *The fall into awareness*; a defining moment in which the individual becomes fully cognisant of the circumstance that presents danger to that individual physically, psychically or both. The next step is (C), *taking stock*; this is represented by a pause in the narrative in which the individual reflects on the situation, assessing the need for action. (D) Crucial to the narrative flow is the *acceptance of personal responsibility*; the narrator has to see that they are in some way responsible for the way that they feel at the moment of crisis or for finding themselves in that situation to begin with; responsibility falls to them for finding a way through their present difficulty. This is a further defining moment from which subsequent action develops and is enmeshed with issues of (E) *control* constituting the next narrative move. The narrator, having accepted personal responsibility, makes the decision to act, but this can only be realised if and when he/she is able to take control of the endangering situation. Whatever the circumstance – which stems from either the threatening behaviour of others or from the physical environment – the locus of control moves from an external force to one that becomes interiorised, a movement that marks, and is essential to, the next narrative stage.

What can be seen in the narratives examined is that the process of internalisation – when the individual takes ownership of the predicament – is vital to the movement towards self-realisation. However fundamental this shift from outer to inner is, of equal importance is the next stage which is marked by an externalisation, a shift which moves the drama outward signalled by *thoughts of significant others*. This is stage (F). Having called on inner resources, the protagonist draws on the importance of relationships with those closest to them in order to activate the inner resources located during stages (C) through (E). This recognition, or acknowledgement, of interpersonal relations acts as a catalyst, or the call, enabling stage (G), *action*.

It is worth pausing for a moment to consider the way in which stage (F) is handled during the shows. Whilst action is obviously integral to any individual narrative in particular, and to the structure of *Oprah* in general, less emphasis is placed on the activity itself – the how and where of the drama – than on the activating factors: the calling on inner selves and the call to significant others. In the case of the latter, the presence of those consequential others may be a physical reality or an imagined presence.

Either way, what is relevant is the empowering force that is brought to bear on the narrative through the consideration of others, placing the individual in a wider familial and social context. Isolation has the possible correlation of inaction and is therefore a force which is seen as counter to productive action. This is most graphically exemplified through Jenny's narrative ('Date Violence') in which both she and her family pay the ultimate price: we can only assume that Jenny remained isolated in her difficulties, that she did not or could not travel from stage (A) to (E). Failing to do so, Jenny dies and her family is sentenced to a life of bereavement. Mark, Jenny's murderer, also pays the price for not taking personal responsibility for his damaging behaviour and has to spend the remainder of his life in prison, isolated from his own family and from the rest of society. Although absent from the show, Mark's own family provide a further shadowy echo of this message. Mark attributes his behaviour towards Jenny to his (unspecified) troubled family life and difficult childhood. What is implied here is that neither Mark nor his parents were able or willing to take stock, accept responsibility, or to control their (apparently) dysfunctional environment. They too, as Mark states to Jenny's parents, feel that their son has died, that they have suffered an extreme loss.

Isolation, whether a physical actuality or a psychic position, is the demon prohibiting self-realisation. That demon is shouted down once the protagonist calls upon meaningful relations with others. We can recall how the women representing the chorus of voices in 'Real Life Dramas' were only able to construct a meaningful narrative around the loss and fear that was born from the fire that devastated their school, their families and their community, once they had formed a group that provided a safe haven for the articulation of their fears and their loss. For 35 years each remained isolated, locked in their own frightening and disabling space until they drew on each other in order to utter the experience which was both an individual and a collective story.

This latter example leads us to the penultimate narrative stage (H), *reflection*. This mirrors (C) in that once the action has taken place, the individual takes stock of what has happened and reflects anew on his or her life and the meaning of others within that life. The period of reflection leads to the final stage (I), *self-realisation*. The self that is realised is the one that is narrating the journey, the self that has successfully negotiated the difficulties, has triumphed over the odds and can claim completion. This self may not be wholly centred as self-realisation is not a static position; the selfhood that is serially presented in *Oprah* shows is part of a dynamic between the individual self and significant others be they a marital partner, family members or social groups. But the vital lesson, and this is important, learnt on the journey is the value of those others as well as a new sense of self-respect and self-worth. It appears as if the journey represents the acquisition of a language through which a rich and purposeful life can be realised, and through this language, life is enhanced or even transformed.

The shows analysed in this section represent a series of testimonials that work to configure a self that is removed from victim status, is active, and is located within meaningful social networks. The narratives that I have called 'ongoing' and 'commencement' can be characterised as confessional.

Ongoing narratives

I now want to examine the narratives that I have called 'Ongoing'. (To remind ourselves, 'ongoing' narratives numbered 7 out of the total 29, two of which are by women speakers and five by male.) In terms of the schema outlined above, I would position these narratives at stage (D) indicating that the orator is in the middle of the process, has identified the problem and is taking *personal responsibility* for it. Facilitating the speakers' progress is the guest expert who contextualises the difficulties, promoting understanding and agency. These stories were all told in the 'Forbidden Thoughts' show (BBC2, 9.11.95) and include anxieties about racist attitudes, fears of harming hyperactive children, confusion over sexual identity. As each speaker confesses his or her feelings of guilt, anger, rage, the emotions are acknowledged as 'normal' responses to trying circumstances by the expert guest (the improbably named Dr Pepper Schwartz, a sociologist), and contextualised: 'just about any thought is normal'. Each participant is applauded for their courage in naming the unspeakable: the woman struggling with racist thoughts is told that she *is* being racist 'but most have these thoughts and it's honest of you. Name it . . . it can be gotten rid of; it can be understood'. The mother of a hyperactive child who often wishes to leave is told, 'This is so honest of you' and is applauded by Oprah – and by extension, all parents coping with children suffering from attention deficit disorder – for coping thus far in such trying circumstances.

Here, Schwartz continually and consistently places the stories into a perspective that validates and normalises the experiences, both the difficulties themselves and the act of disclosure; the latter is especially commended. The act of storytelling here is seen as the way in which individuals are able to make sense of their environment, of their own particular circumstance. As the sociologist says, we have to 'name it, talk about it, deal with it'. These stories are confessional in nature; for the most part, the authority within this power relationship is the expert who seeks to exonerate and redeem the subject who, in turn, is purified through the ritual of telling. Although the *issues* confronting the various storytellers have not been resolved through the act of narration, the integrity of the individual selves is seen as intact. More, they are given enhanced status as courageous, honest, thoughtful – attributes not apparently previously felt by those individuals. These people are 'normal' beings who exemplify the struggle of many others.

By appearing on the show and in standing up to be counted, the narrators here are acting out stages (E), *taking control* and (G), *action*. The responses and interventions made by the guest expert facilitate the move to stage (H), *reflection* and, we assume, to the ultimate stage (I), *self-realisation*. Of course, we, the audience, are only witness to the narrative stages that are presented on the show, but there is an implicit assumption that what is taking place in the studio, through the act of confession and storytelling, represents the process of a journey towards self-realisation that will continue in the actuality of everyday life even if one – or some – of the stages have to be repeated, rehearsed, in the face of adversity. In other words, there is a model that is either articulated in full (narratives of completion) or in part (ongoing narratives) which is called into being and in which the process of attaining self-fulfilment and self-realisation can be activated.

Commencement narratives

Finally, I want to look at those narratives I have labelled 'commencement'. These constitute 4 of the 29 narratives, all involve heterosexual couples, and all are articulated in the show 'Sex' (Channel 4, 21.11.95). These stories involve couples who are at stage (A), *isolation* but who are, by dint of appearing on the show, moving towards stage (B), *fall into awareness*. Although this show is entitled 'Sex' the title might actually be 'Dysfunctional Heterosexual Relationships'.

These are stories of difficulties actively experienced in the present, and as such mark the beginning of the process towards enlightenment.

The potential for the individual to develop their inner self is marked by the activity of narration and facilitated through the intervention and guidance from a guest expert, Dr Barbara De Angelis, and through interjections from Oprah. Confirmation and validation of this process is often given by members of the audience who recount similar experiences of their own.

What differentiates these narratives from the 'ongoing' described above is the speakers' initial non-recognition of the cause of their difficulties. At this stage in the show they are only able to define the form in which their problems exist: they see the symptom – a sexual problem – rather than the cause of that difficulty. Although each story belongs to a couple, the protagonists within that couple are isolated from one another, locked into a misunderstanding which has produced and reproduces that isolation. However, in presenting themselves as a storytelling pair, they signal concern for significant others, along with their desire and willingness to *take stock* (C), *accept personal responsibility* (D), and to *take control* of the situation (E).

Oprah introduces this show's subject matter by justifying and explaining the rationale behind the decision to have sex as a topic of discussion. 'We thought long and hard ... So many people had written and asked us to do this show.' A series of images of 'loving couples', shown along with still photographs of numerous examples of 'How To' manuals, videos and magazines, prompts Oprah's words, 'Why, after all this are people still unhappy? ... I know it's bad for a lot of you out there. The flame has gone, there's just a few ashes left.' 'It' being sexual dissatisfaction, the 'flame' and 'ashes' stand as metaphors for a redundant relationship. But, 'Now here's the good news.' Barbara De Angelis has published a book called *Are You the One for Me?* and is here in the studio to coach a few representative couples in the art of understanding one another's physical and – importantly – psychological needs. Oprah's endorsement ('I really recommend it') is recognition of this expert's validity and the legitimacy of this show's subject matter playing down the sensational at the same time as promoting the book as a commodity.

The four couples are serially presented, each seated on the stage. The expert is also on the stage at some distance from the couple whose turn it is to speak. The manifestation of each dysfunction varies and is a reflection of that which is the source of the problem specific to each relationship. De Angelis hears and responds to the stories in a non-judgemental and reflective manner, looking for the meanings that give rise to the narratives rather than focusing on the narratives themselves.

In common with the ongoing narratives, these stories take the form of a confessional.

Rob and Virginia are here to look at 'what's gone wrong with their sex life'. After seven years of marriage, Virginia had an affair with one of Rob's colleagues, an incident that has left Rob 'devastated'. Cindy and David, married for four years, have two children, work different shift patterns and are 'too tired to make love'. Cindy feels 'consumed by the children'; David states that the 'desire for intimacy' is there but 'not the time'. Babs and Sam have a 'wonderful marriage' of 14 years; although Babs 'takes control' over the frequency of sex, she has never 'realised sexual gratification' which is the source of hurt and confusion for Sam. Carolyn and Jim have been married for six years and have 'good sex' but this couple too has children, are often tired and struggle on a daily basis. The difficulties in this relationship are made manifest through Carolyn's sexual fantasies which place Jim in a 'controlling position'.

As each couple recount their problem, the expert defines the cause of that difficulty, simultaneously situating her as the authority to whom the confession is made and as a voice within the narrative itself. The stories do not actually belong to De Angelis of course, but her ability to reflect, take stock, is that which guides the narratives to the next stage. Repeatedly we are told that the problem is 'not about sex'; rather, sex is a mirror reflecting the dynamic between the two people who constitute a couple. Virginia had an affair because Rob never acknowledged her; she looked outside the marriage for 'love and affection'. Rob 'will do anything to fulfil Virginia's desires [but] does not know what she wants'. Communication, affirmation and intimacy are all inextricably bound as De Angelis delineates the focus of each dilemma. These rather abstract issues are demonstrated through enactments called upon by De Angelis. Rob and Virginia, Cindy and David are, in turn, asked to face one another, hold hands and communicate in an intimate fashion. Rob and Virginia are asked to tell each other, 'One of the things that you could do to make me feel loved is . . .'. Cindy and David are asked to tell each other, 'What I really like about making love to you is . . .'. As each couple comply they are rewarded with applause and a series of 'ahs' from the audience.

The anticipation of the enactment of intimacy between Cindy and David is momentarily breached by a brief exchange between Oprah and De Angelis:

Oprah: 'Holy Toledo! I didn't know you were going to ask them that!'
De Angelis: 'You can edit it for the show.'

Despite its brevity, this exchange highlights the paradox of making private, intimate declarations in a very public sphere. 'You can edit it for the show' demonstrates a conscious awareness of the apparent inappropriateness of the subject for television; the fact that it was not edited for the show foregrounds the validity of conducting such dialogue in the realm of the public. As if to confirm this, once the couple have articulated their feelings, De Angelis turns to Winfrey and says that 'obviously' this is TV and not a bedroom 'but can you feel this energy? This is called intimacy'.

The remaining two couples are not asked to demonstrate intimacy in such a graphic way. Rather, the dynamics of their own specific relationship are discussed, placing issues of control, trust and intimacy at the heart, moving the focus from the outer expression of dysfunction to a move which is inner-directed. With reference to Carolyn's control fantasies for example, we are told that 'fantasies do not create intimacy', that eroticism is external while intimacy is internal, is a state generated from within the individual.

All these couples present examples of commencement narratives. Stages (C), (D) and (E) are reached during the show – or at least, are represented on the show – as each takes stock, accepts personal responsibility and takes control of their situations. The importance and recognition of significant others is an integral part of the process as dialogue is called upon, is either enacted in front of the camera or to be carried out at a later time. The aim is to realise a shift towards stages (H) and (I), completion.

Irrespective of the focus of each individual narrative, talk itself is central; as we have seen, the narrational strategy hinges on confessional or testimonial discourse. The former exists within those narratives labelled commencement and ongoing; the latter is the process through which narratives of completion are articulated.

Mimi White considers the confessional dynamic in television game shows. Drawing on Foucault's paradigm of power relations in the confessional process, White (1992) argues that:

> According to the logic of television's therapeutic discourse, confession is rewritten as a dialogic and multivocal process ... For the confessional couple speaks with two voices, from two bodies. The position of interlocutor is also multiplied and dispersed ... since the role officially held by the program host/authority is shared by members of the studio and home audiences.[16]

White's identification of dispersed authority needs to be expanded to include the talk show expert in the list of authority figures on *Oprah*. I would further add to this the presence of the camera as it problematises the conception of a monolithic audience by splitting the studio and home audiences, further dissipating authority. Members of the studio audience often alter their status as they engage in the process through interjections and confessions of their own, while the position of the home audience remains immobile (in our imaginations at least). During the ongoing and commencement narratives, the expert is the authority who judges, forgives, consoles and reconciles before activating the audience's participation in the process. As I have discussed in the previous chapter, the question of Oprah's authority is complex and slippery. She frequently repositions herself in relation to her guests, moving from authority/interlocutor/host to become the confessing subject, displacing the status – even if only momentarily – of the original confessor. The guest expert and studio audience members remain fixed as the authority unless and until they choose to participate through disclosure. The home audience remains a shadowy witness, an unknown participant.

The locus of power constantly migrates and is reorganised; but yet, the original narrative voice(s) claim a self-recognition through the means of testimony and the ownership of their narratives as they remain specific to them.

To conclude: on *Oprah*, testimony provides a different function from that of confession. The testimonial is the defining feature of the completion narratives signalling the end of the journeying process. Although part of the narrative may concern feelings of worthlessness, fear or shame, the expression of this is not confessional in nature as redemption and exoneration are neither sought nor offered. The speakers stand and bear witness to the healing powers of self-renewal and regeneration.

A further point that I want to draw attention to in the guests' narratives is the possibility of transcendence. On many occasions, we hear the name of God invoked, of the power of love and respect for the self and others as the means by which transcendence over terrible difficulties is obtained. The need to surmount crisis is enmeshed with a theme recurrent in all the narratives examined: control. As stated, the taking of control is integral to the narrative structure. Frequently, our storytellers' dilemmas are located in the control exerted over them by others or by the physical environment. In order for the story to move forward, and not become stuck like Jenny's narrative, control has to be taken from the individual who uses it for malignant purposes to turn it into a benign force, freeing the individual from captivity. Control acts as the fulcrum for all of these stories, marking (E), the mid-way point of the narrative: stages (A) through (D) signal recognition of the control exerted externally; stages (F) through (I) mark the taking of control for the sake of one's self and self-realisation. Narratives become fractured, faulty, and incomplete when we are presented with illustrations of individuals not taking control and personal responsibility: Jenny, Mark and Randy all exemplify this. The protagonists have all been faced with a choice: either to cede power to the person or physical environment or to appropriate that power for themselves. Appropriation of control constitutes empowerment.

One final aspect of these shows that I want to reflect on is that of the written word. I have discussed the power inherent in writing one's own story in Chapter 2; and in Chapter 3 considered the enabling function of publicly displaying private documents – be they letters or diary extracts. Talk shows are about talk, and it is through the activity of talk that individuals define their stories. But I would argue that in the case of the narratives analysed here, empowerment also arises from the act of writing. It is usual that the guest expert flags a recent publication – the sales of which is immediately boosted by and through Oprah's endorsement – and this is the case in four out of the six sample shows. Alongside the overt commercialism of an author advertising his or her product, the act of writing, of authorship, mirrors the authorship of the spoken texts that both complement and are complemented by the book of the day. The act of writing need not take the form of a polished, edited, and published text; writing personal diaries and memoirs are often endorsed on the show as another means by which communication can fruitfully take place.

I have already indicated the power that Jenny's sister's letter exerts on Jenny's story, offering another dimension in the form of an absent but vital protagonist in the narrative. This power, or rather, the empowering nature of writing, is explicitly foregrounded in 'Girl Power'. The show takes its name from a book that is a collection of the stories chronicled by the girls who appear as guests along with others who do not appear but whose extracts are simultaneously read and displayed at intervals during the show. Following the presentation of the stories, Hilary Garlip, the editor of *Girl Power*, endorses 'the healing power of writing' as a means to empowerment: 'Sometimes paper is the only thing that will listen.' Although communication of the verbal kind is seen as essential to well-being, 'communication of any sort is very helpful for girls of this age . . . the great thing about self-expression in writing is that anyone can do it'. These words hold a forceful resonance as we recall the empowerment experienced by Sarah as she expresses herself through the publication attached to the 'Riot Grrrl' group; in the same programme, Tommi Jo pays homage to her mother by means of a letter dedicated to the older woman's generosity and courage. As I stated at the beginning of my examination of these shows, the stories of the guests are spoken and heard through the filter of Winfrey's celebrity persona.

It is beyond the limits of this book to explore the role of the expert in great detail but it can be stated that the voice of expertise contributes to the heteroglossic formation of the show. Expertise forms a part of the 'official' discourse that endorses the monogamous, heterosexual, marital relations which provide the framework for the majority of narratives on *Oprah*. These normative, 'official' discourses are facilitated by and through the conventions adopted by the television industry and which, in the 'elite' cultural criticism, is seen to (re)create fracture, dislocation, isolation; the postmodern subject. On the other hand, we also have evidence of the 'unofficial' discourses that are the inner life of the participants expressed in ways that are similar to those found in the black American literature discussed in Chapter 2. The call and response paradigm of *Oprah*, the accent on the vernacular, the use of writing as a means to self-definition represent aspects of black folk culture made available in a mass popular form.

It is in thinking through the *combined* impact of these processes and discourses that Bakhtin's formulations are of use. Firstly, his model of dialogism is connected to issues of agency and empowerment because it does not espouse the 'top-down' paradigm of power. Rather, the folk constitutes an active force which, in carnival, combines with the official discourse of order to create something new. *The Oprah Winfrey Show* does not have the unruly 'bagginess' of Bakhtin's carnival; the show is constrained by air time, its place within the television flow, the demands of advertisers and the conventions of TV broadcasting. However, it is precisely the commercial project – for 'market place', read 'popular television' – that enables the 'ordinary', everyday individual to act as author of his/her own story rather than being the passive subject of official order.

Whilst the processes of commercialism and commodification are evident on the show, so too is the model of agency found in the black American literature discussed in Chapter 2. The narrativisation of one's self indicates an empowerment that arises from the excavation of one's own history and in the public pronouncement of selfhood. In addition, the key to the transformations narrated in the stories examined here, lies in significant familial and social relations. The social networks in which individuals locate themselves are central to the formation of a positive self-identity so that the stories we hear on the programme are not just those belonging to individuals, but are also those of the community to which the narrator belongs. This, together with the emphasis on lived experience as legitimate knowledge, denotes the agency that supplies the connection with the African American tradition of thought and selfhood that I discussed in Chapter 2.

Whilst Bakhtin's work focuses on the Mediaeval and Renaissance period, his assertion that every age brings about its own official speech lends a flexibility to his idea of the carnivalesque that enables a critique of contemporary cultural practices.[17] 'A new type of communication always creates new forms of speech or a new meaning given to old forms.'[18] I am not proposing here that *Oprah* is the re-creation of a televisual carnival, but that carnivalesque principles are in play on the show enabling a folk language to predominate because of *and* despite the restrictions present in official discourse. This is particularly important when we consider the body of Oprah that is at the centre of this aesthetic activity and which is the focus of the next chapter.

5
The Oprah Persona

In the previous chapter, I expanded my analysis of *Oprah* by investigating the narrative structure of the stories spoken by guests, and the emergence of self-realisation that forms the overarching meaning of the programme. In addition, I demonstrated how the version of self that is articulated is inextricably bound with significant others providing meaningful points of reference for the individual. My argument at the conclusion is that the show is a heteroglossic form in which the antagonistic clash of both 'official' and unofficial' discourses works to produce something new. On the one hand, there are the 'official' normative discourses of the heterosexual family unit, and the therapeutic discourse that serves as an available means for the construction of self. This is facilitated by the conventions of television entertainment with all the attendant concerns of commercial viability, of display and spectacle. On the other hand, we also have the construction of self through a narrative structure that has resonance with a body of black American literature in which self is recoverable. This discourse of self is one in which the individual, through recognition of a past, is able to make coherent sense of the present. This coherence is lent weight through the individual's existence within a network of meaningful relationships that reside in the family and/or in the community.

The ambivalence that marks *Oprah* is also that which is embodied by Oprah. If we think of *Oprah* as carnivalesque, we can discuss Oprah in terms of the grotesque: the symbolic imagery of carnival. 'Grotesque realism', Bakhtin (1968) insists, is 'deeply positive' and contains the principles of growth and regeneration which are articulated not through the biological individual or bourgeois ego 'but in the people who are continually growing and renewed'.[1] Ambivalent in its imagery, carnival is the affirmative articulation of the dual processes of death and becoming.

As we have seen, the stories spoken on *Oprah* point to the possibility of transformation through the degeneration/regeneration paradigm that forms the overarching narrative. So, the Oprah persona can be seen as the grotesque embodiment of death and renewal that is articulated in her autobiography as well as in the narratives of the guests. Thus, Oprah's body contains all of the contradictions that constitute the show by the very fact of her success, wealth and celebrity – with all of the connotations of consumption and commercialism – whilst being simultaneously considered 'down home'.

Thus far, my focus has primarily been with the guests and the ways in which they relate to the show's host in order to determine the discursive structures of *The Oprah Winfrey Show*. However, this only represents one side of the dynamic. All of the voices heard on the show, and the form that their articulations take, are facilitated by and filtered through the persona of Oprah Winfrey whose own authority resides in her life experiences, her struggles to overcome difficulties and in the notion of authenticity signalled through her practice of adopting the confessional position. This chapter will explore the nature of that persona and the attendant relationship between Oprah Winfrey and her guests. My investigation will hinge on two key issues: the management of celebrity and the negotiation of 'race'. I will be considering the ways in which the Oprah persona works to contain the centrifugal forces of (a) the inevitably wide range of topics, approaches and discourses that make up this long-running show, (b) the gap between herself as celebrity and the 'ordinary folk' who make up the audience, and (c) the ways in which the idea of grotesque realism reveals meanings inherent in both Oprah and her show. I argue that the show's participants – who are often drawn from home audiences – are implicated in the celebrity persona through the apparent closing of the gap between the star self and the personal self. What prevents this dynamic from being merely a case of individuals seeking their 15 minutes of fame is the direction in which power moves and what that power is predicated on. Rather than the participants seeking to transcend their 'ordinariness' by emulating the persona of a celebrity, it is the 'ordinary' and everyday experience of Oprah which works to validate the personal stories recounted by the guests. In other words, those who speak on the show, and who participate through viewing at home, do not position themselves within the aura of a persona anchored in a glamour that for the majority is unattainable; rather, empowerment is located within the realm of everyday life.

This chapter will, then, explore the relationship between the commercial interests of talk shows and the construction of the host's persona.

Theories of celebrity and their application to Oprah will form a part of my work here, followed by an examination of the ways in which this works on the programme.

Throughout this book, I have been referring to *The Oprah Winfrey Show* as a commodity; this has an important bearing on the ways in which Oprah is constructed. Shattuc (1997) demonstrates the financial importance of talk shows to production and syndication companies.

> To understand the economic importance of these talk shows and their women audiences to their syndication company, one can look at the contract-renewal dispute between *Oprah* and King World in spring 1994. At the time, *Oprah* was seen in 10.1 percent of households... King World's 1993 Annual Corporate Report had touted *Oprah* as the number one rated talk show for [five years]. The show outranked the nearest competitor by 95 percent. HARPO Productions maintained that King World's distribution fee was too high... The loss of *Oprah* might have led to a drop in King World's stock of 30% in one day... The syndicator negotiated set five-to-seven year contracts [after which] *Oprah's* 1994 contract jumped King World's stock by 5.8%; more than 950,000 shares changed hands on March 18, 1994, five times the stock's daily turnover.[2]

But, as Shattuc points out, talk shows are a cultural product, and cannot therefore be reduced to a standardised commodity; this is made evident by the difference that exists between the various shows. However, a degree of standardisation is inevitable in the face of a winning formula. Shattuc's own investigation of a range of talk shows reveals how topics are duplicated across the genre with only minimal local inflection: 'ministers who rape versus cops who rape'.[3] This characteristic, Shattuc points out, evidences 'problems of innovation in the mass-production system'.[4] What distinguishes one show from another then is the persona of the host whose images are tightly controlled by publicists. The host's image, once constructed, is then maintained over years and often shored up through features in magazines and underpinned by the production of autobiographies that work to reinforce the screen persona. In addition, 'a well-timed confession or event on a talk show can be an effective business tool' providing a boost in interest and/or viewing numbers.[5] A key characteristic of Oprah is a pliability that then lends weight to her often repeated statement of being 'Every Woman', signalling an inclusiveness that informs the management of the guests' stories as well as speaking to the corporate desire to appeal to the largest possible audience. The unifying element throughout the series of *Oprah* shows is Oprah: irrespective of the topic of the day or the treatment through which that topic is handled, Oprah's performance is guaranteed to be inclusive, (generally) non-judgmental, (often) humorous, and (almost always) empathic.

Theories of celebrity

Frequently, *Oprah* shows draw on correspondence from viewers asking for help, stating a point of view, or giving feedback on a particular programme or on the way in which a topic was addressed. We saw in Chapter 3, how some of this correspondence describes viewers' relationship with Oprah. This relationship can also be observed by looking at a sample of responses on fan websites where viewers post messages that describe their feelings about Oprah. For example, the 'Gifts From the Heart'[6] website stands as testimony to the significance of Oprah to some of her fans: 'Oprah, you have touched my heart, and made me search my soul for what it means to be me. I have watched you through the years, and I admire your strength, love and compassion'; 'Oprah, you are certainly a person to look up to. I can feel your strength and caring in everything you do. Accept this little gift from me as my appreciation for all you do... You are an amazing woman! Love, Kristie Bigliazzi'; 'Oprah, Thank you for many years of growing and learning. I've watched all the talk shows over the years, and Oprah is the only one that has been a constant for me... Laura'; 'Because you have touched my heart so many times and in so many ways, I offer a part of my heart to you. Dixie Lady From the Heart of Dixie'. These responses indicate a powerful sense of connection between the viewers at home and a persona that is known to them only through a screen. The affective experience recounted by these fans does not appear to be diminished by the mediated nature of their relationship with Oprah; the impact that she has had on the lives of these respondents appears to be very real. I want to consider the nature of this relationship in the context of some of the ways in which celebrity has been theorised.

P. David Marshall defines celebrity as a position of distinction and success and imbued with a certain discursive power. 'Within society, the celebrity is a voice above all others, a voice that is channelled into the media systems as being legitimately significant.' Marshall (1997) argues that while the audience, who represent the subordinate group, constructs any meaning that is attached to a celebrity, the *process* of making sense is constrained by the cultural forms produced by the dominant culture. So, 'the celebrity is simultaneously a construction of the dominant culture and a construction of the subordinate audiences of the culture ... providing a bridge of meaning between the powerless and the powerful'.[7] However, the sign of celebrity is ambiguous; a symbol of individualism and success, celebrity is also 'ridiculed and derided because it represents the centre of false value'. Cleaved from its 'use value', celebrity is an articulation 'of the individual as commodity'.[8] Transient and transferable, the celebrity complex with its built-in obsolescence becomes integral to the systematic promotion of consumption, a mobilisation of capitalist forces. But, in a culture characterised by consumption, by the endless play of images divorced from any inherent meaning, and by depthlessness, celebrity also indicates a compulsive search for the 'real'.[9] The suggestion of an anxiety attached to the meaning of celebrity indicates a sense of cultural fragility that echoes the 'elite' discourse discussed in Chapter 2 and which Joshua Gamson formulates. He argues that the celebrity tours around the homes of the famous in Beverly Hills indicate in part the 'excitement of proof', the desire 'to confirm and re-confirm that the surfaces have something, in this case, someone, beneath them'.[10] This is a link that is frequently articulated on *Oprah* shows through her practice of adopting the confessional mode of address that apparently reveals the 'truth' of her personhood.

This link between celebrity and the search for the 'real' is foregrounded more explicitly in Richard Dyer's *Stars*, an examination of the phenomenon of stardom which pre-dates Marshall's work.[11] Dyer (1979) conceptualises stardom as a contradiction that concerns the stars-as-ordinary and stars-as-special, that paradoxically, 'ordinariness' is the hallmark of the star that has been rewarded for his/her specialness and/ or talents. The 'ordinariness' of an extraordinary figure can, Dyer argues, be explained by seeing stars as people who live expensively but who remain essentially untransformed by this. The programme analysed in Chapter 3 demonstrates this point very clearly: it will be remembered that the woman correspondents who appeared on the show all articulated a sense of betrayal and disappointment when Oprah breached this code of appearing untransformed by her wealth by employing a diet chef and a personal trainer to help facilitate weight loss. This disappointment was registered by the fact that some of the women claimed to no longer watch the programme – although they clearly remain sufficiently engaged to write letters in order to record their disgust. Dyer suggests that this notion of ordinariness as a mark of a special status offers another way with which to think about the 'charisma model'. This model, based on the website responses cited above, presents a useful paradigm for the examination of Oprah.

Drawing on the work of E.A. Shils, Dyer posits that the charismatic quality of a personality exists within a cultural or historical specificity which in turn determines his/her relationship with society. So, the attributes ascribed to the charismatic individual arise from the historical and/or cultural moment. Of particular interest here is Dyer's further assertions – which are based on the observations of Max Weber – that the charismatic personality is particularly effective 'when the social order is uncertain, unstable and ambiguous and when the charismatic figure or group offers a value, order or stability to counterpoise this'.

The idea of a promise of stability held out by the charismatic figure is useful in thinking about the cultural significance of *Oprah* in the age of late capitalism. In Chapter 2, I pointed to an anxiety expressed by a number of critics over the ways in which selfhood has become decentred, fragmented in our image-saturated contemporary culture, and we have seen the ways in which this is made manifest in the show. I argue that it is the apparent fragility of present-day life that presents the social and historical context within which Oprah Winfrey has achieved her level of celebrity. The frequently cited objection to the show on the grounds that it fails to address larger political and social issues is, as I have stated earlier, justified. However, if we accept that the post-industrial age is characterised by, among other things, a lack of trust in political structures, it is not surprising that solutions to problems are located at the level of the individual and formulated in terms of personal experience. It is this aspect of daily life that *Oprah* relates to. Nevertheless, further qualifications have to be made before we can go further with an analysis of Oprah-as-celebrity.

So far, I have been using the terms 'star' and 'celebrity' interchangeably. Dyer's work looks at stars within the film industry whereas Marshall explores the specific ways in which celebrity is constructed through the various media of film, television and popular music. Marshall argues that the concept of a film star holds a different construction of power from the celebrity. Where the star is a 'publicly organized identity that arises from fictional film',[12] the celebrity:

> is specifically an engagement with the external world. ... The public subject may be produced by the cinematic experience and may derive its originary power from the film text's construction of an ideal self; however, the celebrity element of the star is its transcendence of the text in whatever form.[13]

This notion of a transcendent quality that arises from an engagement with the material world is the most useful in a consideration of the

Oprah persona which is predicated on her 'down home' quality and is shored up by Oprah-as-film-star which emphasises the ambiguity of star-as-ordinary/star-as-exceptional discussed by Dyer. Marshall's conceptualisation advances Dyer's position by separating the two terms, offering a way of thinking about the differing nature of the star and the celebrity persona. The suggestion of the presence of an aura that is created through the star's engagement with the ordinary, most profitably describes the power inherent in the Oprah persona which has evolved more through her position as talk show host than as a film star – although she is that also. For this reason, Oprah is more accurately defined as a celebrity than as a star.

As Marshall points out, 'the film celebrity plays with aura through distance [whereas] the television celebrity is configured around conceptions of familiarity...[and] embodies the characteristics of...mass acceptability'.[14] I will look at this more closely in relation to Oprah shortly; for now I want to also consider the ways in which the engendering of this familiarity has been theorised.

Marshall argues that the power inherent in what he calls the celebrity system lies in its organisation of an individual and collective subjectivity. Meaning is generated through the celebrity's embodiment of their 'industrial/institutional setting as well as [in] the expression of an audience/collective that attaches meaning to the public figure'.[15] Central to the power of the celebrity is *affect* that both supplies attachment to a figure and provides a unifying thread with other public personalities. Marshall bases his employment of the term 'affect' on psychological discourse which describes it as:

> the middle ground between cognition and behaviour: the affective realm is connected to this chain of causality between something experienced and the formulation of a reaction to that experience...
> [T]he celebrity represents a site for the housing of affect in terms of both the audience and the institutions that have worked to produce the cultural forms that have allowed the celebrity to develop.[16]

Affect then is that which supplies meaning and significance to a cultural text, facilitated through the system of celebrity. As an exemplar of success and individuality, celebrity organises representations of a subjectivity that is both individual and collective. This rather complicated idea suggests the link between the appearances of celebrities on *Oprah*, Oprah herself and the audience. The Oprah as celebrity other is simultaneously Oprah as 'one of us' thus providing a bridge between the audience and the stars, including Winfrey herself. The meaning created in *Oprah* emerges in the movement that closes the gap separating the audience from those who exist on the screen. This is realised through the affective response that provides the emotional currency that is bound up with the Oprah persona – so often underscored by overt emotional expression – which itself is predicated on disclosure, intimacy and inclusion. The perception of authenticity does not reside in evidence presented in any one show but, rather like the overarching narrative structure discussed in Chapter 4, is suggested over a number of shows through which the Oprah persona provides a unifying link.

Another way of describing the dynamic between celebrity and audience and the ways in which intimacy develops is through the idea of the para-social relationship. We have seen, in Chapter 3, how some women have related to Oprah through her struggles with weight gain and loss; their para-social identification with the show's host is premised on knowledge of her as a person and is a vital aspect of the show. The notion of a para-social relationship is one that has been developed by Donald Horton and R. Richard Wohl and describes the process by which viewers feel that they have come to know a television personality. Familiarity with that personality is engendered by 'direct observation and interpretation of appearances, gestures and voice, conversation and conduct in a variety of situations. Viewers are thus invited to feel that they are involved in a face-to-face exchange rather than a passive observation'.[17] However, Horton and Wohl (cited in Peck, 1996) further characterise para-sociality as an interaction that is 'one-sided, non-dialectical, controlled by the performer, and not susceptible to mutual development'.[18] Langer (cited in Peck, 1996) further defines this process. 'The television personality system ... is most prominent in "factual" program forms ... where TV personalities play themselves and are represented as "part of [daily] life", are accessible on a regular basis, and work to construct intimacy and immediacy.'[19] So, although viewers experience intimacy as real, the notion of para-social relationship constructs this as illusory. As Peck (1996) argues, 'the gap between the TV persona and the actual person behind it ... ensures that the viewers' relationship with talk show hosts remains bounded by para-sociality'.[20] I would argue that the effectiveness of Oprah resides in the ways in which she works to close the gap between celebrity and viewer. This appearance of accessibility, her apparent ordinariness, contributes to her 'down home' appeal that is then shored up through her exceptional status as celebrity. The ways in which this gap is managed is the focus of the following section.

The Oprah persona and the management of celebrity

The Oprah Winfrey Show opens with a sequence of images, moving and still, that depicts Oprah Winfrey in a variety of positions and among a diversity of people. She is seen laughing, crying, adopting glamorous poses and under stress whilst running; she is seen hugging others and waving to a cheering audience. As each image fades into the next, the signature tune is played. For the 1996 season of shows, the music is accompanied by a Paul Simon song that marks the tenth anniversary of *Oprah*: 'Ten years have come and gone so fast/I Might as well be dreaming/Sunny days have burnt a path/Across another season/Speak until your mind's at ease . . .'. The 1995 season opened with an instrumental version of Chaka Khan's anthem 'Every Woman'. The visual sequences combine with the title music to construct the frame within which we are to understand the Oprah persona: intimacy, connection with others, and transformation are signalled, introducing the central premise around which the show coheres.

Although there is clearly a gap between the Oprah persona and the person behind it, Oprah works to efface the sense of that gap. We have seen how guests share their stories with Oprah and how the display of emotion is integral to the construction of *Oprah's* meaning. The appearance of a shared experience lends the sense of intimacy and substance to Oprah which is composed around an ellipsis that disguises the actuality of performance. Frequently, the notion of a mutual development is evoked through Oprah's willingness to take viewers' opinions and perceptions into account. For example, my analysis of the show 'Lose Weight, Lose Friends' in Chapter 3 demonstrates the way in which viewers' conception impacts on Winfrey's performance; the letters sent in by a number of women who complained about the apparent change in the Oprah persona constitute a significant section of the show and was stated by Oprah to have resulted in a lessening of references to her own weight loss. A willingness to disclose aspects of her own personal struggles is the hallmark of Oprah and constitutes the dynamic on which the show is premised. This discursive structure is underpinned by the ways in which Oprah works to close the gap between her celebrity self and, the guests and audience.

Frequently, shows open with a pronouncement of a personal nature that defines the tone and sets the agenda for the topic of that programme. 'Teachers' Salute' (BBC2, 17.10.95) – the show referred to at the beginning of the Introduction – opens with the declaration: 'we are saluting teachers because it is the second toughest job in the world we believe. Parenting is the first I believe'. The pronoun 'we' connotes inclusion, placing Oprah as one of a number of individuals while her statement that *she* believes parenting to be the most difficult job is a personalised sentiment that speaks to an even larger number of individuals in the audience. The didacticism of the pronouncement that 'teachers today get no respect and no pay. We've really got to do better America, we really do' is undercut by a swift shift to the personal and emotional declaration that 'One of my all time favourite *Oprah* moments was a show we did years ago, my reunion with my 4th grade teacher'. We see a clip from that show in which Winfrey is reunited with the influential teacher, followed by hugs, kisses and tears: 'It was a mascara runnin' kind of day!' The retrospective glance and the statement that follows both validate the repetition of the show's topic and brings Oprah into alignment with her guests as they too salute their favourite teachers.

Similarly, the gap between the person and the persona is breached in 'Oprah's Diets' (Channel 4, 28.11.95). The programme opens with Oprah speaking to the camera – signalling intimacy – and saying: 'this is what I wrote in my journal on the night of 15 November 1988: "I had such emotion and anxiety pulling out that wagonload of fat. I can't believe those jeans!"' This is accompanied by the video footage of the now famous episode in which Winfrey appears with a trolley which is loaded with packets of fat equivalent to the weight she had lost while simultaneously drawing attention to the tight-fitting jeans that she is now able to wear. The entire first segment of 'Oprah's Diets' is devoted to a reading of Winfrey's journal entries written over a period of two and a half years; what we hear is a catalogue of the food eaten and not eaten, expressions of anguish and self-loathing as the lost weight returns.

> Control. Controlled by it. Trying to regain the control God gave me. Where is it? ... Stedman says I'm not even close to my full potential as a human being. But I let my weight be a barrier ... Sometimes I can feel the connection between my own fears and my weight. So what are my fears? The answer can set me free.

The remainder of the show pivots on the necessity for facing one's fears as a way of gaining control over one's life, the fat body symbolising the out-of-control psyche. Exercise and the cultivation of healthy eating habits are presented as secondary to the process of attaining the desired body size; exploration of, and engagement with the cause of one's distress are the primary means through which self-respect is engendered and is the premise for developing the 'good' body.

This degree of personal disclosure, which is Oprah's signature, problematises the formulation of the para-social relationship outlined above. Although these confessions are a constitutive part of the *Oprah* brand, they also appear to be generated by the person who is Oprah Winfrey. It is difficult to maintain a cynical distance from the revelations of the journal entries as they appear to represent aspects of Winfrey's self and not artefacts specifically constructed for display on the show. While the entries are being heard, extracts of the text appear on the screen. At intervals, images that have appeared (and been derided) in the press are shown along with footage of Winfrey at television award ceremonies. The contradiction that exists within the person and the persona is made manifest through the visual images of a successful woman collecting an award juxtaposed with a contemporaneous diary extract proclaiming shame and self-hatred for becoming so large. This exemplifies one of the series of contradictions that circulate around the figure of Oprah Winfrey. An icon of therapeutic culture, Oprah and her show engage with discourses of therapy; at the same time, her public biography situates her *personally* within the same cycle of social trauma and confession that her guests inhabit. Of course, we do not have access to or direct evidence of the actual person behind the persona, but Winfrey's decision to display extracts from her journals works towards creating a sense of authenticity through which we develop a sense of knowing who she is and which is integral to her persona. The show continues with a list of her fears that include disapproval, the inability to confront and to say 'no'. These are contextualised within a gendered reading when she says: 'like most women, we are raised to please'. The two overweight women guests who embody the psychic dilemma are told that change is possible but only over a period of time, that it took Oprah Winfrey 15 years to reach her current stage of physical and mental well-being. 'But do you see what I am talking about, do you understand, do you make the connection?'

The connection here is between the inner turmoil and the bodily manifestation of that dysfunction. But there is another connection sought and that is the one between Oprah and her audience. Despite her own powerful position that enables her to speak 'to millions of people every day, in my life things were different'. And the aim of this show 'is to make the connection' that dieting is 'not about will power, it's about the truth'. Oprah's degree of candour is what lends the degree of intimacy that is absent from some other talk show hosts such as

Ricki Lake and Jerry Springer who both adopt a stance that separates them from the guests, acting more as facilitators for the display and spectacle that is the revelation of others. Oprah's adoption of the confessional position reduces the otherness of others despite the acknowledged fact of her power and position of authority.

Winfrey's own negotiation of her celebrity status and her 'down home' appeal represents another of the contradictions embodied in her Oprah persona which occupies something like a middle ground between the many stars who appear on her show and the everyday experiences of the viewers. Despite the fact that Oprah has 'talked to some of the biggest stars in the world', with some 730 having appeared on the show ('Oprah's Celebrity Hall of Fame', Sky1, 17.7.96), only a small proportion of my sample – 2 out of the 58 – of *Oprah* shows are devoted entirely to an interview with a celebrity. One of these interviews is with the clothes designer Donna Karan (BBC2, 2.4.96), the other with country stars, The Judds (BBC2, 5.12.95); these shows offer differing demonstrations of the way in which the celebrity status of the guests is mediated. Karan's stratospheric status is signalled when she is introduced as 'one of the most successful clothes designers in the whole world'. Both she and Winfrey are seated on the stage, both wearing chic black – the subject of some conversation later – and both are flagged as celebrating 10 years in their respective industries. Despite Oprah's overt positioning of herself with another who is one of the greatest 'in the whole world', this show is really a showcase for Karan's current collection underpinned with tributes – via a video screen – from other stars such as Barbara Striesand, Donald Sutherland, Dyon Cannon and Tom Hanks all of whom have worn or are wearing Karan's clothes; Oprah herself merely acts as facilitator. 'Good friend' Linda Gray joins Karan and Oprah on the stage. The purpose for this is unclear other than providing for a spectacle of friendship characterised by lots of giggles and whispers – at one point Oprah has to stop them chatting to each other in order to get on with the show. The demonstration of an emotional bond between two major stars stands as an enactment of the testimony of the stars who appear on the video screen: Shirley McClaine says of a Karan dress, 'It's like your friendship y'know? It's beautiful, it's flexible, and it's always there.' Emotional attachment between individuals provides an anchorage to the verbal testimonies which appear to be demonstrating the 'real' person behind the celebrity image. But, other than when Karan and Gray were asked to stop chatting, a moment when Oprah was able to assert her own position of authority as host, Winfrey's sycophancy preserves the gap between the 'real' and the serially displayed personas despite the tone of chummy informality. By this I mean that the presence of sycophancy signals awe for the personalities present on the show. By underlining the elevated status of her guests in this way, Oprah maintains the gap between the exceptional nature of the personas on her stage and the audience. However, this places Oprah in alignment with the audience members rather than with the other celebrities present, and so the gap between her own persona and the audience is eclipsed.

'The Judds', however, is a much more complex negotiation of celebrity. As in the Karan interview, the Judds are seated on the stage with Oprah and there is no audience participation apart from applause. The rapturous applause that accompanies the Judds' introduction signals their star status, but we are also told that they are 'three women who might be on *The Oprah Winfrey Show* even if they were not the famous superstars they are. Their stories, painful and heartbreaking and tender and full of *lots* of hope. A lot like a country song actually'. So the Judds' credentials lie in significant part in their private emotional lives; this is more like the Oprah persona than is the celebrity of Donna Karan. Further, the three women are a mother and her two daughters so that we have a family group, the dynamic of which mirrors those others frequently visited on *Oprah* – conflictual but also intimate and supportive. *Oprah* is further signalled as the dominant frame of reference because 'today marks the first time ever [they have appeared] together on TV! [audience whooping, whistling and screaming] It's a first! It's a first!' The marking of *Oprah's* status as special – 'it's a first' – inverts the way in which stars are more traditionally displayed, as in 'Donna Karan', by implying that the stars who appear on the show are stars because they too are like the 'ordinary' folk who more often appear and on whom the show depends. Or, at least, these celebrities have much that is fundamentally important in common with many of the other 'ordinary' guests who appear on the show.

What makes this particular show interesting is the fact that a TV film has just been made of the Judds' lives – the mother and one daughter are the singing stars, the second daughter is an actress. The show hinges around the three women discussing the film, their feelings about the ways in which they have been portrayed and the number of inaccuracies in that representation. This allows for the revelation of personal details that are concealed in the filmic construction of their lives; again, their stories mirror those of many other *Oprah* guests. A sense of the authentic is created by and through the women's consideration of the degree to which they had approved or disapproved of the project, of the experience of watching their filmic selves and the extent to which they had become personally involved. The inclusion of a number of clips from the film allows for the 'real' to be held up in comparison to the apparently real. Although this display is for television and is, therefore, as heavily mediated as the TV film, the opportunity taken by the stars here to discuss their portrayal appears to close the gap between the actual and the representation of the actual.

Celebrities are, at times, used to endorse or to demonstrate a particular point of view that is central to the topic rather than appearing as products themselves. 'Should Gay Marriage be Legalised?' (BBC2, 4.6.96) deals with the contentious issue of the legal rights – or rather, the lack of them – of homosexual couples. The outrage expressed by the members of the audience who oppose homosexual unions is set against the reasoned debate from those who are advocates of legalised same sex marriage. The prevailing cultural, social and legal norm is brought into question as attitudes of bigotry are set against the more thoughtful debate of those seeking legal recognition. This is underlined by an exchange between a woman in the audience and Oprah. The woman – who believes acceptance of homosexuality to be an abomination that will surely lead to an acceptance of child abuse – says: 'I've listened to all this hypocritical claptrap! I've had it up to here!' Oprah: 'You know what I've had it up to here with? I've had it up to here with heterosexual men raping and sodomising children!' [wild applause from the audience]. Immediately following this, Cher's daughter, Chastity Bono, is brought onto the stage [more wild applause], introduced and then recounts her own experiences of dealing with homosexuality: being 'outed' by the tabloid press, her parents' response, her activism concerning legal rights within homosexual relationships. Bono's proximity to celebrity through her parentage affords her a platform – 'we as gays and lesbians need to set an example' – but also serves to legitimise Oprah's earlier response to the woman who is 'fed-up with all this claptrap'.

The authentic is gestured through celebrity guests whose presence on the show is a mark of endorsement of *Oprah* and which is (usually but not always) underpinned through their revelation of a private self, often characterised as a transformation through adversity. An exception to this appears in the show 'Surrogacy' (Sky1, 27.7.96) which looks at the experience of soap opera star Diedra Hall and which has itself been made into a TV movie. Here, notions of authenticity become very slippery despite the central premise that even beautiful and wealthy television stars are susceptible to the slings and arrows of outrageous fortune. The show opens with a clip of the film in which Hall plays herself as the television star whose 'real' self undergoes the trauma of infertility, her subsequent search for a surrogate mother and the eventual birth of her son. This is further complicated by the inclusion of clips from the home video taken of the actual birth and shown on the programme but not in the film. While the video provides testimony of authenticity for the narrative contained in the television film, the dizzying result is akin to looking at an image of the actress constructed in a hall of mirrors each one reflecting and inflecting that representation. In addition, we have the actual presence of the star on the show offering verbal testimony to the struggles narrativised on film. Again, Oprah's sycophantic approach to her guest works to reinforce the gap between the person and the persona thereby setting Hall at a distance from both Oprah and the audience. On the birth of the baby, Hall says that she said 'Call Heaven, there is an angel missing' to which Oprah replies 'What you say is so profound'. Oprah's response does not conceal the theatrical sentimentality expressed by Hall – even when accompanied by evidence of 'real' emotion, and there are plenty of tears on this show. Dislocation is engendered through the distance between the celebrity guests and the audience, and enhanced through the act of watching video representations of their lives. The suggestion of intimacy signalled through Hall's, her husband's and the surrogate mother's disclosures is negated by the awe and flattery with which Oprah treats her guests on this show.

Paradoxically, the shows that are devoted to makeovers in the image of a star actually work to maintain the gap between celebrity and a 'real' person: 'Oprah in Beverly Hills' (BBC2, 27.3.96) circles around the 'Hollywood event of the year' which is the opening of the Planet Hollywood restaurant and the accompanying celebrity party. Ten viewers are taken along for the ride and are on the guest list for the celebrations. The show contains footage of the journey to Hollywood (all excitement and cheer), interviews with resident stars, and the guests being schooled by celebrities on what to wear and how to act in the company of stars: 'don't ask money questions; don't ask for autographs'. On the one hand, the boundary between celebrity and the everyday is blurred through their juxtaposition, by the insertion of the viewers – who are representative of the viewers at home – into this world of stardom, and through Oprah's mediation. Early on in the programme, she goes on a shopping trip for clothes accompanied by Cindy Crawford. 'I'm shopping with Cindy Crawford, can you believe that? [whispers to camera] Talk about a test for your self-esteem.' None of the viewer-guests are present, this remains an exclusive coupling, albeit one that serves to underline

Oprah's self as ordinary. Nonetheless, Crawford's 'real' attributes are the subject of discussion. Asking 'how being so pretty' has affected Crawford's life, Oprah says 'You're pretty secure with yourself at 29 [years of age].' The former responds by saying that this is due to her MidWest upbringing. Later, she says that she 'just wants to excel at being a mother'. At another point in the show Ellen Degeneres is seen talking with Oprah and a number of viewer-guests. When a woman discloses that, like Degeneres, she too is from the South, Oprah says 'And I'm from Mississippi.' Degeneres to Oprah: 'Do you know that you're my hero? You're the wind beneath my wings actually.' Oprah: 'No kidding!' Oprah's apparent amazement that she should exist as an icon for another again works as an understatement of her influential position, but this is a sentiment often articulated by the famous when in Oprah's company and so the declaration from Degeneres will come as no surprise to the audience or, presumably, to Winfrey. The suggestion, triggered by a viewer, of a shared geographical origin is sufficient to imply a bond that transcends more superficially constructed boundaries and serves as the catalyst for the declaration of hero-worship. However, the narrative that suggests that celebrities are like us who are like celebrities is undermined by the viewers' obvious delight at being in such close proximity to the famous and through their (the viewers') self-conscious performance in adopting the celebrity stance.

Earlier, I discussed Dyer and Marshall's conceptualisations of celebrity in relation to issues of authenticity and the search for the real. Basing my argument on their formulations, I would argue that the specific resonance of Oprah lies in its appearance of closing the gap between the celebrity persona and the actual person engendering a sense of the authentic. Part of the work of the TV persona is to reveal the actuality of the 'someone' beneath the surface of the image. As Marshall points out, Richard Dyer emphasises that the nature of celebrity is not wholly formed by manipulative media companies in the pursuit of pecuniary gain, but is the result of a negotiation between the public, the celebrity and the media for whom the star acts as an economic guarantee. Taking this formulation a step further we can see that not only does a public 'buy into' an acceptance of Oprah, but also that that public is implicated in the gap closure, that is, Oprah's mark. The specificity of *Oprah's* intimacy depends on the dialectic relationship between the guests – who stand in for the viewers – and Oprah. The audience forms a part of that bridge of meaning between the powerful and the powerless and can, therefore, share some of the aura that is Oprah.

The Oprah persona and the management of 'race'

Oprah is constructed around the notion of ordinariness despite the fact of her spectacular success; as a black American and as a woman, her attainments within a culture that has historically been deaf to the voices of black Americans in general and of black women's voices in particular, are even more noteworthy. The questions that arise from this are: how does Oprah negotiate the 'problem' of 'race' within a show that is made to attract the widest audiences? How does Oprah work to make the show non-threatening to a white audience when she simultaneously and repeatedly foregrounds her racial identity? On one level, Oprah's mediation of celebrity is through the emphasis on the ordinary in the progression to notability. But as a black celebrity, Oprah has an additional series of negotiations to make. These are also inextricably bound with her persona.

Marshall offers a convincing argument concerning the construction of the Oprah persona and its relation to a mass audience: familiarity with the programme's structure and narrative repetition combine with Winfrey's biography of transformation that is extended to the audience through a reciprocal relationship. Winfrey's blackness and womanhood both signal her marginality while, as a celebrity sign, Oprah represents success and achievement. According to Marshall, Oprah's body is the vehicle through which she has been able to make herself known, over time, to her audience. Cataloguing the series of weight gains and losses, Marshall argues that Oprah's large frame represents a challenge to mainstream dominant codes of acceptable beauty and femininity, while her blackness underlines her challenge to a 'mediascape dominated by white culture'.[21] This perhaps is an understatement. Young (1999) has pointed out that there are three main cultural representations of black women none of which cohere with idealised constructions of beauty: the desexualised mammy who is allowed to nurture slave-owners' children; the duplicitous 'tragic mulatto' who can 'pass' for white; and the lascivious, hypersexed woman. 'None of these images of black femininity have been conducive to allowing women of African descent to share the position on the pedestal of transcendental beauty with white women on equal terms.'[22] Nonetheless, it is Oprah's body size rather than colour that is the focus of Marshall's discussion of her public battle with weight gain and her relationship with the ordinary: 'complementary to the show's content' of human issues, 'Oprah's body image built her authenticity and reinforced perceptions of her sincerity.'[23]

Oprah's body then is constructed as an object of concern in her shows, as we have seen in Chapters 3 and 4, and exists as an extratextual issue up for debate in numerous magazine and newspaper articles. While I would concur with Marshall that Winfrey's emphasis on her weight forms an emotional link with her audiences, the subject of her blackness is more complex. Clearly, as an African American and a woman, Winfrey's position of wealth and power does register a successful challenge to hierarchical structures that place white men as the most influential in the order of things. However, Herman Gray has remarked that in a culture which assigns blackness a 'negative value',[24] 'African-Americans are constructed as invisible and hence ordinary as long as they conform. They become 'black' and thus dangerous when they transgress'.[25]

Gray's argument is that 'race' organises the discursive terms through which social, cultural and moral boundaries are constructed and maintained in America. In an age of celebrity and media saturation, 'race' is used as a sign that renders visible those who violate boundaries as well as drawing attention to the discursive structures themselves. Blackness, Gray (1997) argues, is a sign of excess that works to denote the limits of that excess thereby maintaining cultural and social stability. For instance, Rodney King was repeatedly arrested for frequenting prostitutes after he gained notoriety as victim of police brutality whereas Hugh Grant, also the subject of scandal as a result of using a prostitute, became a feted talk show guest able 'to dismiss the entire episode as a harmless case of bad judgement'.[26] Prominent black politicians who, having been caught and charged with having illegal sex with under-age girls or dealing in drugs, are excommunicated from their professions and elevated social positions while white politicians caught in similar circumstances face far lesser penalties.[27]

I have been arguing that Oprah's 'ordinariness' is a mark of her persona and operates as the bridge that supplies meaning between celebrity and audience; her African American identity is frequently foregrounded. Gray's formulation is that blackness is only visible when it threatens to reveal a culture in crisis, struggling with privilege and its attendant inequities. This position taken in relation to Winfrey would suggest that what is offered on her show is a safe and therefore acceptable version of blackness, that normative codes are upheld in the celebration of this exemplar of the American project – life, liberty and the pursuit of happiness for all. Certainly, this is one possible reading of Oprah (and *Oprah*): that the subversive potential is made safe and contained through the discourses of television that in turn shape and determine the content of the shows.

Indeed, Shattuc has pointed out that despite the fact that Winfrey is a 'race'-conscious black woman who hosts and owns the production company whose staff is 'dominated by people of color', it would be difficult to describe *Oprah* as an African American institution.[28] She argues that the genre depends on the use of representatives of social or personal conflict while commercial imperatives disallow the possibility of complex debate in which conflicts can be situated within a historical or social context. One-dimensional discussion is shored up through the use of racial stereotypes in a programme format that can only deny the subtleties of 'race' issues which themselves are constrained by Western racial discourses – as indicated by Gray above – in order that the broadest possible audience is reached. But then, in the next breath, Shattuc says of the black intellectuals who sometimes appear on the show, 'the show's imperatives as a capitalist institution must be separated from the discourses of the intellectual or expert as well as audience members'.[29] The question of *why* this must be is not addressed. And if intellectuals, experts and audience members are to be separated out from the capitalist imperatives of television, who is it that appears as the (African American) racial stereotype? The only other characters are the guests and the host. But the host of *Oprah* does not conform to any of the three stereotypes outlined by Young, nor does she appear constrained by the controlling images of black women in American culture delineated by Patricia Hill Collins and discussed in Chapter 2.

However, it is clearly important to acknowledge that these 'types' do exist in popular culture and need to be considered in relation to Oprah's screen persona. To do this, I will take a look at shows in which 'race' itself constitutes a part or whole of the show in order to examine how the issue is handled, bearing in mind the necessity of appealing to a broad and racially mixed audience.

'Oprah On the Road' (BBC2, 18.6.96) represents a series of reflections of shows that have been broadcast while 'on the road'. The opening clip is from the first road show recorded after five months of *Oprah* being on air; the date is February 1987. The location is Georgia, Forsyth County, an overtly racist town in which no blacks live. Oprah states that in going there 'I was a little scared myself I can tell ya. Do you wanna stay the night? Nooo ma'am!' Footage is shown of white members of the population shouting 'nigger go home'. Oprah's earlier declaration of being afraid underscores the atmosphere of hostility that she encounters when she confronts one of the men shouting 'nigger go home': 'do you mean the entire black "race"?' to which the reply is heard: 'You have blacks and you have niggers. The blacks stayed at home and the niggers went on the march.' This man's formulation that a 'nigger' is one who has the temerity to demand a voice, whilst the 'black' accepts the subjugated position forecloses the possibility of any further discussion, absolutely. Oprah maintains control of the proceedings, but only just. As the clip ends, we are returned to the studio when Oprah offers an update: the declaration that 'some African Americans are living there now in peace' is supported by testimony from a number of audience members, and we are told that Ku Klux Klan membership has fallen.

On its own, this slice of *Oprah* history bears out Shattuc's criticism concerning the lack of complex debate or historical contextualisation. We certainly do not hear too much from the black population about the everyday reality of living in a community steeped in racial bigotry. And we are left with no impression of the actual material living conditions, how wealth and poverty are distributed, what education and employment opportunities are offered or denied. The somewhat tidy conclusion that things have improved for blacks in the area forecloses a broader discussion of these indices of in/equality; and certainly it speaks to the narrative of completion to which the shows generally adhere. However, the context in which this clip is seen supplies additional meaning to that which is actually and openly articulated. From the advantage of hindsight, knowledge of Winfrey's popularity and cultural significance frames the speech we have heard on the clip, and to a degree works to undermine the odious nature of the messages delivered by the white supremacists. The clip that follows demonstrates this point. It is of a show in which an entire audience was taken from Chicago, home of Harpo Productions, to Philadelphia, because as Oprah says: 'You all know I like to have fun!' We see the planeload of audience members, all wearing 'Oprah' T-shirts and all apparently having the time of their lives. During the journey individuals are introduced, one of whom appears as a guest on a subsequent show. On the one hand, this slice of 'memory lane' offers a huge endorsement of Oprah's popularity, while on the other it obliterates any sense of unease that may have been evoked during the previous clip.

After revisiting Oprah's show in her Tennessee home, when we see the shop in which she first worked, and meet her father – 'Dad, meet the people' – and after seeing the homes of celebrities who 'opened their doors to our cameras', we have a clip of 'one of the most gripping shows ever'. It is a clip from the show broadcast from LA in the wake of the riots that followed the Rodney King beating. Summarising the complexity of the issues that arose during and after the social upheavals of LA in 1992 Oprah says, 'Easy solutions are sometimes hard to come by. Our next update comes from one of the biggest stories of the decade and one of our most gripping shows ever. The aftermath of the 1992 riot exposed the raw and stunned emotions of its citizens.' This pronouncement is followed by clips from the show in which white, black and Asian individuals speak of their horror and anger at what took place during the riots. This is the show that has been criticised by Robert Ferguson and Janice Peck (see Chapter 1) for its inadequate address of damaging and socially divisive issues. Ferguson (1998) argues that Oprah and the guests are so constrained by the discursive boundaries of commercial television that real debate is precluded, emptying the show of political meaning. Peck (1994) argues that the white liberal model around which the show is constructed works against the possibility of any racial identity being asserted other than (off) white trailer park trash.[30]

It is difficult to fully assess the show from LA on the basis of the brief segment shown here. However, like the earlier clip from Georgia, the audience is offered a reminder of an inflamed atmosphere that was then, juxtaposed with a greater sense of calm that is now, through the provision of testimony from members of the original audience who supply an update for the current programme. When one Asian man states that despite having taken three and a half years to rebuild his business, 'all is forgiven', Oprah replies 'All is forgiven. Is it though? But we're happy that hope has risen from the ashes.' Both the question left hanging and the faint glimmer of hope comprise the full stop to this particular section. This then is followed by excerpts from more road shows featuring: celebrities (lots of them); survivors of Hurricane Hugo; a couple who married on the bridge at Madison County (the woman referred to it as Oprah's bridge); 2000 followers of an Oprah diet . . .

The potential for expansive debate gestured at the opening of the show is closed down by the eclectic offerings that make up the entirety of the programme. The audience members from the town in Forsyth County and from LA remain present for the duration of the show but only represent a fleeting reference to the issues indicated in the respective highlighted clips. These are sandwiched between much more benign images of Oprah 'having fun' on the road at various locations and with various different people. There is a way in which this show can be viewed as a microcosm of the way *Oprah* operates across all programmes. Shows that contain topics of political and social significance are broadcast and circulated among others that are light-hearted and represent, simply, entertainment. There are two ways that this can be read. Firstly, that the force of the politically orientated shows becomes dissipated amongst the debris of the 'fun' shows. Or, secondly, that the existence of programmes that deal with light-hearted topics allows for an acceptance of the treatment of more potentially divisive issues while Oprah's celebrity status, with her non-threatening 'down home' appeal allows for a space to be opened in which contentious issues may be explored.

In my sample, only one show is dedicated to the subject of 'race' relations in America. 'The Color of fear' (BBC2, 15.1.96) is based on a film of the same name made by a man, Lee Mun Wah, whose Chinese mother was murdered by a black man in a racist attack. The show opens with still and moving images of violence that has occurred during 'race' riots. Bloodied individuals are shown in close-up while Oprah's voice tells us that 'Today in our studio we are going to do a bold experiment. Today we are not just going to talk about racism, we're going to *try* to do something about it.' This statement echoes the argument I made in Chapter 4 about the narratives supplied by the guests have an accent on taking action rather than on exploring the social and political frameworks in which difficulties arise. However, in the context of this programme, this (self-serving) declaration implies that *The Oprah Winfrey Show* is the arena in which centuries of 'racial' inequity is not only acknowledged but can be corrected (although it is difficult to believe that Winfrey does actually consider it possible that ages old, deep-rooted bigotry can 'have something done about it' on her talk show).

As the images in the *Color of Fear* continue we are told that 'they could not be clearer, they could have been taken a century ago or they could have been taken this morning'. The suggestion of a timeless situation stands in for a more complete historical, political and social contextualisation; but the graphic images of individuals of different ethnic origins hurting and being hurt in mob violence is shocking. In this programme, racial conflict is signalled as being more complex than a white/black dichotomy, but the footage shown from the *Color of Fear* focuses on the dialogue between a white man and a black man in an encounter group run by Mun Wah. The latter's fury at the treatment he and other black men receive in America is, initially, met with complete incomprehension by the former who feels that all have access to the same opportunities in American society. The black man (later introduced as Victor) addresses the white man (later introduced as David).

Racism is looked at as a black problem. And it is not. It's essentially a white problem... You think you can survive without me, but you can't, man... There is no American ethnicity! You throw away ethnicity to become American. And we're dying from it. You're dying from it too, but you don't know it. I'm not willing to trust you as long as you are unwilling to be as changed by my experience as I am by yours.

The camera is focused on Victor throughout this speech which is yelled at David. Later Victor says 'White people talk about themselves as human beings, as if it's the same thing... What does it mean to be white?' The palpable and raw power of this discourse effectively dislodges David's complacency as he acknowledges that he has never considered the question 'what does it mean to be white?'

This clip is followed by a return to the studio where all the male participants of the film are seated on the stage. Mun Wah tells us that Victor and David 'actually get on great now'. So we return to the more familiar *Oprah* narrative of conflict resolution. The remainder of the show centres on the workshop involving the entire audience as they are invited to think about and question their assumptions concerning others that are a different colour. This is comprised of individuals seeking other audience members of a different ethnic origin, approaching them and spending some time in conversation. The results are typified by Heidi who reports that she chose to talk to a young black man who she normally would have been afraid to speak to because of his blackness – she found that he is really very nice. One by one, individuals offer their thoughts in relation to the workshop experience which has generally resulted in an opening of dialogue. Oprah's remark to one of the pairs: 'you're looking like an interracial couple' produces laughter as well as underlining the stated aim of this show. Although Oprah states repeatedly that 'race' issues involve more than black and white in conflict, the clip from *The Color of Fear* and the subsequent discussion does, in fact, focus on this one specific area. More precisely, the show's focus is actually on the racism of white people. But this emphasis is deflected from Oprah whose position of neutrality is maintained through her statements suggesting a mutual responsibility for 'racial' disharmony leaving the actual conflict to be enacted by others – this is a highly skilful way to manage a subject that may alienate her viewers. This allows her to then ask: 'What's it like being white? Is being white something you take for granted?' and again, later when she says that 'For years I have tried to do these shows on racism. My question to you [whites] is how can you *not* feel superior when you are raised in a society that tells you that other people are not equal to you? That is my question.' It is a question that remains unanswered.

This question is a rhetorical device intended to promote a self-reflexivity in line with the stated aim of the show. As one of the other participants in *The Color of Fear* says, while change at an institutional level is unlikely, there needs to be acceptance of the fact that 'everyone is racist and the only way we can deal with racism is to accept all the parts of ourselves, not just the shiny wonderful parts... We can stay unconscious... and nothing will ever change'. The potential for transformation is, as seen in Chapter 4, the underlining narrative structure around which *Oprah* coheres, and Oprah's persona is as marked by this ideology as by a 'racial' grouping.

I have stated that Oprah's 'racial' identity is often foregrounded, but this takes place most commonly outside any political frame of reference. 'Where Are They Now' (BBC2, 28.1.96) looks at the 'most memorable faces of yesteryear' and to see where they are now. The show opens with Oprah telling us that when young she 'wanted to look like this model'. A 1964 magazine cover showing a white girl is held up; the audience laughs. 'You all might recall that before *Essence* magazine there were no black models.' This white girl 'was as close to black as any body I saw. [more audience laughter] She has a pug nose... so I thought there was some hope. I used to adore her'. The girl, now a married woman is introduced and explains that she has spent the intervening years being a wife and raising two daughters [rapturous applause from the audience] before Oprah asks: 'Do you have any black blood?' [laughter from the audience]. 'Trading Places' (BBC2, 18.1.96) is about married couples who swap hobbies for a weekend but the show opens bizarrely with a parade of Oprah look-a-likes. These are eight women who have written in to the show to say how they resemble Oprah; one of them is white. Five of the eight are put to the test and sent out to canvas public opinion, and the white woman fails. There is no point to this especially other than setting the humorous and upbeat tone for the remainder of the programme.

These are two examples of the way in which Oprah commonly draws attention to her blackness. While this is devoid of substantive political comment, Oprah's constant self-references as a black woman deny the possibility of effacing her own racial identity and so is self-consciously an integral part of her persona. The unifying narrative theme and the relative constancy of Oprah enable both the mediation and containment of tricky, and possibly unpopular, programme topics. As stated earlier, the Oprah persona does not cohere with any of the three main representations of black women outlined by Young above. She is not the tragic mulatto, nor is she lascivious and her position of power, of ownership of her show also undercuts the mammy image: mammy's self is constructed around the fulfilment of others. Oprah also presents a challenge to Gray's formulation that blackness is visible only as a sign of deviance. It is the case that potentially divisive issues are contained and made safe through Oprah's negotiation of them, as seen in the examples cited above. Nonetheless, *Oprah's* vacillation between the socially contentious and the banal has enabled the (albeit partial) exploration of 'race' relations within the context of a mass media text.

More importantly, Oprah Winfrey has made repeated direct connections between herself and a number of key African American women writers whose project has been discussed in Chapter 2. This aspect of Oprah's persona is of fundamental importance as it embeds the idea of who she is within a tradition that has its origins in the civil rights movement and which has become increasingly visible over the past twenty years. Winfrey's acting roles in the films *The Color Purple* (1985) and in *Beloved* (1998) as well as in movies made for television provide intertextual references that work to cement her identification with an African American tradition of thought. The underlying narrative structure that drives *Oprah* reflects the potential for recovery that is characteristic of much black American literature while Oprah is the embodiment of that world view. The majority of stories articulated by the guests not only stand as testimony to this possibility, but the means through which transformation occurs is a reflection of the paradigm found in black literature. Namely, that recovery is premised on recognition of self through the excavation of a history which is at once individual and collective. Significant others that constitute one's family, social and community groups and who share that history act as a source of strength and are integral to individual fulfilment and completion. So, although the making of a self during an *Oprah* show is inscribed by a mass subjectivity that is marked by corporate and commodity culture, it is, in turn, heavily inflected by an African American discourse of the self.

If we are forced to adopt a name that encapsulates Oprah's public character, the term 'othermother' as discussed in Chapter 2 more accurately fits the Oprah persona. Central to the process of self-reclamation, the othermother figure empowers others as she is empowered in turn. We have seen how Oprah works to empower through the confessional mode of discourse and through the narration of selfhood. Further to this, as a powerful, self-made woman, she also mounts a challenge to the controlling effect of stereotypes discussed by Patricia Hill Collins (see Chapter 2) and the images outlined by Young. In this light, the argument posited by Gray, that blackness only becomes visible when transgression occurs, becomes more problematic. It is possible to argue that the sign Oprah is constructed through the discursive apparatus of commercial television which reflects and regenerates the subjectivity of the dominant culture. This formulation would indicate that Oprah's blackness is rendered invisible and therefore harmless. But if we look at a show such as 'The Color of Fear', I would argue that the meaning inherent in the question 'what does it mean to be white' is politically charged in ways that would not be possible if the host were white. This is true also on the other occasions when 'race' is explicitly dealt with.

Another example: the show 'Letters from Children' (Sky1, 22.7.96) ends with a letter from a group of 6th grade children who have responded to an earlier programme that marked the birthday of Martin Luther King Jr. The latter show had focused on the reunion between individuals who as children had been caught up with the civil rights struggle 35 years before when white students had actively opposed the integration of black students into their institution. What had struck the children watching this programme were the scenes from contemporaneous news footage laying bare the degree of hostility and abuse directed at black activists. Also, the way in which one particularly vociferous white girl, now a woman, professed feelings of shame and a desire to re-meet the schoolgirl who had been the object of her derision. In time-honoured *Oprah* fashion, a reunion was staged, followed by declarations of forgiveness. Jennifer, one of the (white) children who appear on 'Letters', states that 'I learnt so much from you' and that the programme had taught her more about the civil rights movement than did her lessons at school, prompting Oprah to say that she is 'very proud' of her job. This very tidy conclusion to both the earlier show with its reunion, and the present show with its child commentators, could be laid out as an example of the ways in which real issues are circumvented in favour of televisual sentimentalism with Oprah acting as tom.[31] Likewise, 'The Color of Fear'. This position becomes difficult to sustain, however, when Oprah is placed in the broader context of black feminist debate with which she has aligned herself and which she draws into her shows through the promotion of books by black feminist authors in her Book Club and through her film performances.

As discussed in Chapter 2, Collins (1991) argues that 'black feminist thought encompasses theoretical interpretations of black women's reality by those who live it'.[32] Oprah does not offer theoretical analysis of black women's lives, nor can her life be said to be typical of many other women – black or white. But her particular form of celebrity is characterised by her engagement with the everyday thus enabling a conflation of her 'down home' attributes and her TV and movie star self. Add to this the model of the othermother whose role is considered central to the formation of a self-reliance that is inextricably linked to roots and community (see discussion of Stanlie M. James in Chapter 2), and we can see the ways in which *Oprah* insinuates aspects of black culture within mainstream popular culture. As Stanlie M. James makes clear, denied access to traditional sources of power, othermothering empowers the women who practice it and those who are benefited by it. The othermother also coheres with Walker's (1983) term 'womanist' which signals an African American woman who is 'committed to survival and wholeness of an entire people, male *and* female. Not a separatist... Traditionally Universalist'[33] (emphasis in original). The non-separatist stance occupied by Oprah is necessarily adopted in the construction of a cultural artefact that speaks to a large and ethnically diverse audience. But it is also a position that does not automatically signal the turning away from a cultural heritage in order that the commercial imperatives of a television show are met. It is this womanism, and all the 'racial', historical, and political implications of the term, that generates an affective attachment to the sign Oprah and which underlies the narrative structure of *Oprah*. Those who appear on the show represent, generally, the disempowered and/or those who traditionally lack a public voice. Appearing as a guest on *Oprah* does not in itself signal an immediate move from powerlessness to powerfulness, and the updates demonstrate how often promises of fulfilment indicated on one show do not have a lifespan beyond the studio. More accurately, the shows offer a version of selfhood that is attainable through the pathways displayed in the repeating narrative structure. This is combined with Oprah's othermother role to create the affective response of the guests and audience and which supplies the meaning between cognitive understanding of a situation and the reaction to it. The degree of Oprah's popularity is indicative of a charismatic personality that is forged within the historical specificity of late capitalism with all its attendant instabilities, uncertainties and fragmentation. That the majority of audience members are women, and that those who appear on the show are often marginalised individuals, act as confirmation of Dyer's argument that some of the strongest attachment between celebrities and their audience arises from within the disenfranchised and at times of uncertainty. I want to conclude this chapter by furthering my arguments by returning to the idea of Oprah-as-grotesque. Looking at Oprah through the frame of Bakhtin's formulations of grotesque realism and carnival will, I believe, reveal meanings that underline Oprah's performance as talk show host, and the show itself.

The 'grotesque body' and Oprah

To explain more fully why I am ascribing the characteristic of grotesque to Oprah, I will give a brief account of the grotesque as formulated by Bakhtin (cited in Dentith, 1995). Grotesque imagery stands at the symbolic heart of carnival, offering the means of overcoming the cosmic terror ('the fear of that which is materially huge and cannot be overcome by force').[34]

> The downward thrust of bodily imagery in folk culture, which associates the procreative belly with the earth as womb, combats such [cosmic] fear. The body itself comes to represent the cosmos and in the hyperbolic comic images... terror is mocked, transformed and mastered.[35]

Cosmic and universal, grotesque imagery is 'a point of transition in a life eternally renewed, the inexhaustible vessel of death and conception'.[36] Thus, the grotesque body and the carnival spirit, freed from the restrictions of official life point to the possibilities of transcendence and the creation of new meanings. The possibilities of renewal and change are inextricably linked to protection against terror through the transforming power of laughter. This bodily imagery of the folk stands in contrast to the smooth, rounded, finished and closed 'classical' body that represents the rules and restrictions of official culture and which is 'unable to express the regenerative potential of the grotesque body of folk culture'.

I do not wish to take 'laughter' to imply merely that which is comic. Rather, I extend my use of the term to include the act of transgressing codes, the activity of shouting down or a disavowal of officially determined boundaries of taste that is characterised on *Oprah* through the verbal violation of taboos in speaking the unspeakable and in the nonverbal expressions of emotion. Through this laughter, the struggles and anxieties of daily experience are challenged and to an extent, defeated (even though it may also induce horror).

The terror of the cosmos that mediaeval carnival spoke to is transformed, in contemporary American culture, to the sense of an all-pervading but unspecific anxiety delineated by the 'elite' cultural criticism discussed in Chapter 2 and which is both made manifest in *Oprah*, and of which the show is a manifestation. The rise of technology with its threat of nuclear annihilation, the negation of self through (over) consumption of images along with the inexhaustible desire for consumer goods that is fed by image saturation in contemporary culture, positions the individual within an inescapable loop. This is apparent in *Oprah*, as is the 'official' discourse of therapy which contributes to the discursive nexus that informs the show. As in Bakhtin's carnival, *Oprah* is not free from the official discourses that surround it. Rather, they combine with the folk – or, popular – to form the grotesque display of inner life, and in the process produce something new in the form of a utopia that stands counter to the despair that gives rise to the guests' narratives.

One strand of African American thought, along with the call and response dynamic of the black church, is the element of folk that provides the energetic bulwark against fear and oppression. The importance of history and memory is, as we have seen in Chapter 2, crucial to the process of self-definition for a number of black writers. Likewise, Bakhtin insists on the importance of historicity in carnival and the grotesque body:

> [T]he image of the ancestral body is merged with the people's vivid awareness of historic immortality. We have seen that this awareness forms the very nucleus of the entire system of popular-festive imagery. The grotesque conception of the body is interwoven not only with the cosmic but also with the social, utopian, and historic theme, and above all with the theme of the change of epochs and the renewal of culture.[37]

The accent on ancestry and the historical is seen not only in Winfrey's own autobiographical position within the history of a people recounted in black American writing which stresses ancestral links and posits a hope for cultural renewal, but also in the ways in which the stories of the show's guests are formed. As we have seen, the uncovering of personal and private histories, the ways in which the stories are articulated with their inflection on the importance of family and friendship ties, are mediated by Oprah. She is the grotesque embodiment of that which takes place on the show.

However useful, Bakhtin's model, it would be too crude to apply it wholesale in the consideration of Oprah's body; it does not fully address the gender issues that are present in the presentation of grotesque images. Mary Russo argues these images 'have suggested a positive and powerful figuration of culture and womanhood to many male and female writers and artists'. But it is also an 'easy and perilous slide from these archaic tropes to the misogyny which identifies the hidden inner space with the visceral. Blood, tears, vomit, excrement – all the detritus of the body that is separated out and placed with terror and revulsion ... on the side of the feminine'.[38] Not only is Oprah concerned with 'the hidden inner space' of herself, but that of her guests and audience also; this latter category of participants are implicated in the proceedings through her frequent – face to camera – appeals to 'America'. Further, she is – or rather, was – fat. Her oscillation between fat and sleek offers another instance of the ways in which she embodies *both* the commodifying culture of capitalism *and* its exclusions. Russo (1995) cites Maud Ellman who writes that:

> The fat woman, particularly if she is non-white and working class, has come to embody everything the prosperous must disavow: imperialism, exploitation, surplus value, maternity, mortality, abjection and unloveliness. Heavier with projections than with flesh, she siphons off this guilt, desire, and denial, leaving her idolized counterpart behind: the kind of woman one sees on billboards, sleek and streamlined like the cars she is often used to advertise, bathed in the radiance of the commodity.[39]

Ellman's formulation encapsulates the problem that the body of Oprah represents in contemporary American culture with its problems of excess, denial and guilt. In this schema, Oprah's big and black body stands at the centre of her show representing the antithesis of the white, smooth, rounded, finished classical bodies that populate advertising images and which stand in service to bourgeois capitalism.[40] Thus, Oprah-as-grotesque irritates the processes of commodification and commercialism that also inform the show. However, Oprah's concern over her 'too large' body signals a conflict in Oprah-as-grotesque in that she does not revel in it. Her continual struggle with her large body forms the basis of many *Oprah* shows. Therefore, her desire for the sleek, controlled, classical body represents a further expression of the ambivalence that she embodies. In addition, in this context it is important to recall that Winfrey also straightens her hair. Whilst she does not dwell on this aspect of her bodily experiences, she has drawn attention to the fact by stating, on occasion, that visiting the hairdresser is a trial. The subject of hairstyles and the identity that is signalled through them is a complex issue that will not be explored here; I merely wish to point it up in relation to the ambivalence she embodies.

As a big, black American woman, Oprah's body stands as the antithesis of the smooth, sleek, white and finished body that represents the ideal. However, fatness is only one expression of the grotesque. Besides the grotesqueness of one's being – such as fat – there is also the grotesque performance characterised by risky behaviour and seen by Mary Russo as a form of 'stunting'. Citing Amelia Erhart and her aerial acrobatics as an example, Russo identifies stunting as an activity that positions the stunters as exceptional or abnormal, and explores the relationship between stunting, liminality and the grotesque. Stunting, characterised by Russo as grotesque performance, engenders an ambivalence that marks it as risky.

> On the one hand, they [grotesque performances] perpetuate the blaming, stigmatization, and marginalisation of groups who ... are seen as 'high-risk' groups; on the other hand, they elicit 'risk-control' tactics which characterise risk as almost entirely negative, seeking to out-regulate (or make invisible) those performances and groups which enact or embody such double riskiness.[41]

On the other hand, stunting also draws admiration for the risk taker from those witnessing the spectacle. Equating stunting with Michel de Certeau's theorisation of 'tactics' – a logic of action for the displaced; a temporal rather than spatial category – Russo argues that stunts demonstrate what is possible in the moment, so that stunting points to *possibility* rather than to progress.

Russo offers a formulation that enables a view of participation on *Oprah* to be seen as a form of stunting and which is marked by risk. The risks taken by Oprah and the shows' participants include the potential reinforcement of their existing marginality, ridicule and stigmatisation for publicly airing private issues and concerns. In addition, despite and because of making a spectacle of themselves, *Oprah* performers risk being rendered invisible by those who deem them reprehensible. However, participation on the programme also points to the inherent possibilities of becoming and of renewal (as is evident in the narratives of both Oprah and her guests).

The activity of both stunting and spectating the stunts holds both participant and viewer in the same liminal moment in which the possibility of transformation is signalled by and embodied in Oprah. Marx (1986) has pointed out that in American pastoralism, the liminal character is one who stands at odds with the dominant culture and who underpins the need to mediate between the constraints of society and the constraints of nature.[42] But whereas the pastoral figure makes the sophisticated *choice* to step outside, Oprah is always already positioned as liminal by the fact of her African Americanness. Her liminality is then maintained through her ties with black America and references to folk culture, both implicitly and explicitly, and is reinforced by the grotesque performance of taking risks through self-revelation, of 'making a spectacle' of herself. Oprah's activity draws the participants into the same liminal space as she mediates between that which codifies the dominant culture – black women as other, the conventions of commercial television and commodification – and the everyday, inner experiences of her guests.

The liminal space, the borderzone, that is *Oprah* extends to include the studio audience as they contribute to the performance and to audience members at home as they watch. As Russo points out, for Bakhtin, spectacle is the antithesis of the carnivalesque as it assumes the 'partitioning of space and a creation of discrete sightlines'.[43] Arguably, watching television is an activity that particularly speaks to the partitioning of space. However, this implies a passivity that we cannot take for granted and which is anyway undermined by the show's inclusion and use of so many letters sent in by home viewers in response to this or that programme. In addition, watching television positions the viewer betwixt and between the material, everyday world that is suspended while the screen offers temporary admission to an alternative space.[44]

Further, I would argue that in sharing a liminal space, guests and audience members also constitute a grotesque body as they personally and psychically identify with the host. However, this is problematised by the fact that the regenerative possibility of transformation is not always an inevitable reading of the show; rather the abject is also signalled when viewers form an identification with Oprah through body size. The self-loathing articulated by Oprah in her journal extracts displayed on 'Oprah's Diets' stands parallel to the degree of disappointment articulated by the viewers who appear as guests on the show 'Lose Weight, Lose Friends' discussed in Chapter 3. On this occasion, it will be remembered, a number of women express anger over Oprah Winfrey's contemporaneous weight loss and their subsequent perception that she was no longer like them. What is evident here is a slippage from the positive and affirming 'laughter' of grotesque imagery and performance to the misogyny that positions the abject as feminine. In none of the shows in my sample is the cultural practice of degrading large bodies – such as that outlined by Ellman above – discussed. Restriction and subjugation through conventional standards of beauty is only fleetingly referred to by one participant on 'Girl Power' (see Chapter 4) and is not broadened into a debate that might work to reposition fat girls and women as desirable. In addition, as stated earlier, Winfrey's continual and public struggle to control her weight gain indicates a conflict between the powerful potential of the unofficial grotesque and the official bourgeois ideal of the rounded, controlled, sleek and finished classical body with all the limitations that it implies. In fact, it would appear that the classical side of the ambivalence has won out as Winfrey has maintained something closer to her ideal body size, culminating in her triumphalism at appearing on the cover of *Vogue* magazine in 1998. In achieving a body to match her class status, she positions herself as the object of the gaze and its patriarchal relations of power.

Self-realisation through transgression

It is unsurprising that Winfrey is gleeful in attaining a body that stands in accord with idealised images of female beauty. As Russo points out, 'fat women, particularly in America, are repositories of shame and repressed desire'. However, this work of abjection 'constitutes a hard and hidden work – a work that is easily misrecognised as the very over consumption it is designed to hide'.[45] Positive and exuberant as Bakhtin's model is, there are dangers for women and other excluded and marginalised groups within carnival, the 'double jeopardy' recognised by Russo that suggests 'an ambivalent redeployment of taboos around the female body as grotesque ... and as unruly when set loose in the public sphere'.[46]

The dangers lie in the inherent misogyny in the idea of woman as carnivalesque. As Russo argues, the central presence of women and other marginalised groups in carnival signals those groups as 'quintessentially dangerous ... In other words, in the everyday indicative world, women and their bodies, certain bodies, in certain public framings, in certain public spaces are always already transgressive – dangerous, and in danger'.[47] The structural view of carnival is that the transgression of boundaries in liminal states reinforces the social structures and norms that are temporarily overturned. So, even as the transgressive effects of the grotesque free them, women are so tied to dominant discourses concerning physical appearance, they remain separated from its liberatory possibilities.

The grotesque bodies of Oprah and *Oprah's* participants articulate the ambiguity of the dangerous and the endangered. While offering up possibilities of transgression through progression, the show also attracts vilification, a response to the unruly that is an attempt to reassert normative social frameworks (see Chapter 1). A site of conflict and contradiction, *Oprah* offers an unstable representation of 'low' others – the mark of popular culture – that the 'top', or 'high' attempts to reject or expel in the interests of maintaining status and prestige. Stallybrass and White (1986) argue that out of the ambivalence of carnival a pattern emerges in which the top repulses the low other only to discover:

> that it is frequently dependent on that low-Other ... [and] also that the top *includes* that low symbolically ... The result is a mobile, conflictual fusion of power, fear and desire in the construction of subjectivity: a psychological dependence on precisely those Others which are being rigorously opposed and excluded at the social level[48] (emphasis in original).

This formulation stands parallel to Toni Morrison's argument in *Playing in the Dark* (1992) in which she writes that the black body has historically been othered in the service of a white American self-definition.[49] Not only is Oprah's body positioned as grotesque because of its size, but as a *black* woman she is always a part of and apart from a cultural tradition that seeks to expel or rather, deny, the existence of the otherness that is also a constituent aspect of the white, male self.

Thinking about Oprah in terms of the female grotesque is, in my view, more productive than simply engaging in a discussion around whether or not her body size undermines idealised images of beauty or reinforces the mammy stereotype. Consideration of her within the framework of the grotesque supplies complexity, texture and depth of analysis that allow for a discussion of the importance of the folk. I would argue that the sense of loss and disenchantment expressed by the women participants in the show 'Lose Weight, Lose Friends' – discussed in Chapter 3 – is not simply the perception that Oprah can no longer identify and be identified with their own struggles in terms of acceptable body size. The degree of estrangement expressed is premised on the apparent demise of Oprah's 'down home' persona that has hitherto made para-social identification a powerful experience. The down homeness of Oprah is an articulation of the folk/unofficial discourse and the suggestion of possibilities of transformation and regeneration that act as a buffer against 'cosmic terror'.

The ways in which Oprah manages the conflicting and contradictory forces that comprise *Oprah* is made especially clear when, as this chapter has done, we look at the nature of her own celebrity and the ways in which she negotiates this to form relationships with the guests on the show. Her affiliation with, and articulation of, a particular mode of African American thought is that which produces the possibility of transformation that marks the show. This is facilitated by the cultural acceptance of the therapeutic and the recognisable conventions of television entertainment – along with the attendant anxieties about the self – which are made manifest in the programme as well as the programme being a manifestation of them.

Conclusion

This book has used *The Oprah Winfrey Show* as a case study of a popular cultural phenomenon that has achieved iconic status. In turn, an exploration of the programme has enabled an analysis of Oprah's celebrity persona and of her significance to viewers. In particular, I have focused on the representations of selfhood and explored the ways in which self is constructed through the programme. My central questions have concerned what version(s) of selfhood are serially represented on *Oprah*. What kinds of cultural practices and traditions give rise to such a phenomenon as this show? Related to this, I have asked the question of how we explain both the popularity of this programme and its condemnation as trash TV by a large number of critical commentators. Specifically, I have explored the show within the context of American culture. The show is immensely popular in a number of countries however; to explore the programme in transcultural terms is another – larger – project. This book has therefore explored the discursive cultural practices that give form and meaning to *Oprah* within the culture of its origin.

There are other questions that I have not addressed but which could well be asked to further understanding of this show as a cultural phenomenon. For instance, in terms of the talk show debate as a whole, it would be of use – and interest – to explore the differences between talk shows. I have argued that meanings generated by a talk show are heavily inflected by the persona of the host. Whilst I have explored this with specific reference to Oprah Winfrey, I have not examined any other talk shows to see the ways in which the host's position affects the processes. In order to make this claim more generally, therefore, further work would need to be carried out to explore the impact of talk show hosts on their programmes and to consider characteristics individual to them, marking them as different from other shows within the genre.

Also, although I have identified two distinct traditions of thought for my analysis of *Oprah*, I am aware that there are other discourses available for understanding the programme. For example, the impact of the 1960s and 1970s feminist movement on *Oprah* is relegated to the margins in this book. This is partly because this work has already been carried out, and partly because in my view, the specifics articulated within the black feminist tradition that I have isolated here have a more prominent role than has hitherto been acknowledged. However, the impact of the wider feminist movement is not an insignificant factor in the phenomenon of *Oprah*. Given that many of the show's guests, experts and studio audience members are men and boys, the ways in which feminist debates have informed performances of the male participants would be worth further study. Similarly, further work could be carried out to examine how issues of class and race impact on the representation of guests.

It would also be fruitful to conduct a closer examination of the expert voice which makes a significant contribution to the official discourse articulated on the show. Frequently, the expert is a psychologist, or some other mental health professional such as a family therapist, who mediates the guests' narratives. There is a connection here between the display of emotional life and the desire to understand emotional complexity that is a part of self-identity. This would constitute a whole different project, but there are clear links between the emotional content of talk shows and the rise in the use of mental health professionals to explain the behaviour of participants on reality television shows across a range of genres.

So, this book represents an attempt at understanding *Oprah* from within a limited set of frameworks. Throughout, I have argued that the meaning(s) generated by the show hinge on a representation of selfhood that is (has to be) recognisable to a large and varied audience, and which has a particular resonance for contemporary viewers. However, this version of self is a complex and ambivalent construction that is the product of conflicting and contradictory cultural discursive practices. Further, I argue that the Oprah persona is the embodiment of these contradictions, and performs as the conduit for expressions of self that emerge on the programme. As an African American woman, whose public biography of abuse, rejection and self-loathing – articulated through her perception of her (large) body – Oprah is the antithesis of that which is considered desirable in official discourse. At the same time, however, Oprah-as-celebrity epitomises success, wealth and power, and stands as a testimony to the possibility of renewal, regeneration and self-realisation. This aspect of her persona is used to underpin what I have called the narrative of completion – an individual's story of a journey from loss and isolation through to self-realisation. These features are shared by the majority of narratives in the shows I have examined. These conflicting properties result in a persona that is complex, ambivalent and open to multiple readings.

Ambivalence is also evident in the critical debate that surrounds the programme and the genre of television talk shows more generally. As it stands, the debate is polarised. As is discussed in Chapter 1, talk shows are seen on the one hand to represent a social harm, a symptom of the worst excesses of commercialism – trash TV – in which the individual is emptied of meaning through the process of commodification. On the other, they are regarded as a public platform from which marginalised voices speak; talk shows are treated as a discursive site in which the self is constructed as empowered. At times, the ambivalent nature of talk shows is recognised, but this remains undeveloped in the existing literature. This, in my view, offers the most interesting and productive starting point for my own case study.

The vacillating nature of the debate is, I have argued, a reflection of the ambivalence inherent in *Oprah* and is a product of the intersection of diverse traditions of thought concerning selfhood. Chapter 2 explored the constructions of self formed through 'elite' cultural criticism that is marked by nihilism, and an African American version of self that suggests an active agency in the formation of self-respect. These differing constructions of self emerge from the two distinct histories of ideas and different lived experiences of distinct social groupings. On *Oprah*, these combine to form a carnivalesque play of 'unofficial' and 'official' discourses producing something new. Further, I have argued that at the heart of this carnivalesque play is Oprah's grotesque persona which embodies all of the contradictions inherent in the show itself. The method adopted for this study is premised, then, on my argument that in order to understand the processes at work in *Oprah*, there is a need to move beyond the range of positions employed within media studies, which has adhered to the talk show-as-empowering/talk show-as-trash binary. I have, therefore, looked to alternative systematic discursive practices through which to read *Oprah*.

Of interest to me is the disjunction between the success of *Oprah* and the (largely) negative evaluation of it in the academy. The social harm/ trash TV position, discussed in Chapter 1, links with a history of ideas articulated in the canon of American cultural criticism. This, in turn, is linked to the Frankfurt School's position that mass culture operates to the detriment of social, cultural and political life. By tracking the ways in which self has been formulated within this tradition, as I have in Chapter 2, it becomes apparent that there is a series of cultural practices that give rise to an anxiety about selfhood in America. The foci of concern are commodification and consumerism, popularisation of the therapeutic and technological advance. The relationship between these practices forms the culture of consumption in which an appeal to the therapeutic both perpetuates, and is perpetuated by, the fragmentation, dislocation and emptiness that follow in the wake of an excess of consumption. The self in this tradition of thought is one that is subjugated by and through mass mediated images, practices of consumption and the popularisation of the therapeutic.

In tracking this history of ideas, it becomes possible to recognise an anxiety about selfhood that appears embedded in American culture and to see that *Oprah*, as a commercial enterprise, operates as a manifestation of this. This body of critical thought, therefore, provides an available language with which to make an evaluation of the programme. However, as well as operating as a *manifestation* of cultural malaise, it is evident that fragmentation, isolation and concerns about self also perform a narrative function within the show itself. This becomes particularly evident through my analysis of *Oprah's* – and Oprah's – confessional mode of operation and management of voices in Chapter 3. The confessional practice lends a distinctly therapeutic hue – the truth heals – to the programme in which a series of guests reveal intimate aspects of their lives and contemporaneous troubles. Oprah's own practice of confessing offers validation of the guests' stories as well as providing a frame through which the show is structured.

In Chapter 3, I also discussed the ways in which processes of commercialism and commodification are revealed in the show's structure which is based around (usually) five segments separated by a series of advertisements. The guests' stories are, then, sutured into a succession of commercial breaks that are themselves signalled by Oprah's pronouncement that one is about to occur, or by her reference to what has happened, off air, during the preceding break. Further, the display of intimate disclosure is made spectacular by the accompanying video/succession of still photographs that illustrate and underpin the spoken narrative. Frequently, these are images of transformation – from fat to thin, youth to adulthood, from child to parent, and, occasionally, from healthy to beaten/bruised. The presentation of visual evidence of the verbal story mirrors the convention employed in television commercials in which the product and its uses are displayed as proof of the claims made in the narrative. As I argued in Chapter 3, the display of the guests' transformation is closely bound with the desire for the new self that is an articulation of American Dreaming. Lentricchia (1990) writes that the object of television advertising is 'the foreplay of desire' so that 'to buy is merely an effect, but to dream is a cause – the motor principle, in fact, of consumer capitalism'. Sitting in front of our TV sets is like a 'perpetual Atlantic Crossing' in which the old self is left behind in favour of the new: 'a new self because a new world'.[1]

As we watch the video representations of *Oprah* guests, we see the Dream realised, though this is not without problems. Firstly, whatever the transformation presented, it is rarely the case that the individual is represented as trouble-free: they would not be on the show in the first place if they were. Or, if the participant *is* held up as an exemplar of success, he/she is presented within the context of whatever it is that is troubling for others. Secondly, as stated, some of the visual transformations witnessed are those of degradation rather than regeneration. However, trouble and degeneration operate as a driving force that perpetuates the show. By this I mean that the commercial viability of *Oprah* is dependent on a succession of personal troubles to be displayed and talked about. Crucially, for the commercial logic of the programme, no narrative is completely closed: there is frequently another set of problems to be opened up. However, this occurs without disturbing the overarching narrative of completion in which the ideal self is realised.

The discursive formations of self that are produced in the 'elite' critical tradition are evident in *Oprah*, both through the construction of the show – which is premised on commercial interest, technological availability, imagery, and cultural acceptance of the therapeutic – and within the show itself. This is facilitated by the Oprah persona that is constructed by and through the system of celebrity which, as Marshall (1997) states, is integral to the systematic promotion of consumption and the mobilisation of capitalistic forces: celebrity is an articulation of the 'individual as commodity'.[2] Thus far, the conventions of television entertainment that form the show, and the ways in which individuals are displayed/display themselves, lends *Oprah* to a reading that emerges from the cultural pessimism in which selfhood is subjugated by and through the processes of commercialism.

However, this does not represent the totality of the programme. My structural analysis of the guests' stories in Chapter 4 reveals a pattern in which a positive and active sense of self emerges, and which identifies an inner locus of control. This stands in contradistinction to the external forces – of commodification and technological advance – that form the constructions of self articulated within the 'elite' critical position. Through an examination of a small number of shows, it is evident that *Oprah* participants formulate their versions of self in relation to significant others and to their community. Particularly striking is the insistence of the guests' concern for those they consider closest to them and through whom their lives derive meaning. It is this connection with others that is the frequently cited force that drove the individual into taking action in the face of difficult circumstance.

Further, the exploration of stories in Chapter 4 revealed that testimony performs an important function within the overarching narrative of *Oprah*. In the majority of shows, it is clear that the guests are not seeking absolution through confessional speech, but are stating the 'truth' of their lived experiences and of their positions that emerge from this experience. In doing so, the guests act out an empowered sense of self, frequently gaining expressions of approval from Oprah and the studio audience for their 'honesty' and 'courage' in speaking out. Thus, guests are making claims about themselves and for themselves in a public arena, a space that is ordinarily denied to them. This signals a move from the show's therapeutic emphasis which is more evident when the mode of confessional is adopted.

During my analysis, I identified three main narrative structures, and these I called commencement, ongoing and completion. What becomes apparent is that the narratives of completion form the majority in my sample, shaping the meaning of *Oprah* over time; those that I named commencement and ongoing represent the earlier stages in the overarching narrative (of completion). Whatever the narrative form, the reading aloud of a diary extract or a letter is a much-used strategy that has several functions. Firstly, publicly reciting material that is a private form of communication signals a move from an inner dialogue to an outer display that, secondly, flags an intimate relationship with the addressee – and, by extension, the audience. Thirdly, autobiographical material is the means through which a narrative is often introduced, and constitutes an excavation of a personal history that grounds the narrative. As well as providing the context for the story, the rehearsal of a personal history works as a refusal of subjugation. Here, I make a connection with the ways in which some African American writers and black feminist scholars make use of the past in order to rewrite that past, reinscribing themselves as active agents through the formation of their self-definition.

This connection is key to some of the meanings generated in *Oprah*, and is made on the grounds that Oprah Winfrey frequently positions herself in alliance with prominent black feminist writers through her film performances and her endorsement of their work in her book club. This is not to suggest that the tradition of autobiography has its genesis in black American literature, or that it is the sole province of African American writers: this is clearly not the case. But the ways in which story telling has been used in an African American tradition of thought, and the place of the self within it, can be seen to be reflected in the story-telling activity that takes place on *Oprah*. I have discussed the ways in which the fiction and non-fiction of writers such as Alice Walker and Toni Morrison articulate a selfhood that is constructed through meaningful relations with significant others, and through the communities to which an individual belongs. Further, the past represents a storehouse of voices and experiences that shape and define the present. Recognition of this past, and the reconfiguration of self in relation to it, is an essential part of the process towards self-realisation. This construction of self is also found in the feminist literature of writers such as Patricia Hill Collins, bell hooks and in the historical project of Darlene Clarke Hine that uncovers the contribution made to communities by unsung black American women.

In this tradition of thought, the emphasis is on everyday lived experience as the cornerstone for developing ideas of what constitutes selfhood and self-esteem. The personal–political argument that emanates from this version of selfhood lies in talking back and speaking out, in claiming a place for oneself. The accent on everyday experience (and which is reflected in the language used in this literature) is that which marks the speech of *Oprah* participants. These are ordinary individuals, who, while sometimes facing extraordinary circumstances, locate the narratives of their lives in the realm of the everyday, and who use their experiences as a legitimate form of knowledge as opposed to expert advice. The relationship that non-celebrity guests have with Oprah is premised on precisely this ordinariness that is seen as her trademark.

As I have argued throughout, Oprah's persona is central to the meaning(s) generated by the show; and as we saw in Chapter 3, it is the audience perception of her 'down home' characteristic that enables the para-social identification to take place. For me, what is extraordinary about this relationship is the ways in which Oprah's celebrity appears to be effaced in the participants' desire to 'read' Oprah as 'ordinary folk'. As a successful and wealthy film star, television producer and talk show host, Oprah is the exemplar of the individualism and pecuniary success that represents the American Dream. Yet these are attributes that are somehow denied by the audience as they relate to her 'down home' self. I have also argued that Oprah's role on her show is something akin to that of the 'othermother' identified by Stanlie M. James and Collins as a woman who, in black communities, takes care of others, empowering and becoming empowered in the process. It is Oprah's appearance of ordinariness together with her apparent concern for those who take part on her show, that (appears to) make her an authority on the everyday. Her performance as talk show host places an emphasis on her own (past and present) life difficulties rather than on the successes achieved in her professional career. However, this also raises the question: would the audience relate to Oprah, and appear to trust her word, if she were *not* the extraordinary figure that she is? The answer to this has to be speculative. But I would suggest that the system of celebrity that produced Oprah is a complex mechanism that has a powerful cultural resonance, offering an available means through which audiences make identifications with the celebrated individual. The contradiction between Oprah's extraordinary professional success and her 'ordinary' self can, therefore, be contained through a cultural acceptance of the processes that produce the show and her persona, while the focus of attention is simultaneously placed on her everyday life experiences that are shared by the participants.

The call and response dynamic of *Oprah*, with its connotations of talking back and speaking out, of 'gittin ovuh', along with Oprah's frequent use of black vernacular suggest links with aspects of black American folk culture that are tied to ways in which marginalised and subjugated voices make themselves heard. In *The Oprah Winfrey Show*, this dynamic facilitates the carnivalesque play of official and unofficial discourses, neither of which are cancelled out, but which combine to form something new. This is embodied in Oprah who simultaneously endorses the normative values of heterosexuality and monogamy, success and individualism, whilst her black, large, female body and her use of black vernacular positions her with a historically marginalised and subjugated group in America. Unofficial discourse is, then, articulated through her 'down home' persona, but which is also shored up through her celebrity – and iconic – status.

As the site of conflicting discourses, and with the emphasis on regeneration and renewal, Oprah can be characterised as grotesque. As I have discussed in Chapter 5, according to Mikhail Bakhtin, grotesque imagery 'is a point of transition in a life eternally renewed, the inexhaustible vessel of death and conception'.[3] The grotesque body, and the carnival spirit it represents, is freed from the restrictions of official life, and points to the possibilities of transcendence and the creation of new meanings. Bakhtin (cited in Dentith, 1995) argues that the transforming power of laughter engendered by the grotesque is linked to protection against terror of the cosmos and to the possibilities of renewal and change.

As I demonstrated in Chapter 4, *Oprah's* overarching narrative is one of completion in which the individual charts his/her journey to self-realisation through a process of change and renewal. I have also argued that in publicly speaking the unspeakable, the show's participants risk ridicule and further ostracism. That this is the case is evident in the review of literature on talk shows carried out in Chapter 1. In order to think through the risk-taking activity that is displaying the self on *Oprah*, I have drawn on Mary Russo's conception of stunting.[4] Russo (1995) suggests that risk-taking is a stunt that attracts an ambivalent response: on the one hand, those performing stunts take the risk of becoming further stigmatised, blamed and ridiculed, while on the other hand, stunters also draw admiration from those witnessing the performance. Stunting is an act of transgression, an act that I argue characterises the performances of *Oprah* participants.

Stallybrass and White (1986) contend that despite the significant impact that the 'rediscovery' of the carnivalesque figure has had on the political unconscious, transgression can only carry political transformation when and if major sites of discourse are challenged and changed.[5] This implies that the presence of the carnivalesque alone is insufficient to register political change. If *Oprah* is considered in terms of its potential for political and social transformation (or otherwise), I believe that our understanding of what is taking place on the screen remains limited to the binary that marks the current debate on talk shows. Nonetheless, there is an empowerment that arises from, and is evident in, the testimony of the guests' stories. Testifying to life experiences on *Oprah* not only stakes a claim for the individual, but also communicates a condition shared by others. Expressions of self-esteem premised on experience are then shared with a wider community, some members of which have encountered similar circumstances. Thus, testifying and confessing – stunting – on *Oprah* constitute a political act.

However, rather than attempting to locate political activity *per se*, it is my argument that Oprah's (and *Oprah's*) success lies in the interplay of discourses that have meaning within a particular historical moment. In Chapter 5, I discussed Dyer's argument (1979) that celebrity status is linked to the 'charismatic model' in which specific attributes of an individual are particularly effective in forming a relationship with the rest of society when 'the social order is uncertain, unstable and ambiguous'.

It is at these moments in time that the charismatic personality 'offers a value, order or stability to counterpoise this'.[6] The instability and anxious uncertainty that marks the 'elite' cultural position not only offers an available model through which to read expressions of selfhood displayed on *Oprah*; the programme itself is a manifestation of this set of ideas on contemporary American culture. The figure of Oprah, however, offers the possibility to think through the fragility of self-formation within the postmodern context. Oprah, with her celebrity status and her insistence on her 'ordinariness', encapsulates two distinct traditions of thought in which self is respectively posited as fragmented and as recoverable. It is this ambivalence that accounts for her popularity *at this particular moment in time*. In the context of contemporary culture with its attendant uncertainty, social fragmentation and mass mediation, Oprah's grotesque body offers the possibility of renewal and regeneration while *Oprah* operates as a borderzone in which identity can be rehearsed. *The Oprah Winfrey Show* then, operates as a liminal space in which those who participate – as host, guests, audience and home viewers – are bound up in a performance that has a dynamic closely aligned with elements of carnival. This process is facilitated by a (grotesque) persona that incorporates those participants into the spectacle through a para-social identification. The self that is thereby constructed is one tied to community, friendship and familial networks, placed in a historical context and capable of contesting oppressive social forces.

Appendix

Show title	Channel and date of broadcast	Subject matter of show
How Could You Not Know?	BBC2, 7.10.95	Women who were unknowingly married to paedophiles
Teachers' Salute	BBC2, 17.10.95	Celebration of inspirational teachers
Over-Indulgent Parents	BBC2, 21.10.95	Problems caused through over-indulging children
Date Violence	Channel 4, 24.10.95	Teenage girls in abusive relationships with their boyfriends
Men and Women Communicating	Channel 4, 31.10.95	Gender differences and their impact on communication
Real Life Dramas	BBC2, 4.11.95	Individuals overcoming life-threatening scenarios
Forbidden Thoughts	BBC2, 9.11.95	Everyday thoughts that cause guilt and anxiety
Girl Power	BBC2, 15.11.95	Interviews with teenage girls who have overcome adversity
Sex	Channel 4, 21.11.95	Heterosexual couples in crisis
Oprah's Diets	Channel 4, 28.11.95	Diet and fitness advice; includes psychological approaches to weight loss
The Judds	BBC2, 5.12.95	Celebrity interview
Are We Better Off Today?	BBC2, 9.12.95	A debate on the position of women in the 1990s
Welfare Reform	BBC2, 13.12.95	A debate concerning the advantages and disadvantages of the welfare state
Undercover Agents	BBC2, 14.12.95	Camcorder revelations of undesirable practices
Women for Women	BBC2, 16.12.95	Women musicians plugging their fund raising for breast cancer
Friends Falling Out	BBC2, 20.12.95	Psychotherapists offer advice to women who have difficult friend relationships

Show title	Channel and date of broadcast	Subject matter of show
Men Who Con Women	BBC2, 21.12.95	A number of women who have fallen prey to the deceptive practices of one man
Lose Weight, Lose Friends	BBC2, 23.12.95	Relationship difficulties that result in the wake of an individual's loss of weight
Teenage Sex	BBC2, 9.1.96	Teenagers who have taken a vow of celibacy
Mothers in Prison	BBC2, 11.1.96	Mothers who have turned to crime for money in order to supplement the family income
Single Parents Without a Date	BBC2, 17.1.96	Single parenthood and (the lack of) romance
Trading Places	BBC2, 18.1.96	Couples swap hobbies for a weekend
Letters From Children	BBC2, 19.1.96	Responses to letters sent in by child viewers
Fertility Scandal	BBC2, 24.1.96	Embryo theft in a fertility clinic
The Color of Fear	BBC2, 15.1.96	Video and workshop addressing racial bigotry
Where Are They Now?	BBC2, 28.1.96	Popular stars from the past and their current status
The Roadmap Out	BBC2, 1.2.96	Advice for women on how to get away from domestic violence
Women Over 40	BBC2, 3.2.96	A celebration of older women
Unruly Children	BBC2, 7.2.96	Families in crisis
Reaching Boiling Point	BBC2, 7.3.96	Problems caused by impatience
Consumer Wrapping	BBC2, 14.3.96	The in/accuracies of product description on packaging
How To Be A Star	BBC2, 16.3.96	Makeovers in the image of a star
Oprah In Beverly Hills	BBC2, 27.3.96	Celebrity event in Hollywood with a number of *Oprah* viewers as guests
Donna Karan	BBC2, 2.4.96	An interview with the designer and a display of her current collection
Time Warp Objects	BBC2, 4.4.96 Sky1, 27.2.96	The peculiar artefacts from the past that people hoard

Estranged Families	BBC2, 8.4.96	First steps to reconciliation for families that are fractured
Dog Extravaganza	BBC2, 22.5.96	A celebration of all things canine with particular focus on Winfrey's pets
Reunion Updates	BBC2, 23.5.96	A retrospective of reunions on other shows; some of which failed, others were more successful
Hidden Camera Highlights	BBC2, 29.5.96	A candid camera retrospective
Anti-Social Behaviour	BBC2, 30.5.96	The do's and don'ts of social etiquette
How to Make A Million	BBC2, 3.6.96	'Ordinary' people who have made millions of dollars
Should Gay Marriages Be Legalised?	BBC2, 4.6.96	Debate on same-sex marriage
Special Effects	BBC2, 5.6.96	Techniques used in film and television advertisements
Anorexia	BBC2, 17.6.96	The problems of and treatments for eating disorders
Oprah On The Road	BBC2, 18.6.96	A series of clips from previous *Oprah* road shows
Summer Movie Review	BBC2, 19.6.96	Film critics review current films
Lost First Loves	Sky1, 5.7.96	Tracking down and meeting up with old flames
Fat Camp	Sky1, 8.7.96	Three teenage girls at a slimmers' camp
Great Job!	Sky1, 9.7.96	Surprise salutes to those deemed to have done 'a great job'
Tipping Anxiety	Sky1, 11.7.96	Advice on appropriate tips and gifts for service providers
Second Chance	Sky1, 12.7.96	Deserving cases receive a 'second chance'
Unusual Letters from Viewers	Sky1, 15.7.96	Surprising requests from viewers
Sleeping Disorders	Sky1, 16.7.96	The problems of insomnia and other sleep disorders
Oprah's Celebrity Hall of Fame	Sky1, 17.7.96	A retrospective look at the celebrities who have appeared on the show

Show title	Channel and date of broadcast	Subject matter of show
Letters from Children	Sky1, 22.7.96	Children writing to the show at times of crisis and a look back at earlier letters sent in
Cookery Contest	Sky1, 25.7.96	Viewers demonstrate their culinary skills and compete on the show
House Detectives	Sky1, 26.7.96	What an individual's home reveals about them; includes some celebrity homes
Surrogacy	Sky1, 27.7.96	Issues concerning the practice of surrogacy

Notes

Introduction

1. Throughout, I employ the name 'Oprah' – as distinct from Winfrey – to signal the construct that is her TV persona.
2. Jane Shattuc. *The Talking Cure: TV Talk Shows and Women*. New York: Routledge, 1997. p. 1.
3. See for example, Tammy Johnson's online article 'It's Personal: Race and Oprah' in which she argues that despite her influence, Winfrey still cannot transcend the 'boundaries of race and power in America... she safely reduces all things racial to the personal, sidestepping the hard questions of institutionalized racial oppression and white privilege'. In *Colorlines*. Vol. 4(4), Winter 2001–2002.
4. Message posted March 14, 2003, http://members3.boardhost.com/Oprah/msg/1612.html [accessed 12.03.2003].
5. http://mitglied.lycos.de/Oprah/ [accessed 20.03.2003].
6. Garth Pearce. 'When It's Not So Good To Talk'. *Sunday Times*. 7 February, 1999. p. 10.
7. Shattuc. p. 53.
8. Shattuc. p. 2.
9. Pearce. pp. 10–11.
10. Although the viewing figures cited above show that *Oprah* has an appeal that extends beyond the United States, it is beyond the scope of this study to address its attraction in a global context.
11. Foucault. *The Will to Knowledge: The History of Sexuality*. Vol. I (Trans.) Robert Hurley. London: Penguin Books, 1978. p. 63.
12. Susannah Radstone. 'Social Bonds and Psychical Order; Testimonies'. *Cultural Values*. Vol. 5(1), January 2001: pp. 59–78.
13. Pam Morris. *The Bakhtin Reader: Selected Writings of Bakhtin, Medvedev and Voloshinov*. London: Arnold, 1994. p. 12.
14. Morris. pp. 248–49.
15. Voloshinov cited in Morris. p. 9.
16. Bakhtin, 1968. It is recognised that his writing presents a critique of Stalinist Russia of the early 20th century; his dissertation on Rabelais remained unpublished until 1965. See Morris, *The Bakhtin Reader* and Simon Dentith, *Bakhtinian Thought: An Introductory Reader*. London: Routledge, 1995.
17. Bakhtin. p. 16.
18. In order to signal an awareness of the slippery and problematic usage of terms such as 'race', I frame the word with inverted commas.
19. Paul Gilroy. *The Black Atlantic: Modernity and Double Consciousness*. London: Verso, 1993. p. 3.
20. Gilroy, 1993. p. 4.
21. Gilroy, 1993. p. 15.
22. Mikhail Bakhtin cited in Gilroy, 1993. p. 226, n2.

23. This is with reference to Philip Rieff's influencial *The Triumph of the Therapeutic: Uses of Faith After Freud*. London: Chatto and Windus, 1966.
24. Mimi White. *Tele-Advising: Therapeutic Discourse in American Television*. Chapel Hill: University of North Carolina Press, 1992. p. 20.
25. These shows are all the copyright of Harpo Productions and syndicated by King World. When the shows are broadcast in Britain they do not contain the title ascribed by the production company and so I have assigned the titles myself based on a frequently used tag line that is pertinent to any one show. So, 'Second Chance' is the name of the show that appeared on Sky1, 12.7.96, during which viewers were given a second chance to do something that they had failed at the first time around – such as a woman who missed her own graduation ceremony, or another whose father had been too ill to attend her wedding ceremony. The situations were all re-staged in order that they get 'a second chance'. Further, the broadcast dates that I have signalled are in relation to the shows that are aired on British television; there appears to be only two or three months between the taping of the show and its distribution to other countries. In one of the shows dedicated to children's letters shown in Britain on 22 July 1996, we have a group of children who had responded to an earlier programme that was aired to mark the birth date of Martin Luther King Jr – 15 January – from which a clip is shown. The copyright date on both of these shows is 1996, so we can assume that following its broadcast in America, a show will be seen as part of its international syndication very shortly after. This is verified by a show, which is not in my collection but was viewed by me during the time of Bill Clinton's impeachment hearing in 1998, that discussed the (in)advisability of conducting affairs with work colleagues in direct reference to Clinton's own conduct.
26. Michel Foucault. *The Will to Knowledge: The History of Sexuality*. Vol. I (Trans.) Robert Hurley. London: Penguin Books, 1978. pp. 58–63.
27. White, 1992. p. 8.
28. Foucault, 1978. p. 59.
29. Foucault, 1978. pp. 61–62.
30. White. p. 183.
31. Shattuc. p. 130.
32. bell hooks. 'Talking Back' in Russell Ferguson, Martha Gever, Trinh T. Min-ha and Cornel West (eds). *Out There: Marginalisation and Contemporary Cultures*. Cambridge, MA: MIT Press, 1990. p. 340.
33. Vladimir Propp. *Morphology of the Folktale* (1928). (Trans.) Lawrence Scott. USA: University of Texas Press, 1968.
34. Mikhail Bakhtin. *Rabelais and His World*. (Trans.) Helene Iswolsky. Cambridge, MA: MIT Press, 1968. p. 19.

About television talk shows

1. Jane Shattuc defines the newer breed of talk shows thus: 'Topics moved from personal issues connected to a social injustice to interpersonal conflicts which emphasised only the visceral nature of confrontation, emotion and sexual titillation. The expert disappeared as the number of guests proliferated... Everything also got younger.' in Jane Shattuc. 'Go Ricki: Politics, Perversion

and Pleasure in the 1990s' in Christine Geraghty and David Lusted (eds). *The Television Studies Book*. London: Edward Arnold, 1998. p. 212.

2. Jane Shattuc. *The Talking Cure: TV Talk Shows and Women*. New York: Routledge, 1997. pp. 3–5.

3. The high culture/low culture dialectic is that which marks the dichotomous structure that frequently characterises debates within cultural studies.

4. There is a body of work conducted on audience responses to television. See for example Sonia Livingstone and Peter Lunt (1994). *Talk on Television: Audience Participation and Public Debate*. London, Routledge; John Tulloch (2000). *Watching television: audiences cultural theories and methods*. London, Arnold; David Morley (1992). *Television, audiences and cultural studies*. London, Routledge; Duncan Petrie and Janet Willis (eds) (1995). *Television and the household reports from the BFI's audience tracking study*. London, BFI.

5. Debbie Epstein and Deborah Lynn Steinberg. 'Twelve Steps to Heterosexuality? Common-Sensibilities on *The Oprah Winfrey Show*'. *Feminism and Psychology*. Vol. 5(2), 1995: 275–80. Jane Landman. 'The Discursive Space of Identity: *The Oprah Winfrey Show*'. *Metro*. Vol. 103, 1995: 37–45. Landman. 'Identity on Trial: Narration, Gossip and Confession on the Daytime Chat Show'. *Australian Journal of Communication*. Vol. 23(1), 1996: 1–14. Lisa McLaughlin. 'Chastity Criminals in the Age of Electronic Reproduction: Reviewing Talk Television and the Public Sphere'. *Journal of Communication Enquiry*. Vol. 17(1), Winter 1993: 4–55.

6. Barbara Cruikshank. 'Revolutions within: self-government and self-esteem'. *Economy and Society*. Vol. 22(3), August 1993: 327–44.

7. Jane Shattuc. *The Talking Cure: TV Talk Shows and Women*. New York: Routledge, 1997. Jane Landman. 'Identity on Trial: Narration, Gossip and Confession on the Daytime Chat Show'. *Australian Journal of Communication*. Vol. 23(1), 1996: 1–14. Joshua Gamson. 'Why Do They Like *Jerry Springer?'* *Tikkon*. Vol. 13(6), 1998: 25–28.

8. Theodore Adorno is central within the Frankfurt School and his position has been summarised by J.M. Bernstein. 'While Adorno nowhere identifies the culture industry with the political triumph of fascism, he does imply, both directly and indirectly, that the culture industries' effective integration of society marks an equivalent triumph of repressive unification in liberal democratic states to that which was achieved politically under fascism'. Deploring mass culture, Adorno argues that high art keeps faith by its 'freedom from the ends of a false universality' while the illusionary (false) universality is that art of the culture industry which only provides easy amusement as relief from labour in order to begin it again. 'Culture is no longer the repository of a reflective comprehension of the present in terms of a redeemed future; the culture industry forsakes the promise of happiness in the name of the degraded utopia of the present.' What might appear as individuality is not so; it is immediately integrated and repressed. So, the effectiveness of the culture industry lies in the removal of the idea that there is any alternative to the status quo which is monitored and maintained by presenting a 'benign image of society requiring only conformity'; a conformity which is endorsed by the stars of film, television and advertisements who say 'it is thus', and through showing the individual in a position of power to make choices. See Theodore W. Adorno. *The Culture Industry: Selected Essays on Mass Culture*. J.M. Bernstein (ed.). London: Routledge, 1991.

9. Teresa Keller. 'Trash TV'. *Journal of Popular Culture*. Vol. 26(4), Spring 1993: p. 195.
10. These are descriptors that characterise 'reality TV'. For a full treatment of this subject see Jon Dovey. *Freakshow: First Person Media and Factual Television*. London: Pluto Press, 2000.
11. Keller. pp. 204–05.
12. Eva Illouz. 'That Shadowy Realm of the Interior: Oprah Winfrey and Hamlet's Glass'. *International Journal of Cultural Studies*. Vol. 2(1), 1999. p. 110.
13. Illouz. p. 111.
14. Illouz. p. 110.
15. Illouz. p. 119.
16. Illouz. p. 119.
17. Illouz. p. 127.
18. Vicki Abt and Mel Seesholtz. 'The Shameless World of Phil, Sally and Oprah: Television Talk Shows and the Deconstructing of Society'. *Journal of Popular Culture*. Vol. 28(1), Summer 1994.
19. Abt and Seesholtz, 1994. p. 187.
20. Abt and Seesholtz, 1994. p. 173.
21. Abt and Seesholtz, 1994. p. 181.
22. Hal Himmelstein. *Television Myth and the American Mind*. New York: Praegeer, 1984. p. 183.
23. Joshua Gamson. 'Publicity Traps: Television Talk Shows and Lesbian, Gay, Bisexual and Transgender Visibility'. *Sexualities*. Vol. 1(1), 1998. p. 26.
24. Joshua Gamson. 'Do Ask, Do Tell: frank talk on TV'. *The American Prospect*. Vol. 23, Fall 1995. p. 49.
25. Gamson, 1995. p. 50.
26. Aaron Fogel. 'Talk Shows: On Reading Television'. In Stephen Donadio, Stephen Railton and Ormond Seavey (eds). *Emerson and His Legacy: Essays in Honor of Quentin Anderson*. Carbondale: Southern Illinois University Press, 1986. p. 150.
27. Donal Carbaugh. *Talking American: Cultural Discourses on* Donahue. New Jersey: Ablex Publishing Corporation, 1989.
28. Carbaugh. p. 28.
29. Carbaugh. pp. 2–28.
30. Wayne Munson. *All Talk: The Talk Show in Media Culture*. Philadelphia: Temple University Press, 1993. p. 1.
31. Munson. p. 12.
32. Munson. p. 138.
33. Munson. p. 83.
34. Barbara Grizzuti Harrison. 'The Importance of Being Oprah'. *New York Times Magazine*. 11 June, 1989. p. 28.
35. Munson. p. 145.
36. Paolo Carpignano, Robin Anderson, Stanley Aronowitz and William Difazio (eds). 'Chatter in the Age of Electronic Reproduction: Talk Television and the "Public Mind"'. *Social Text*. Vol. 25(26), 1990. pp. 33–55.
37. Lisa McLaughlin. 'Chastity Criminals in the Age of Electronic Reproduction: Reviewing Talk Television and the Public Sphere'. *Journal of Communication Enquiry*. Vol. 17(1), Winter 1993. p. 43.
38. McLaughlin. p. 48.
39. McLaughlin. p. 51.

40. McLaughlin. pp. 53–55.
41. Donal Carbaugh, cited in Sonia Livingstone and Peter Lunt. *Talk on Television: Audience Participation and Public Debate*. London: Routledge, 1994. p. 40.
42. Livingstone and Lunt. *Talk on Television: Audience Participation and Public Debate*. London: Routledge, 1994. pp. 93–132.
43. Patricia Joyner Priest. *Public Intimacies: Talk Show Participants and Tell-All TV*. New Jersey: Hampton Press, 1997. pp. 214–16.
44. Joshua Gamson. 'Why Do They Like *Jerry Springer?' Tikkon*. Vol. 13(6), 1998. p. 26.
45. Gamson, 1998. p. 27.
46. Gamson, 1998. p. 28.
47. Carpignano *et al*. pp. 50–51.
48. Himmelstein. p. 297.
49. Vicki Abt and Mel Seesholtz. ' "The Shameless World" Revisited'. *Journal of Popular Film and Television*. Vol. 26, 1998. p. 43.
50. Abt and Seesholtz, 1998. p. 44.
51. Abt and Seesholtz, 1998. p. 44.
52. Abt and Seesholtz, 1998. pp. 44–45.
53. Laura Grindstaff. 'Media Protest is Just a Lot of Talk'. Editorial. *Philadelphia Enquirer*. 16 May, 1997.
54. Abt and Seesholtz, 1998. p. 47.
55. Abt and Seesholtz, 1994. p. 18, nn2–3. The postion adopted by these writers will form a part of my discussion in the following chapter.
56. Debbie Epstein and Deborah Lynn Steinberg. 'American Dreamin': Discoursing Liberally on *The Oprah Winfrey Show'. Women's Studies International Forum*. Vol. 21(1), 1998. pp. 77–93.
57. Epstein and Steinberg, 1998. p. 77.
58. Epstein and Steinberg, 1998. p. 84.
59. Epstein and Steinberg, 1998. p. 85.
60. Epstein and Steinberg, 1998. pp. 84–86.
61. Epstein and Steinberg, 1998. p. 78.
62. Epstein and Steinberg, 1998. p. 92.
63. Epstein and Steinberg, 1998. p. 92.
64. Jane Landman. 'Identity on Trial: Narration, Gossip and Confession on the Daytime Chat Show'. *Australian Journal of Communication*. Vol. 23(1), 1996. p. 1.
65. Landman. p. 12.
66. Landman. p. 13.
67. Landman. p. 10.
68. Donal Carbaugh. *Talking American: Cultural Discourses on* Donahue. New Jersey: Ablex Publishing Corporation, 1988.
69. Landman. p. 1.
70. Landman. p. 2.
71. Michel Foucault. *The Will to Knowledge: The History of Sexuality*. Vol. I (Trans.) Robert Hurley. London: Penguin Books, 1978. p. 45.
72. Landman. p. 11.
73. Landman. p. 11.
74. Landman. p. 12.
75. Linda Martin Alcott and Laura Gray-Rosendale. 'Survivor Discourse: Transgression or Recuperation?' In Sidonie Smith and Julia Watson (eds). *Getting*

A Life: Everyday Uses of Autobiography. Minneapolis: University of Minnesota Press, 1996. p. 199.

76. Alcott and Gray-Rosendale. p. 208.
77. Alcott and Gray-Rosendale. p. 211.
78. Shattuc. p. 112.
79. Shattuc. p. 112.
80. Shattuc. pp. 112–13.
81. Shattuc. p. 111.
82. Shattuc. p. 113.
83. Shattuc. p. 114.
84. Gloria Jean Masciarotte. 'C'mon Girl: Oprah Winfrey and the Discourse of Feminine Talk'. *Genders*. Vol. 11, Fall 1991.
85. Masciarotte. p. 82.
86. Masciarotte. p. 83.
87. Henry Louis Gates Jr. *The Signifying Monkey: A Theory of African-American Literary Criticism*. New York: Oxford University Press, 1988.
88. Masciarotte. pp. 83–84.
89. Masciarotte. p. 89.
90. Masciarotte. p. 89.
91. Masciarotte. p. 100.
92. Masciarotte. p. 104, n9.
93. Corinne Squire. 'Empowering Women? *The Oprah Winfrey Show*'. *Feminism and Psychology*. Vol. 4(1), 1994. p. 65.
94. Squire, 1994. p. 65.
95. Squire, 1994. p. 75.
96. Squire, 1994. p. 69.
97. Squire, 1994. p. 70.
98. Debbie Epstein and Deborah Lynn Steinberg. 'Twelve Steps to Heterosexuality? Common-Sensibilities on *The Oprah Winfrey Show*'. *Feminism and Psychology*. Vol. 5(2), 1995. p. 276.
99. Masciarotte. p. 103.
100. Robert Ferguson. *Representing 'Race': Ideology, Identity and the Media*. London: Arnold, 1998. p. 86.
101. Janice Peck. 'Talk About Racism: Framing a Popular Discourse of "Race" on *The Oprah Winfrey Show*'. *Cultural Critique*. Vol. 27, Spring 1994. p. 89.
102. Peck, 1994. p. 92.
103. Peck, 1994. p. 119.
104. Peck, 1994. p. 120.
105. Corinne Squire. 'Who's White? Television Talk Shows and Representations of Whiteness'. In Fine, Michelle, Lois Weis, Linda C. Powell and L. Mun Wong (eds). *Off White: Readings on 'Race', Power and Society*. London: Routledge, 1997. p. 243.
106. Squire, 1997. p. 243.
107. Squire, 1997. p. 245.
108. Squire, 1997. p. 248.
109. Patricia Mellencamp. *High Anxiety: Catastrophe, Scandal, Age and Comedy*. Bloomington: Indiana University Press, 1992. p. 161.
110. Carpignano *et al*. pp. 51–52.

Anxiety and agency: *Oprah* and constructions of self

1. Jane Shattuc. *The Talking Cure: TV Talk shows and Women*. New York: Routledge, 1997.
2. Shattuc. p. 34. Shattuc offers a comprehensive overview of the origins of issue-orientated daytime talk shows tracing them back, before the advent of television, to the journalistic tradition of 19th century tabloid newspapers with their emphasis on the personal and the sensational (see Chapter 2).
3. Shattuc. p. 113.
4. Teresa Keller. 'Trash TV'. *Journal of Popular Culture*. Vol. 26(4), Spring 1993: 195–206. Vicki Abt and Mel Seesholtz. 'The Shameless World of Phil, Sally and Oprah: Television Talk Shows and the Deconstructing of Society'. *Journal of Popular Culture*. Vol. 28(1), Summer 1994: 171–91. Abt and Seesholtz. 'The Shameless World Revisited'. *The Journal of Popular Film and Television*. Vol. 26, 1998: 42–48.
5. However, I need to state that I am doing so in the knowledge that discourses do not exist as closed, unitary and discrete units of meaning; discourses contain elements of other discourses, and they change over time.
6. I am not suggesting that the critics *themselves* are anxious (although they might be), rather that their work delineates aspects of contemporary life that they are anxious about.
7. Neil Postman. *Amusing Ourselves to Death: Public Discourse in the Age of Show Business*. London: Methuen, 1985. p. viii.
8. Postman. pp. 88–95.
9. Postman. p. 108.
10. Roland Barthes. *Camera Lucida: Reflections on Photography*. (Trans.) Richard Howard. London: Vintage, 1993. pp. 118–19.
11. Zygmunt Bauman cited in Robert Ferguson. *Representing 'race': Ideology, Identity and the Media*. London: Arnold, 1998. p. 5.
12. I have stated that I will be dealing with critics writing in and about post-Second World War America, but a new critical tradition did not suddenly come into being in 1945, and much of what has been written is a continuation of a theme, or a number of concerns, that has preoccupied American intellectual thought since the Puritans landed in the 17th century.
13. T.J. Jackson Lears. 'From Salvation to Self-Realization: Advertising and the Therapeutic Roots of the Consumer Culture, 1880–1930'. In R.W. Fox and T.J. Jackson Lears (eds). *The Culture of Consumption: Critical Essays in American History 1880–1980*. New York: Pantheon, 1988.
14. Sherry Turkle. *Psychoanalytic Politics: Jacques Lacan and Freud's French Revolution*. London: Burnett Books, 1979. p. 4.
15. Turkle. p. 7.
16. This observation of Turkle's is in relation to American culture. She observes that although student radicals in 1969 and 1970 France also turned to psychoanalysis in the face of the failure of the revolutionary activism of 1968, there are two main differences, both of which highlight the American inflection of a discourse that might appear to be universal. Firstly, in France the turn was towards a highly theoretical psychoanalysis 'rather than to the medley of more mystical and more visceral therapies popular in America'. Secondly, the student radicals were turning to a highly subversive discourse as a gesture of

considerable force 'because they, unlike their American counterparts, had grown up in a general intellectual culture that was markedly hostile to psychoanalytic ideas'. Turkle. pp. 8–10.

17. Turkle. p. 29.
18. Turkle. p. 34.
19. Nathan Hale cited in Turkle. p. 30.
20. Turkle. p. 43.
21. Lears. p. 4.
22. Lears. p. 4.
23. Lears. p. 7.
24. Lears. p. 6.
25. Lears. p. 19.
26. Philip Rieff cited in Lears. p. 21.
27. Philip Rieff. *The Triumph of the Therapeutic: Uses of Faith After Freud.* (1966) Chicago: University of Chicago Press, 1987. p. 13.
28. Rieff. p. 10.
29. Rieff. p. 11.
30. David Riesman cited in Lears. p. 8.
31. David Riesman. *The Lonely Crowd.* New Haven: Yale University Press, 1961. p. xiv.
32. Riesman. p. xxxix.
33. Riesman. pp. 21–22.
34. Riesman. p. 25.
35. Riesman. p. xli.
36. Riesman. p. 25.
37. Riesman. pp. 25–26.
38. Theodore Roszak. *The Making of a Counter Culture.* London: Faber and Faber, 1970. p. 5.
39. Roszak. p. 6.
40. Christopher Lasch. *The Culture of Narcissism: American Life in an Age of Diminishing Expectations.* New York: WW Norton & Company, 1979. p. xv.
41. Lasch, 1979. p. xvi.
42. Lasch, 1979. p. xviii.
43. Christopher Lasch. *The Minimal Self: Psychic Survival in Troubled Times.* London: Pan Books, 1985. p. 15.
44. Lasch, 1985. pp. 15–16.
45. Geoffrey Gorer. *The Americans: A Study in National Character.* London: The Cresset Press, 1948. p. 50.
46. Gorer. p. 40.
47. Gorer. pp. 40–41.
48. Gorer. p. 45.
49. Gorer. p. 49. In particular, Gorer concerns himself with the feeding habits engendered by the American mother: sweet foods such as candy and ice cream are given as tokens of love and come to assume a symbolic importance as a loved person becomes equated with a loved food. Extrapolating from this, Gorer makes the rather startling observation that the feeding habits of babies have given rise to 'the very great erotic fetishist value given to women's breasts. The addiction American men have of drinking milk is possibly of huge symbolic as well as nutritional importance' (p. 56). However amusing

this observation may seem, it is followed by a more ominous one: that the mother's neurotic fear and anxiety around the issue of nutrition has led to a nation of obese children. 'The anxiety of the mothers has lost touch with reality' (p. 36).

50. Gorer. p. 105.
51. Lasch, 1985. p. 26.
52. Lasch, 1985. pp. 27–28.
53. Lasch, 1979. pp. 31–32.
54. Lasch, 1979. pp. 50–51.
55. Other cannonical work within this tradition includes Robert N. Bellah. *Habits of the Heart: Individualism and Commitment in American Life.* London: University of California Press, 1985; Herbert Marcuse. *One Dimensional Man: Studies in the Ideology of Advanced Industrial Society* (1964). London: Routledge, 1991; Richard Sennett. *The Fall of Public Man.* New York: Alfred A. Knopf, 1997.
56. Herbert Marcuse. *One Dimensional Man: Studies in the Ideology of Advanced Industrial Society* (1964). London: Routledge, 1991. p. 23.
57. Marcuse. p. 90.
58. Lasch, 1979. pp. 67–68.
59. Lasch sees the language of the ghetto as a manifestation of the violent actuality of everyday existence, an 'everyday speech that ... connects sex with aggression, and sexual aggression with highly ambivalent feelings toward mothers'. By aligning hatred of 'mothers' with the language of the ghetto, Lasch places the misogynist tendency within black culture thereby distancing it from his own despite his argument that the position of mothers, and their relationship with their children, is situated at the core of this narcissistic culture. It is in this context that the language of violence and degradation is expressive of 'highly ambivalent feelings toward mothers'. To support his argument, Lasch refers to the slogan 'Up against the wall, Motherfucker!' adopted by white radicals in the late 1960s. This, 'like other black idioms ... and in slightly expurgated form, has become so acceptable that the term 'mother' has everywhere ... become a term of easygoing familiarity or contempt'. Lasch's argument is that language is a means through which everyday experience is both expressed and perpetuated. This much is difficult to argue against, but with specific reference to 'motherfucker', I think that if any ambivalence is being articulated, it is towards Oedipus, not Jocasta.
60. Fredric Jameson. *Postmodernism, or, the Cultural Logic of Late Capitalism.* London: Verso, 1991. p. xxi.
61. Jameson. p. 318.
62. Jameson. p. 319.
63. Don Delillo. *White Noise.* London: Picador, 1984. p. 285.
64. Delillo. pp. 104–05.
65. Delillo. p. 162.
66. I would like to thank Lola Young for this suggestion.
67. John Docker. *Postmodernism and Popular Culture: A Cultural History.* Melbourne, Australia: Cambridge University Press, 1994. pp. 127–32.
68. I am not making the claim that *all* black Americans subscribe to this one position. Rather, I am exploring the discourse that is manifested in *Oprah* and to which Winfrey draws attention in her performance as talk show host.

69. Martin Kettle. 'Oprah's Jurors Reject Ranchers Beef'. *The Guardian*. 27 February, 1998. p. 1.
70. Andrew Duncan. 'People'. *Radio Times*. 27 February–5 March, 1999. pp. 17–19.
71. I would like to thank Richard Maltby for suggesting this phrase.
72. This statement was made by Angelou during an informal conversation and reported to me by Richard Maltby.
73. Patricia Hill Collins. *Black Feminist Thought: Knowledge, Consciousness and the Politics of Empowerment*. New York: Routledge, 1991. p. 92.
74. Collins. p. 22.
75. Paul Gilroy. *The Black Atlantic: Modernity and Double Consciousness*. London: Verso, 1993. p. 52.
76. Gilroy. p. 53.
77. Gilroy. p. 219.
78. Gilroy. p. 5.
79. Collins. p. xi.
80. bell hooks. 'Women and Men: Partnership in the 1990s. A Dialogue Between bell hooks and Cornel West'. In *Yearning: 'Race', Gender and Cultural Politics*. London: Turnaround, 1991. p. 205.
81. hooks, 1991. pp. 207–08.
82. hooks, 1991. pp. 209–10.
83. hooks, 1991. p. 210.
84. hooks, 1991. p. 212.
85. hooks, 1991. p. 213.
86. Michael Wood. '*America in the Movies*' or, '*Santa Maria, it had slipped my mind*'. New York: Columbia University Press, 1989. pp. 41–42. I should clarify that Wood is discussing 'America in the movies' rather than supplying a cultural critique *per se*. However, it is not too contrived to draw on Wood's conceptualisations now because he asserts that movies exist as fragments of cultural myths rather than as fully articulated stories. As such, they do not have to *solve* the dilemma that the myth is addressing; rather, movies give that myth a run, they exercise it. 'It seems that [film] entertainment is not, as we often think, a full-scale flight from our problems, not a means of forgetting them completely, but rather a rearrangement of our problems into shapes which tames them.' p. 18.
87. hooks, 1991. p. 213.
88. hooks, 1991. p. 227.
89. hooks. *Yearning: 'Race', Gender and Cultural Politics*. London: Turnaround, 1991.
90. hooks, 1991. pp. 218–19.
91. hooks, 1991. p. 220.
92. hooks. 'Talking Back.' In Russell Ferguson, Martha Gever, Trinh T. Minh-Ha and Cornel West (eds). *Out there: Marginalisation and Contemporary Cultures*. Cambridge, MA: MIT Press, 1990. p. 399.
93. Alice Walker. *In Search of Our Mothers' Gardens: Womanist Prose*. London: The Women's Press, 1983. p. 5.
94. Walker. p. 6.
95. Craig Werner. 'Go Tell Old Pharaoh: The Afro-American Response to Faulkner'. *Southern Review*. Vol. 19(4), Winter 1983. p. 716.
96. James Baldwin cited in Werner. p. 717.

97. Ralph Ellison. *Invisible Man*. London: Penguin, 1952. p. 468.
98. Gloria Jean Masciarotte. 'C'mon Girl: Oprah Winfrey and the Discourse of Feminine Talk'. *Genders*. Vol. 11, Fall 1991. p. 89.
99. Walker. p. 13.
100. Walker. pp. 232–33.
101. Walker, 1986. p. 14.
102. See Joshua Gamson, 'Why Do They Like *Jerry Springer*?' *Tikkon*. Vol. 13(6), 1998: 25–28 and Patricia Joyner Priest. *Public Intimacies: Talk Show Participants and Tell-All TV*. New Jersey: Hampton Press, 1997.
103. Russell Ferguson, Martha Gever, Trinh T. Minh-Ha and Cornel West (eds). *Out There: Marginalisation and Contemporary Cultures*. Cambridge, MA: The MIT Press, 1990. p. 9.
104. bell hooks. 'Marginality as Site of Resistance' in Ferguson *et al*. p. 341.
105. Susan Willis. 'Memory and Mass Culture'. In Fabre, Geneveve and Robert O'Meally (eds). *History and Memory in African-American Culture*. New York: Oxford University Press, 1994. p. 187. For more recent work on memory that has been carried out in a broader context, than I am exploring here, see Susannah Radstone (ed.). *Memory and Methodology*. Oxford: Berg, 2000.
106. Toni Morrison. *Beloved*. London: Picador, 1987. p. 95.
107. Gilroy. p. 220.
108. Toni Morrison cited in Gilroy. p. 221.
109. bell hooks. *Ain't I a Woman?: Black Women and Feminism*. London: Pluto Press, 1981. p. 7.
110. Collins. p. xii.
111. Collins. p. 5.
112. Collins. p. 5.
113. Collins. pp. 35–39.
114. Collins. p. 30.
115. Collins. p. 31.
116. Collins. p. 10.
117. Stanlie M. James. 'Mothering: A Possible Black Feminist Link to Social Transformation?' In James, Stanlie M. and Abena P.A. Busia (eds). *Theorizing Black Feminisms: The Visionary Pragmatism of Black Women*. London: Routledge, 1993. p. 44.
118. James. p. 45.
119. James. p. 47.
120. James. pp. 50–51.
121. James. p. 49.
122. Collins. p. 9.
123. Darlene Clark Hine. *Hine Sight: Black Women and the Reconstruction of American History*. Bloomington: Indiana University Press, 1994. pp. xxi–xxv.
124. Kim Marie Vaz (ed.). *Black Women in America*. London: New Sage Publications, 1995. p. ix.
125. Collins. p. 68.
126. Collins. p. 77.
127. Collins. p. 99.
128. Katherine Viner. 'Black Pearls'. *The Guardian*. 24 March, 1998. p. 2. The 'instant success of *Paradise* in America is also 'quite extraordinary' when it's considered in the knowledge that Morrison writes for a black audience, and

that Viner reports Morrison as saying 'I have always wanted to develop a way of writing that was irrevocably black.' p. 3.

129. Geneva Smitherman. *Talkin and Testifyin: The Language of Black America.* Detroit: Wayne State University Press, 1977. p. 105.
130. Smitherman. p. 73.
131. Smitherman. p. 104.
132. Smitherman. p. 87.
133. Smitherman. p. 90.
134. Smitherman. p. 109.

Confessional discourse on *Oprah*

1. *The Oprah Winfrey Show* often addresses this sense of a continuum by showing clips of previous shows and presenting updates that contrasts the then and the now. These often display disappointment, that the management of conflict has not been sustained, as well as offering instances where friction has been successfully resolved.
2. Mimi White. *Tele-Advising: Therapeutic Discourse in American Television.* Chapel Hill: University of North Carolina Press, 1992. pp. 7–8.
3. Michel Foucault. *The Will to Knowledge: The History of Sexuality.* Vol. I (Trans.) Robert Hurley. London: Penguin Books, 1978. pp. 61–62.
4. This will be modified later in this chapter and in the one that follows by refering to the role of testimony.
5. 'Lose Weight, Lose Friends'. *The Oprah Winfrey Show.* Harpo Productions, BBC2, 23.12.95. All quotations in this chapter are from this programme.
6. In this exchange, Lisa, in offering a statement of fact is testifying while it is Sheila who, through her disclosure of 'unacceptable' emotions, confesses. The difference is of importance and will be discussed more fully in the following chapter.
7. While White examines a range of programmes that includes quiz shows and the Home Shopping Club, she does not explore the more overtly staged therapeutic discourse of daytime talk shows.
8. White. pp. 183–84.
9. White. pp. 180–81.
10. White. p. 184.
11. White. p. 184.
12. White. p. 183.
13. Foucault, 1978. p. 62.
14. White. p. 8.
15. There is a large body of material that explores with both letter and diary writing as its subject. For fuller discussion on diaries and letters as tools that offer possibilities for subversion, and that also operate as a means of constructing selfhood, see Harriet Blodgett. *Centuries of Female Days: English Women's Diaries.* Gloucester: Alan Sutton Publishing, 1989; Judy Simmons. *Diaries and journals of Literary Women from Fanny Burney to Virginia Woolf.* Basingstoke: Macmillan Press Ltd., 1990; Ralph Houlbrooke (ed.). *English Family Life, 1576–1716: An Anthology from Diaries.* New York: Basil Blackwell, 1989; Mary A. Favret. *Romantic Correspondence: Women, Politics and the Fiction of Letters.* Cambridge: Cambridge University Press, 1993.

16. White. p. 11.
17. Nancy K. Miller. 'Representing Others: Gender and the Subjects of Autobiography'. *Differences: A Journal of Feminist Cultural Studies*. Vol. 6(1), 1994. pp. 2–3.
18. Susan Stanford Friedman cited in Miller. p. 4. See also Gillian Swanson, 'Memory, Subjectivity and Intimacy: The Historical Formation of the Modern Self and the Writing of Female Autobiography'. In Susannah Radstone (ed.). *Memory and Methodology*. Oxford: Berg, 2000; Nicola King. *Memory Narrative and Identity: Remembering the Self*. Edinburgh: Edinburgh University Press, 2000.
19. Miller. p. 9.
20. William L. Andrews (ed.). *African American Autobigraphy: A Collection of Critical Essays*. New Jersey: Prentice Hall Inc., 1993. p. 1.
21. Andrews. p. 1, n1.
22. Albert E. Stone. 'After *Black Boy* and *Dusk of Dawn*: Patterns in Recent Black Autobiography'. In Andrews. pp. 171–72.
23. Stone. In Andrews. p. 187.
24. Robert B. Steptoe. 'Narration, Authentication, and Authorial Control in Fredrick Douglass' *Narrative* of 1845'. In Andrews. pp. 26–27. For further discussions of this tradition within autobiography, see Joanne Braxton. *Black Women's Autobiography: A Tradition Within A Tradition*. Philadelphia: Temple University Press, 1989; Francois Lionnet. *Autobiographical Voices: Race, Gender and Self Portrait*. Ithica: Cornell University Press, 1989; Edward Said. 'Ideology of Difference'. In Henry Louis Gates Jr. (ed.). *'Race', Writing and Difference*. Chicago: University of Chicago Press, 1985.
25. Donald Bogle. *Toms, Coons, Mulattos, Mammies and Bucks: An Interpretative History of Blacks in American Films*. Oxford: Roundhouse, 1994. p. 6.
26. Clarence Major. *Black Slang: A Dictionary of Afro-American Talk*. London: Routledge & Kegan Paul, 1971.
27. I would like to thank Misha Kavka for this observation.
28. Major. pp. 9–10.
29. Frank Lentricchia. '*Libra* as Postmodern Critique'. *South Atlantic Quarterly*. Vol. 89(2), Spring 1990. pp. 431–53.

Oprah and narrating the self

1. Pam Morris (ed.). *The Bakhtin Reader: Selected Writings of Bakhtin, Medvedev and Voloshinov*. London: Arnold, 1994. pp. 248–49.
2. Mikhail Bakhtin. *Rabelais and His World*. (Trans.) Helene Iswolsky. Cambridge, MA: MIT Press, 1968. pp. 153–54.
3. Bakhtin. p. 188.
4. Bakhtin. p. 7.
5. Morris. p. 12.
6. Morris. pp. 248–49.
7. Vladimir Propp. *Morphology of the Folktale* (1928). (Trans.) Lawrence Scott. USA: University of Texas Press, 1968.
8. Jane Shattuc. *The Talking Cure: TV Talk Shows and Women*. New York: Routledge, 1997. p. 130.

9. Sara Ahmed and Jackie Stacey (eds). 'Testimonial Cultures: An Introduction'. *Cultural Values*. Vol. 5(1), January 2001. p. 2.
10. Ahmed and Stacey. p. 5.
11. Susannah Radstone. 'Social Bonds and Psychical Order'. In Ahmed and Stacey. p. 61.
12. Eva Illouz. 'That Shadowy Realm of the Interior: Oprah Winfrey and Hamlet's Glass'. *International Journal of Cultural Studies*. Vol. 2(1), 1999. p. 117.
13. Illouz. p. 129.
14. This calls to mind Clifford Geertz's assertion made in the context of his exploration of the illegal but frequently staged Balinese cockfight: 'Art forms generate and regenerate the very subjectivity they pretend only to display', see Clifford Geertz. *The Interpretation of Cultures: Selected Essays*. New York: Basic Books, 1973. pp. 450–51.
15. John Gray is (in)famously known as the author of the best-selling, self-help book *Men are From Mars, Women are From Venus* (1992).
16. Mimi White. *Tele-Advising: Therapeutic Discourse in American Television*. Chapel Hill: University of North Carolina Press, 1992. p. 67.
17. It is recognised that Bakhtin's writing presents a critique of Stalinist Russia of the early 20th century; his dissertation on Rabelais remained unpublished until 1965. See Morris, *The Bakhtin Reader* and Simon Dentith, *Bakhtinian Thought: An Introductory Reader*. London: Routledge, 1995.
18. Bakhtin. p. 16.

The Oprah persona

1. Mikhail Bakhtin. *Rabelais and His World*. (Trans.) Helene Iswolsky. Cambridge, MA: MIT Press, 1968. p. 19.
2. Shattuc, 1997. pp. 53–54.
3. Shattuc, 1997. p. 54.
4. Shattuc, 1997. p. 55.
5. Shattuc, 1997. p. 56.
6. http://www.geocities.com/rainforest/1078/oprah/oprah2.html [accessed 26.02.2003].
7. P. David Marshall. *Celebrity and Power: Fame in Contemporary Culture*. Minneapolis: University of Minnesota Press, 1997. pp. 48–49.
8. Marshall. pp. x–xi.
9. Richard Dyer cited in Joe Moran. 'Don Delillo and the Myth of the Author Recluse'. *Journal of American Studies*. Vol. 34(1), 2000. pp. 137–52.
10. Joshua Gamson cited in Moran. p. 144.
11. Richard Dyer. *Stars*. London: British Film Institute, 1979.
12. Marshall. p. 15.
13. Marshall. p. 14.
14. Marshall. p. 119.
15. Marshall. p. 185.
16. Marshall. pp. 73–74.
17. Donald Horton and R. Richard Wohl cited in Janice Peck. 'The Mediated Talking Cure: Therapeutic Framing of Autobiography in TV Talk Shows'. In Smith, Sidonie and Julia Watson (eds). *Getting a Life: Everyday Uses of Autobiography*. Minneapolis: University of Minnesota Press, 1996. p. 137.

18. Peck. p. 137.
19. John Langer cited in Peck. p. 136.
20. Peck. p. 137.
21. Marshall. p. 145.
22. Lola Young. 'Racializing Femininity'. In Jane Arthurs and Jean Grimshaw (eds). *Women's Bodies: Discipline and Transgression*. London: Cassell, 1999. p. 68.
23. Marshall. p. 145.
24. Herman Gray. 'Anxiety, Desire and Conflict in the American Racial Imagination'. In Lull, James and Stephen Hinerman (eds). *Media Scandals: Morality and Desire in the Market Place*. Cambridge: Polity Press, 1997. p. 87.
25. Gray. p. 96.
26. Gray. p. 91.
27. The comparison drawn between Rodney King's treatment following on from his use of prostitutes and that of Hugh Grant's engagement of a black prostitute's services leads me to another observation that is also interesting. King had exposed the malicious and brutal activities of members of an (American) institution – the LAPD – whereas Grant's only real transgression, as far as the media is concerned, is of his own boyish persona and in the tarnishing of the image of his happy, monogamous relationship with the beautiful Liz Hurley.
28. Shattuc. p. 105.
29. Shattuc. p. 106.
30. Robert Ferguson. *Representing 'Race': Ideology, Identity and the Media*. London: Arnold, 1998; Janice Peck. 'Talk About Racism: Framing a Popular Discourse of 'race' on *The Oprah Winfrey Show'*. *Cultural Critique*. Vol. 27, Spring 1994.
31. A 'Tom' is a 'Good Negro' character discussed by Donald Bogle and described as those who 'keep the faith, n'er turn against their white massa, and remain hearty, submissive, stoic and generous, selfless and oh-so-very-kind'. Donald Bogle. *Toms, Coons, Mulattos, Mammies and Bucks: An Interpretative History of Blacks in American Films*. Oxford: Roundhouse, 1994. p. 7.
32. Patricia Hill Collins. *Black Feminist Thought: Knowledge, Consciousness and the Politics of Empowerment*. New York: Routledge, 1991. p. 7.
33. Alice Walker. *In Search of Our Mother's Gardens: Womanist Prose*. London: The Women's Press, 1983. p. xi.
34. Bakhtin in Dentith. pp. 241–42.
35. Bakhtin in Simon Dentith. *Bakhtinian Thought: An Introductory Reader*. London: Routledge, 1995. p. 227.
36. Bakhtin in Dentith. p. 227.
37. Bakhtin in Dentith. p. 232.
38. Mary Russo. *The Female Grotesque: Risk, Excess, and Modernity*. London: Routledge, 1995. pp. 1–2.
39. Maud Ellman cited in Russo. p. 24.
40. Russo states that Western culture has persistently coded the female body as grotesque through the Medusa, the Crone, the Bearded Lady, the Fat Woman . . . She adds that 'we may begin a long list which would add to these curiosities and freaks those conditions and attributes which link these types with contemporary social and sexual deviances'. This brings to mind Ricki Lake's grotesque performance in John Water's film *Hairspray* (1988) prior to her present status as host of a talk show that depends on the serial presentation

of dysfunctional excess. However, Lake's persona does not work to undercut the commodification of the individual because the guests are positioned as representing the undesirable end product of violated social and cultural codes concerning sexuality, family relations and work ethic. The guests on *Ricki Lake* are often pilloried by members of the audience and implicitly through Lake's concluding speech to camera that works to reiterate normative values and beliefs. Here, Lake's grotesque persona acts as an echo of those on the stage before normative values are restored.

41. Russo. p. 22.
42. Leo Marx. 'Pastoralism in America'. In Sacvan Bercovitch and Myra Jehlen (eds). *Ideology and Classic American Literature*. Cambridge: Cambridge University Press, 1986.
43. Russo. p. 38.
44. Of course there is an alternative reading of the show to be made in relation to the dominant culture that regards the show as empty spectacle: the Trash TV discourse. This marks the difference between mediaeval carnival, in which all were involved, and the contemporary television spectacle that allows others to stand outside so they may judge and categorise. However, I am discussing the process through the involvement of the performers and the regular viewing audience.
45. Russo. p. 24.
46. Russo. p. 56.
47. Russo. p. 60.
48. Peter Stallybrass and Allon White. *The Politics and Poetics of Transgression*. New York: Cornell University Press, 1986. p. 4.
49. Toni Morrison. *Playing in the Dark: Whiteness and the Literary Imagination*. Cambridge, MA: Harvard University Press, 1992.

Conclusion

1. Frank Lentricchia. '*Libra* as Postmodern Critique'. *South Atlantic Quarterly*. Vol. 89(2), Spring 1990. p. 433.
2. P. David Marshall. *Celebrity and Power: Fame in Contemporary Culture*. Minneapolis: University of Minnesota Press, 1997. pp. x–xii.
3. Mikhail Bakhtin. In Simon Dentith. *Bakhtinian Thought: An Introductory Reader*. London: Routledge, 1995. p. 227.
4. Mary Russo. *The Female Grotesque: Risk, Excess and Modernity*. London: Routledge, 1995.
5. Peter Stallybrass and Allon White. *The Politics and Poetics of Transgression*. New York: Cornell University Press, 1986.
6. Richard Dyer. *Stars*. London: British Film Institute, 1979. pp. 35–36.

Bibliography

Abt, Vicki and Mel Seesholtz. 'The Shameless World of Phil, Sally and Oprah: Television Talk Shows and the Deconstructing of Society'. *Journal of Popular Culture.* Vol. 28(1), Summer 1994: 171–91.

—' "The Shameless World" Revisited'. *Journal of Popular Film and Television.* Vol. 26, 1998: 42–48.

Adorno, Theodore W. *The Culture Industry: Selected Essays on Mass Culture.* J.M. Bernstein (ed.). London: Routledge, 1991.

Ahmed, Sara and Jackie Stacey (eds). 'Testimonial Cultures: An Introduction'. *Cultural Values.* Vol. 5(1), January 2001: 1–6.

Alcott, Linda Martin and Laura Gray-Rosendale. 'Survivor Discourse: Transgression or Recuperation?' In Smith, Sidonie and Julia Watson (eds). *Getting a Life: Everyday Uses of Autobiography.* Minneapolis: University of Minnesota Press, 1996.

Allen, Robert C. (ed.). *Channels of Discourse: Television and Contemporary Criticism.* London: Methuen, 1987.

Andrews, William L. *African American Autobiography: A Collection of Critical Essays.* New Jersey: Prentice Hill Inc., 1993.

Baker, Houston A. 'Figurations for a New American Literary History'. In S. Bercovitch and M. Jehlan (eds). *Ideology and Classic American Literature.* Cambridge: Cambridge University Press, 1986.

Bakhtin, Mikhail. *Rabelais and His World.* (Trans.) Helene Iswolsky. Cambridge, MA: MIT Press, 1968.

Barthes, Roland. *Camera Lucida: Reflections on Photography.* (Trans.) Richard Howard. London: Vintage, 1993.

Bellah, Robert N. *Habits of the Heart: Individualism and Commitment in American Life.* London: University of California Press, 1985.

Blodgett, Harriet. *Centuries of Female Days: English Women's private Diaries.* Gloucester: Alan Sutton Publishing, 1989.

Bogle, Donald. *Toms, Coons, Mulattos, Mammies and Bucks: An Interpretative History of Blacks in American Films.* Oxford: Roundhouse, 1994.

Born, Georgia. 'Inside Television: Television Studies and the Sociology of Culture'. *Screen.* Vol. 41(4), Winter 2000: 404–23.

Braxton, Joanne M. *Black Women's Autobiography: A Tradition Within a Tradition.* Philadelphia: Temple University Press, 1989.

Carbaugh, Donal. *Talking American: Cultural Discourses on Donahue.* New Jersey: Ablex Publishing Corporation, 1989.

Carpignano, Paolo, Robin Anderson, Stanley Aronowitz and William Difazio. 'Chatter in the Age of Electronic Reproduction: Talk Television and the "Public Mind"'. *Social Text.* Vol. 25(26), 1990: 33–55.

Collins, Patricia Hill. *Black Feminist Thought: Knowledge, Consciousness and the Politics of Empowerment.* New York: Routledge, 1991.

Cruikshank, Barbara. 'Revolutions Within: Self-Government and Self-Esteem'. *Economy and Society.* Vol. 22(3), August 1993: 327–44.

de Young, Mary. 'Breeders for Satan: Toward a Sociology of Sexual Trauma Tales'. *Journal of American Culture.* Vol. 19, 1996: 111–17.

Decker, Jeffrey Louis. *Made in America: Self Styled Success from Horatio Alger to Oprah Winfrey.* Minneapolis: University of Minnestoa Press, 1997.

Delillo, Don. *White Noise.* London: Picador, 1984.

Dentith, Simon. *Bakhtinian Thought: An Introductory Reader.* London: Routledge, 1995.

Dixon, Wheeler Winston. *Distaster and Memory: Celebrity Culture and the Crisis of Hollywood Cinema.* New York: Columbia University Press, 1999.

Docker, John. *Postmodernism and Popular Culture: A Cultural History.* Melbourne, Australia: Cambridge University Press, 1994.

Douglass, Frederick. *Narrative of the Life of Frederick Douglass, an American Slave Written by Himself* (1854). New York: Penguin, 1986.

Dovey, Jon. *Freakshow: First Person Media and Factual Television.* London: Pluto Press, 2000.

Duncan, Andrew. 'People'. *Radio Times.* 27 February–5 March, 1999: 17–19.

Dyer, Richard. *Stars.* London: British Film Institute, 1979.

Ellison, Ralph. *Invisible Man.* London: Penguin Books, 1952.

Epstein, Debbie and Deborah Lynn Steinberg. 'Twelve Steps to Heterosexuality? Common-Sensibilities on *The Oprah Winfrey Show*'. *Feminism and Psychology.* Vol. 5(2), 1995: 275–80.

——'All Het Up!: Rescuing Heterosexuality on *The Oprah Winfrey Show*'. *Feminist Review.* Vol. 54, 1996: 88–115.

——'American Dreamin': Discoursing Liberally on *The Oprah Winfrey Show*'. *Women's Studies International Forum.* Vol. 21(1), 1998: 77–94.

Fabre, Genevieve and Robert O'Meally (eds). *History and Memory in African-American Culture.* New York: Oxford University Press, 1994.

Fairclough, Norman. *Media Discourse.* New York: Edward Arnold, 1995.

Fanon, Frantz. *Black Skin White Masks* (1952). (Trans.) Charles Lam Markmann. London: Pluto Press, 1986.

Favret, Mary A. *Romantic Correspondence: Women, Politics and the Fiction of Letters.* Cambridge: Cambridge University Press, 1993.

Ferguson, Robert. *Representing 'Race': Ideology, Identity and the Media.* London: Arnold, 1998.

Ferguson, Russell, Martha Gever, Trinh T. Minh-Ha and Cornel West (eds). *Out There: Marginalisation and Contemporary Cultures.* Cambridge, MA: MIT Press, 1990.

Fogel, Aaron. 'Talk Shows: On Reading Television'. In Donadio, Stephen, Stephen Railton and Ormond Seavey (eds). *Emerson and His Legacy: Essays in Honor of Quentin Anderson.* Carbondale: Southern Illinois University Press, 1986.

Foucault, Michel. *The Order of Things: An Archaeology of the Human Sciences.* London: Tavistock Publications Ltd., 1970.

——*The Will to Knowledge: The History of Sexuality.* Vol. I (Trans.) Robert Hurley. London: Penguin Books, 1978.

Gamson, Joshua. 'The Assembly Line of Greatness: Celebrity in Twentieth Century America'. *Critical Studies in Mass Communication.* Vol. 9, 1992: 1–24.

——'Do Ask, Do Tell: Frank Talk on TV'. *The American Prospect.* Vol. 23, Fall 1995: 44–50.

——'Publicity Traps: Television Talk Shows and Lesbian, Gay, Bisexual and Transgender Visibility'. *Sexualities.* Vol. 1(1), 1998a: 11–41.

——'Why Do They Like *Jerry Springer?*' *Tikkon.* Vol. 13(6), 1998b: 25–28.

Gates, Henry Louis Jr. (ed.). *'Race', Writing and Difference.* Chicago: University of Chicago Press, 1985.

——*Figures in Black: Words, Signs and the Racial Self.* New York: Oxford University Press, 1987.

——*The Signifying Monkey: A Theory of African-American Literary Criticism.* New York: Oxford University Press, 1988.

Geertz, Clifford. *The Interpretation of Cultures: Selected Essays.* New York: Basic Books, 1973.

Gilroy, Paul. *The Black Atlantic: Modernity and Double Consciousness.* London: Verso, 1993.

——*Between Camps: Race, Identity and Materialism at the End of the Colour Line.* London: Penguin Press, 2000.

Gorer, Geoffrey. *The Americans: A Study in National Character.* London: The Cresset Press, 1948.

Gray, Herman. 'Anxiety, Desire and Conflict in the American Racial Imagination'. In Lull, James and Stephen Hinerman (eds). *Media Scandals: Morality and Desire in the Market Place.* Cambridge: Polity Press, 1997.

Grindstaff, Laura. 'Media Protest is Just a Lot of Talk'. Editorial. *Philadelphia Enquirer.* 16 May, 1997.

Grizzuti Harrison, Barbara. 'The Importance of Being Oprah'. *New York Times Magazine.* 11 June, 1989.

Haag, Laurie. 'Oprah Winfrey: The Construction of Intimacy in the Talk Show Setting'. *Journal of Popular Culture.* Vol. 26(4), Spring 1993: 115–17.

Himmelstein, Hal. *Television Myth and the American Mind.* New York: Praeger, 1984.

Hine, Darlene Clark. *Hine Sight: Black Women and the Reconstruction of American History.* Bloomington: Indianna University press, 1994.

hooks, bell. *Ain't I A Woman? Black Women and Feminism.* London: Pluto Press, 1981.

——'Marginality as Site of Resistance'. In Russell Ferguson, Martha Gever, Trinh T. Minh-Ha and Cornel West (eds). *Out There: Marginalisation and Contemporary Cultures.* Cambridge, MA: MIT Press, 1990.

——'Talking Back'. In Russell Ferguson, Martha Gever, Trinh T. Minh-Ha and Cornel West (eds). *Out There: Marginalisation and Contemporary Cultures.* Cambridge, MA: MIT Press, 1990.

——*Yearning: Race, Gender, and Cultural Politics.* London: Turnaround, 1991.

Houlbrooke, Ralph. *English Family Life, 1576–1716: An Anthology from Diaries.* New York: Basil Blackwell Inc., 1988.

Illouz, Eva. 'That Shadowy Realm of the Interior: Oprah Winfrey and Hamlet's Glass'. *International Journal of Cultural Studies.* Vol. 2(1), 1999: 109–31.

James, Stanlie M. and Abena P.A. Busia (eds). *Theorizing Black feminisms: The Visionary Pragmatism of Black Women.* London: Routledge, 1993.

Jameson, Fredric. *Postmodernism, or, The Cultural Logic of Late Capitalism.* London: Verso, 1991.

Jones, Maldwyn A. *The Limits of Liberty: American History 1607–1980.* New York: Oxford University Press, 1983.

Keller, Teresa. 'Trash TV'. *Journal of Popular Culture.* Vol. 26(4), Spring 1993: 195–206.

Kettle, Martin. 'Oprah's Jurors Reject Ranchers Beef'. *The Guardian.* 27 February, 1998.

King, Nicola. *Memory, Narrative and Identity: Remembering the Self.* Edinburgh: Edinburgh University Press, 2000.

Landman, Jane. 'The Discursive Space of Identity: *The Oprah Winfrey Show'. Metro.* Vol. 103, 1995: 37–45.

——'Identity on Trial: Narration, Gossip and Confession on the Daytime Chat Show'. *Australian Journal of Communication.* Vol. 23(1), 1996: 1–14.

Lasch, Christopher. *The Culture of Narcissism: American Life in an Age of Diminishing Expectations.* New York: WW Norton & Company, 1979.

——*The Minimal Self: Psychic Survival in Troubled Times.* London: Pan Books, 1985.

Lears, Jackson T.J. 'From Salvation to Self-Realization: Advertising and the Therapeutic Roots of the Consumer Culture 1880–1930'. In R.W. Fox and T.J. Jackson Lears (eds). *The Culture of Consumption: Critical essays in American History 1880–1980.* New York: Pantheon, 1988.

Lee, Robert A. *Designs of Blackness: Mappings in the Literature and Culture of Afro-America.* London: Pluto Press, 1998.

Lentricchia, Frank. '*Libra* as Postmodern Critique'. *South Atlantic Quarterly.* Vol. 89(2), Spring 1990: 431–53.

Lionnet, Francoise. *Autobiographical Voices: Race, Gender and Self Portait.* Ithica: Cornell University Press, 1989.

Livingstone, Sonia and Peter Lunt. *Talk on Television: Audience Participation and Public Debate.* London: Routledge, 1994.

Lull, James and Stephen Hinnerman (eds). *Media Scandals: Moraltiy and Desire in the Popular Culture Market Place.* Bodmin, Cornwall: Polity Press, 1997.

Lupton, Deborah. 'Talking About Sex: Sexology, Sexual Difference and Confessional Talk Shows'. In Sigal, Carol and Ann Kibby (eds). *Eroticism and Containment: Notes From the Flood Plain.* New York: New York University Press, 1994.

Major, Clarence. *Black Slang: A Dictionary of Afro-American Talk.* London: Routledge & Kegan Paul, 1971.

Marcuse, Herbert. *One Dimensional Man: Studies in the Ideology of Advanced Industrial Society* (1964). London: Routledge, 1991.

Marshall, David P. *Celebrity and Power: Fame in Contemporary Culture.* Minneapolis: University of Minnesota Press, 1997.

Marx, Leo. 'Pastoralism in America'. In Bercovitch, Sacvan and Myra Jehlen (eds). *Ideology and Classic American Literature.* Cambridge: Cambridge University Press, 1986.

Masciarotte, Gloria Jean. 'C'mon Girl: Oprah Winfrey and the Discourse of Feminine Talk'. *Genders.* Vol. 11, Fall 1991: 81–110.

McLaughlin, Lisa. 'Chastity Criminals in the Age of Electronic Reproduction: Reviewing Talk Television and the Public Sphere'. *Journal of Communication Enquiry.* Vol. 17(1), Winter 1993: 4–55.

Mehl, Dominique. 'The Television of Intimacy'. *Reseaux: The French Journal of Communication.* Vol. 4(1), 1996: 75–84.

Mellencamp, Patricia. *High Anxiety: Catastrophe, Scandal, Age and Comedy.* Bloomington: Indiana University Press, 1992.

Miller, Nancy K. 'Representing Others: Gender and the Subjects of Autobiography'. *Differences: A Journal of Feminist Cultural Studies.* Vol. 6(1), 1994: 1–27.

Mitchell, Jeremy and Richard Maidment (eds). *Culture: The United States in the Twentieth Century.* London: Hodder and Staughton in association with the Open University, 1994.

Modleski, Tanya. *Feminism without Women: Culture and Criticism in a 'Postmodernist' Age*. New York: Routledge, 1991.

Moran, Joe. 'Don Delillo and the Myth of the Author-Recluse'. *Journal of American Studies*. Vol. 34(1), 2000: 137–52.

Morris, Pam. *The Bakhtin Reader: Selected Writings of Bakhtin, Medvedev and Voloshinov*. London: Arnold, 1994.

Morrison, Toni. *Beloved*. London: Picador, 1987.

——*Playing in the Dark: Whiteness and the Literary Imagination*. Cambridge, MA: Harvard University Press, 1992.

Munson, Wayne. *All Talk: The Talk Show in Media Culture*. Philadelphia: Temple University Press, 1993.

Pearce, Garth. 'When It's Not So Good To Talk'. *Sunday Times*. 7 February, 1999.

Peck, Janice. 'Talk About Racism: Framing a Popular Discourse of "Race" on *The Oprah Winfrey Show*.' *Cultural Critique*. Vol. 27, Spring 1994: 89–126.

——'The Mediated Talking Cure: Therapeutic Framing of Autobiography in TV Talk Shows'. In Smith, Sidonie and Julia Watson (eds). *Getting a Life: Everyday Uses of Autobiography*. Minneapolis: University of Minnesota Press, 1996.

Postman, Neil. *Amusing Ourselves to Death: Public Discourse in the Age of Show Business*. London: Methuen, 1985.

Priest, Patricia Joyner. *Public Intimacies: Talk Show Participants and Tell-All TV*. New Jersey: Hampton Press, 1997.

Propp, Vladimir. *Morphology of the Folktale* (1928). (Trans.) Lawrence Scott. USA: University of Texas Press, 1968.

Rabinow, Paul (ed.). *The Foucault Reader*. London: Penguin Books, 1984.

Radstone, Susannah (ed.). *Memory and Methodology*. Oxford: Berg, 2000.

——'Social Bonds and Psychical Order: Testimonies'. *Cultural Values*. Vol. 5(1), January 2001.

Rieff, Philip. *The Triumph of the Therapeutic: Uses of Faith After Freud*. London: Chatto and Windus, 1966.

Riesman, David. *The Lonely Crowd*. (1950) New Haven: Yale University Press, 1961.

Roszak, Theodore. *The Making of a Counter Culture*. London: Faber and Faber, 1970.

Russo, Mary. *The Female Grotesque: Risk, Excess and Modernity*. London: Routledge, 1995.

Said, Edward. 'Ideology of Difference'. In Henry Louis Gates Jr. (ed.). *'Race' Writing and Difference*. Chicago: University of Chicago Press, 1985.

Sennett, Richard. *The Fall of Public Man*. New York: Alfred A. Knopf. 1997.

Shattuc, Jane. *The Talking Cure: TV Talk Shows and Women*. New York: Routledge, 1997.

——'"Go Ricki": Politics, Perversion and Pleasure in the 1990s'. In Geraghty, Christine and David Lusted (eds). *The Television Studies Book*. London: Edward Arnold, 1998.

Simmons, Judy. *Diaries and Journals of Literary Women from Fanny Burney to Virginia Woolf*. Basingstoke: Macmillian Press Ltd., 1990.

Smith, Sidonie and Julia Watson (eds). *Getting a Life: Everyday Uses of Autobiography*. Minneapolis: University of Minnesota Press, 1996.

Smitherman, Geneva. *Talkin and Testifyin: The Language of Black America*. Detroit: Wayne State University Press, 1977.

Squire, Corinne. 'Empowering Women? *The Oprah Winfrey Show*'. *Feminism and Psychology*. Vol. 4(1), 1994: 63–79.

——'Who's White? Television Talk Shows and Representations of Whiteness'. In Fine, Michelle, Lois Weis, Linda C. Powell and L. Mun Wong (eds). *Off White: Readings on 'race', Power and Society*. London: Routledge, 1997.

Stallybrass, Peter and Allon White. *The Politics and Poetics of Transgression*. New York: Cornell University Press, 1986.

Steptoe, Robert B. 'Narration, Authentication and Authorial Control in Fredric Douglass' *Narrative* of 1845'. In William L. Andrews (ed.). *African American Autobiography: A Collection of Critical Essays*. New Jersey: Prentice Hall Inc., 1993.

Stone, Albert E. 'After Black Boy and Dusk After Dawn: Patterns in recent Black Autobiography'. In William L. Andrews (ed.). *African American Autobiography: A Collection of Critical Essays*. New Jersey: Prentice Hall Inc., 1993.

Swanson, Gillian. 'Memory, Subjectivity and Intimacy: The Historical Formation of the Modern Self and the Writing of Female Autobiography'. In Susannah Radstone (ed.). *Memory and Methodology*. Oxford: Berg, 2000.

Turkle, Sherry. *Psychoanalytic Politics: Jaques Lacan and Freud's French Revolution*. London: Burnett Books, 1979.

Vaz, Kim Marie (ed.). *Black Women in America*. London: New Sage Publications, 1995.

Viner, Katherine. 'Black Pearls'. *The Guardian*. 24 March, 1998: 2–4.

Walker, Alice. *In Search of Our Mothers' Gardens: Womanist Prose*. London: The Women's Press, 1983.

——*The Color Purple*. Aylesbury, Bucks: The Women's Press, 1983.

Werner, Craig. 'Go Tell Old Pharaoh: The Afro-American Response to Faulkner'. *Southern Review*. Vol. 19, Winter 1983: 711–35.

West, Cornel. *Keeping Faith: Philosophy and Race in America*. New York: Routledge, 1993.

White, Mimi. 'Ideological Analysis and Television'. In Robert C. Allen (ed.). *Channels of Discourse: Television and Contemporary Culture*. London: Methuen, 1987.

——*Tele-Advising: Therapeutic Discourse in American Television*. Chapel Hill: University of North Carolina Press, 1992.

Willis, Susan. 'Memory and Mass Culture'. In Fabre, Geneve and Robert O'Meally (eds). *History and Memory in African-American Culture*. New York: Oxford University Press, 1994.

Wood, Michael. *America in the Movies or, 'Santa Maria, It Had Slipped My Mind'*. New York: Columbia University Press, 1989.

Young, Lola. 'Racializing Femininity'. In Arthurs, Jane and Jean Grimshaw (eds). *Women's Bodies: Discipline and Transgression*. London: Cassell, 1999.

Index